Decoding Ancient History

A Toolkit for the Historian as Detective

Carol G. Thomas 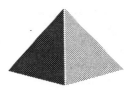 D. P. Wick

PRENTICE HALL, *Englewood Cliffs, New Jersey 07632*

Library of Congress Cataloging-in-Publication Data
Thomas, Carol G.,   (date)-

  Decoding ancient history : a toolkit for the historian as
detective / Carol G. Thomas, D.P. Wick.
     p.   cm.
Includes bibliographical references and index.
   ISBN 0-13-176769-0. — ISBN 0-13-200205-1 (pbk.)
   1. History, Ancient--Methodology.   I. Wick, D.P., (date)-
II. Title.
D56.T48 1994
930'.001--dc20   92-37583
                                                                            CIP

Acquisition Editor: STEVE DALPHIN
Editor-in-Chief: CHARLYCE JONES OWEN
Editorial/production supervision and
   electronic page makeup: ELIZABETH BEST
Marketing Manager: CHRIS FREITAG
Copy Editor: STEPHEN C. HOPKINS
Cover Designer: JOHN THOMAS JUDY
Prepress Buyer: KELLY BEHR
Manufacturing Buyer: MARY ANN GLORIANDE
Editorial Assistant: CAFFIE RISHER

 © 1994 by Prentice-Hall, Inc.
A Simon & Schuster Company
Englewood Cliffs, New Jersey 07632

Printed in the United States of America

10 9 8 7 6 5 4 3 2 1

ISBN 0-13-200205-1 (paper)

ISBN 0-13-176769-0 (case)

Prentice-Hall International (UK) Limited, *London*
Prentice-Hall of Australia Pty. Limited, *Sydney*
Prentice-Hall Canada Inc., *Toronto*
Prentice-Hall Hispanoamericana, S.A., *Mexico*
Prentice-Hall of India Private Limited, *New Delhi*
Prentice-Hall of Japan, Inc., *Tokyo*
Simon & Schuster Asia Pte. Ltd., *Singapore*
Editora Prentice-Hall do Brasil, Ltda., *Rio de Janeiro*

In memory of my mother and my aunt,
whose keenness for learning set this book in motion.
Carol G. Thomas

To Lowell Hagan, who began this road,
and to Mary Lynn, who has made it ever smoother.
D. P. Wick

Contents

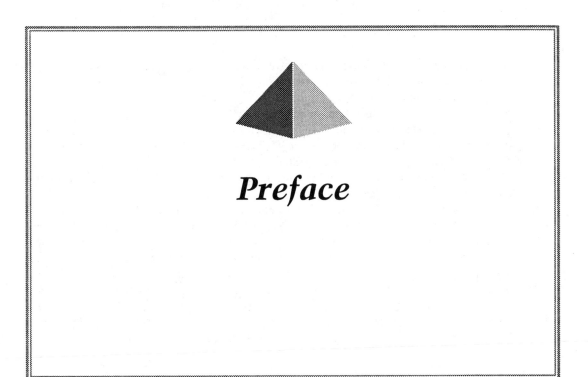

Preface

A particularly pointed student assessment of one ancient history course a few years ago became the tinder that sparked this book. The supplemental reading assigned for that class received a collective "grade"—generously interpreted—of perhaps "D –." The usual adjectives were "scatter-shot," "unfocused," "insignificant issues," and "dull." So clear a dissatisfaction set an alternative goal: readings in ancient history focused tighter on intriguing problems and significant events, aimed at a point higher on the "interest curve." Little came of the search for such a book.

Thus, using two later offerings of that same course, I began to develop a series of case studies aimed at exploring the methods used when studying ancient history. One well-known case would illustrate each method and add another tool to the student's historian "kit." Students would learn specific data about a particular ancient era and problem at the same time that they were learning a new historical "craft." A lever is more interesting when one has something to move with it.

Over time the case studies found their footings in method, multiplied and lengthened. Readers suggested new ideas, fresh angles, and plain improvement. At this point fortune added another element. I was reading a paper written by a doctoral student in the department of history at the time I was considering how the case studies might well be welded into a book. Its author, David Wick, had found just the right evocative language to describe the wistful character of Athens under the rule of Rome. His sense of style struck me as perfect for this book and I was delighted when he agreed to join the venture. His map-making skills, love of time charts, and skill with computer technology were additional boons.

As our labor of merging ideas and words progressed, another touch of fortune intervened. The local representation of Prentice Hall left notices in the mail boxes of our history faculty urging us to contact her if we were pursuing projects the publishers of the College Division might find interesting. We took our "long-shot" to Elizabeth Dedrick Morse and, through her good services, to executive editor, Steve Dalphin, both of them proving gracious as well as interested. The game was afoot. On Mr. Dalphin's advice, we expanded our coverage to include some additional methodologies one could explore using case-studies of Rome. Formal reviews by Brendan Nagle, University of Southern California, and Diane Harris, California State University, Fresno, further spurred by the informal encouragement of our colleague Jon Bridgman, carried the work forward to its culmination and a contract.

We are grateful to each of the individuals who have helped, in one way or another, to create *Decoding Ancient History*. Besides those mentioned above, we owe special debts to a number of others: to Tom B. Jones and the journal *Agricultural History* for permission to reprint his essay "By the Rivers of Babylon Sat We Down"; to the memory of Alan Wace for his insightful analysis "The Evolution of Art in Roman Portraiture" (both accessible and oddly fresh after so many years in which deconstruction has dominated the understanding of ancient art); to Edith B. Burke for the fine comb with which she edited this manuscript and to the Keller Fund whose financial aid eased the cost of editing; to Anne Lou Robkin for the illustrations; to Mary Lynn Wick for the index.

Introduction

Reconstructing the history of the ancient Mediterranean and Near East is no common task; both those who respect and those inclined to smile at the labors of an "ancient" historian are usually inclined to admit that much at least. Materials for building such a history must descend to us from an extremely remote past, and even when they succeed in surviving they are inclined to be troublesome. The richest sources that have come through to us over the millennia since antiquity have been physical things—objects crafted by, treasured by, or even (more often than not) discarded by some ancient culture. Building a "road" across the uncertain landscape of a bygone age is always a tricky thing to do, even when a culture's own historians have left us "maps." The ancient historian must often proceed without such "maps," and with only the rubble of ancient refuse (dangerously mixed with an occasional heirloom) to fill in the unstable places.

Even a chance, and perhaps fragmentary, piece of writing from the pre-classical era is thus a treasure beyond price, and yet we cannot always lean on it too heavily when we have it. When the ancient cultures first came to writing things down, they seem to have concentrated in the beginning either upon getting their bureaucratic records in order or on preserving their accumulated store of oral legend. Neither provide quite the sort of thoughtful eyewitness accounts that a scholar prefers.

And problems multiply. The evidence surviving from antiquity is generally very incomplete. Time has left us a great many randomly pulverized potsherds, but few complete pots. We have bits and pieces of the old bureaucratic records, even when they were originally inscribed on "durable materials." The epic legends most often survive in fragments, perhaps quoted (or misquoted) by later authors, and when we do have a whole work (like "Homer"), scholars are troubled by the thought that something so precious

1

might have been added to or "improved upon" over the years. It is bad enough to build our "road" with so few signposts, but what if they lie?

What would historians of modern Europe do if an entire chapter of their knowledge hung upon the tale told by a single piece of broken pottery? Would they feel much happier if the researchers "eased" their problem by finding a great deal more of the same pottery? Perhaps for this reason really "ancient" history is sometimes dismissed as more a form of guesswork, rather than respected as a real discipline. And while we hope in this book to dispel the illusion that "ancient" history is guesswork, we would be foolish not to learn something from this notion. From the kind of materials scholars of ancient history have available, we must learn precisely as possible how we can and cannot use the information contained in each, appreciating what can be expected from each source of data and also realizing how each is limited.

Learning this kind of thing has always formed the necessary, exacting, and sometimes boring dog-work of ancient history. For those who manage to persevere, toughened, beneath its yoke, the study of antique evidence becomes a fascinating pursuit. Coaxing historical facts from the clues hidden in an artifact can carry a thrill like the thrill of criminal detection. Even when it is neither exciting nor dangerous, the study of the methods for using evidence from the past is the bedrock upon which we must build any reliable "road" into the distant past. It tells us what questions to ask, and (if we are lucky) it may give us a few answers. Like criminal investigation, historical detection is risky. A brilliant, yet inaccurate guess about a few misaligned clues can cloud the truth about an ancient culture for decades. Thus we must use great care in searching for the right questions and their answers.

Several major disciplines form the regular tools we employ when piecing together an account of ancient history. Our strongest emphasis in this book will be upon archaeology, decipherment, and philology, which is the study of literature including grammar, literary criticism, and interpretation. Our attention will be fixed, that is, on evidence contained in material remains and written records that have survived from antiquity. For every major facet of each discipline, we have used as illustration an account of some historical figure whose story depends upon the solution to a particular kind of puzzle presented by the evidence. (A quick look at the table of contents will show that one of the puzzles is actually about a place, not a person—since it comes from an era so ancient that no names of people have survived.)

This book begins in the Old Stone Age and works chronologically forward through human history. Thus the "puzzle without names" is the first one—Lascaux Cave, in France, across whose deeper walls spring ancient painted beasts that still captivate the eye today. An inspection of Lascaux is a study of archaeology alone, for no written records or trustworthy oral traditions exist to shed light for us on that distant chapter of the human past.

We must be content to associate writing with the earliest complex cultures we can discover, dating to around 3000 B.C. Chapter Two uses these accounts: some financial and legal records allow us to follow the fortunes of a Babylonian family as it tries to better itself in the growing economy of one of Mesopotamia's city-states. The discipline that becomes possible is *epigraphy*.

Nestor, who belonged to the Greek "Age of Heroes," and also perhaps to the actual Greek Bronze Age, gives us a chance in Chapter Three to see what comes of combining archaeology with the epigraphy of bureaucratic inscriptional records of the sort we first

FIGURE I-1 The Context of Ancient History

3

found in Mesopotamia. As the mix of evidence increases, the rewards become richer—both in the flavor and the detail with which we can begin to understand a lost culture.

Legend is a source as rich as either archaeology or epigraphy, but trickier to handle. Considered alone, legends provide clues about historical figures and events, especially about why they were remembered—we begin to get near the meaning a culture sees in its own early history, approaching the wise historical goal of letting a culture speak for itself. Chapter Four follows the story of David, the first king of a united Israel. Though he has been the subject of archaeological and even inscriptional reconstruction, his earlier career may provide a case study of the value and limits that are inherent in oral tradition as a historical tool.

Until recently the modern habit has been to regard an ancient culture's store of legend as some form of fiction, but this has begun to change as we understand more and more about oral composition. Although we generally know legends only because they were eventually written down, each was originally only in an oral form—a way of passing the memory of a culture from one generation to the next in an era when the only thing that could be patterned to preserve information was the human memory. As scholars understand more of that process, they can make better use of the evidence left to us, and very often they gain a much greater respect for it. Chapter Five takes a close look at some of the mechanics of oral tradition as it examines the Greek farmer-poet Hesiod, who lived about 700 B.C.

One very specialized historical discipline wrestles with evidence that lies in the borderland between archaeology and epigraphy. Numismatics try to learn everything it can from ancient coins, both as physical relics and as bits of authentic writing. In Chapter Six we take a particular look at Croesus, king of Lydia in Asia Minor in the sixth century B.C., the kingdom where coinage may have originated. Coinage was of course not only artifact and record but also a medium of exchange. It quickened the pace and ease of trade, and as we follow its evidence across regional boundaries, we must pull back and broaden our focus. The context of these studies begins to spread, blending the various "ancient histories" into one.

Socrates, the brilliant gadfly of fifth-century B.C. Athens, could reward the attention of many different disciplines. In Chapter Seven he finds his place in our book not because he was remembered, but because he was remembered in so many different (and perhaps even conflicting) ways. At last we begin to have written and thoughtful accounts that are very nearly contemporary with him. Strangely, however, most attempts to capture his whole personality from the accounts seem to end in frustration. He serves nicely to question the validity of personal testimony.

Chapter Eight is another of those in which we can draw several techniques of reconstruction together into one study. Reputedly royal tombs have now been discovered in Macedonia; one of them may belong to Philip II, the enigmatic military genius who founded the Macedonian Empire. Philip, who died at the height of his career (and provided us with the clues for the first really historical "murder mystery"), turned a comparatively simple, rough-spoken, hill-country nation on the edge of the Greek world into the builders of an empire. What he failed to leave behind were very many clues about himself, and so the question of whether or not archaeologists have indeed found his tomb buried under a grassy hillock at Vergina has a special urgency.

Alexander, Philip's son, almost single-handedly changed the shape of the Mediterranean world. Not surprisingly, we know a good deal more about him than we do about his father. But the few supremely towering, dynamic characters in ancient history offer their own peculiar mystery: how can we come to understand the inner fire that made them what they were? Can we ever truly know their secret motivation? They were "larger than life," and their biographers often seem to describe bits and pieces of them, rather than capturing the whole. Some modern historians with a bent for psychology have turned to a method called psychohistory to cut through the knot which binds the clues. Is this method reliable, or does it tell us only about its inventors?

Chapter Nine has something of the air of nostalgia about it. Athens, which had in Socrates' time been the quintessential city of the Greek world—almost a definition of what it meant to be Greek—had by the later centuries of antiquity become a place of shadows, memories, and regrets. Rome ruled the world, and only Athens' universities, her banks, and her value as a cultural tourist-stop lent her whatever quiet elegance and influence she still retained. Our evidence remains within the realm of collective memory, though it was of a more private and sentimental sort (the world had become a far more literate, and a far larger place): the testimony of private letters and memoirs. Once again we must handle it with care, for as with the biographies of Alexander we are using evidence in which personal feeling has become very closely intertwined with fact.

In Chapter Ten the later Roman world provides the setting for our final tool, portraiture. From an early era in their cultural history, the Romans were able to value realistic portrayals of themselves (even when unflattering). The facial features of Roman sculpted heads emphasize individual traits, even when certain features told hard or humorous truths about the personalities they represented. Can we probe beneath the surface of these images and find the character of ancient persons in the carved stone and metal faces we still can see? And can we watch a change in attitudes over time as the Roman peace of the early empire becomes the tumult of the late empire?

As types of evidence begin to cluster and overlap round a particular person or event, the story grows richer. The most difficult trick to attaining mastery is learning to gain the insights from each kind of evidence without confusing them, or being led astray. What we stand to achieve in the end (with discipline and a little artistry) is a composite, hypothetical, re-created picture of some historical life, or city, or culture, or world. We have some clue that "X" existed: taking all the clues that become possible with an understanding of archaeology, legend, oral tradition, numismatics, reconstructed testimony, psychohistory, deciphered scripts, primary written sources, and the various kinds of literature, we try to build a knowledge of "X" as whole and honest as we can.

Unfortunately, such wealth of evidence seldom exists for any particular event, figure, or situation in antiquity. The key is to find all that is there—missing nothing small, distorting the troublesome clues as little as we can, fitting everything by the right criteria into the best individual answer the question will allow. We have tried to write a guidebook, or at least a casebook, for such exercises. There is nothing in these pages like a precise formula for scholarly success, only some signposts gathered from others who have driven useful roads across the more difficult landscapes of the ancient past.

We have designed *Decoding Ancient History* to be used alongside a narrative history, as a supplement or companion. Even more important, it should be used whenever possible with the appropriate primary source. The fullest evidence for the story of David is to be found in the Old Testament, not in any secondary work. The surest things we can know about Hesiod, his verse and his style, are in his own *Theogony* and *Works and Days*.

Chapter Seven will remain a wilderness foggy with allusions unless the reader sets out with Aristophanes' *Clouds*, Plato's *Dialogues*, and Xenophon's *Memoirs of Socrates* somewhere close at hand.

Our first aim has been to make information about the ancient past more accessible. The examples are concrete ones: the lives of specific people, the feel and fortunes of specific places. We have tried to help students visualize how they might conduct their own first historical investigation. We encourage them each to think about the ways in which their own previous experiences in life may have colored their understanding of history—the effects of their own cultural and historical environment—and to apply these insights as they deal with the past. In a similar fashion, the reader will notice before long how often questions about the nature of biography crop up when we are discussing the earlier, more central historical figures. These instances point up a critical issue: the interrelation of an individual with some culture's collective memory of the past. If we can begin to understand how this relation functions we will have a clue to using historical narratives of all kinds and to the changing memories of cultures across broad reaches of time.

Our fundamental hope is to center the reader's perspective on one question: how have individuals or entire peoples tried to remember, or to understand, both their past and the times in which they lived? Once we know that, we shall be less likely to misunderstand the information that we have inherited from them across the centuries.

Historians in more recent fields, who can so easily draw upon a greater and more varied wealth of data, tend to talk as though the serious pursuit of antiquity were folly, as though the ancient historian were a sort of deluded Hamlet, posturing gloomily among the twilit ruins of impossible eras. Perhaps. Conclusions about the ancient past are fragile, as all historical conclusions are. There was a bit more to Hamlet than the experts thought, too. "Though this be madness," Polonius said, "yet there is method in't" (II, ii, 222).

Chapter One

The Images
of Lascaux

The historians of the more recent times and topics do not often appreciate the wealth of data they have, or can have, ready at their fingertips. Thus, when they watch the scholars of antiquity attempting to wring so much from so few and so meager as the very distant past affords, they are tempted to smile. One can hardly blame them. A skeptic has gone so far as to define the practice of ancient history as a convocation of seven historians clustered, squinting and quarrelling, round a single potsherd. The description is funny. It is also perilously close to being accurate.

History as a discipline may be defined as the recording and interpreting of the human past—it relies, in other words, upon written records. By that definition, of course, the larger part of the tale of humans must be called prehistory. Although we are currently told that the story of human life began between 1 and 2 million years ago (the date seems to march constantly further into the past), we remain forced by the best evidence to place the invention of writing as recently as the end of the fourth millennium B.C. All other things being equal, then, we should be able to have documents only for—at most—one-half of one percent of human history. For that remaining ninety-nine and one-half percent of the saga we shall have to rely upon nonwritten materials.

But all other things are not equal. Such nonwritten materials as a scholar of antiquity needs are very, very scanty for the first million years of human life and development. Populations then would, by necessity, have been very small. Until quite recently, for example, only one human skull dated to earlier than 10,000 B.C. had been found in the whole of Greece. So minuscule a population of the globe will have produced an extremely small number of objects and, allowing for the normal ratio of artifact survival, an even smaller number of those objects will have survived to be studied today.

Remember that we are speaking of the Old Stone Age: the material world was a far less complex one during that first long age of human culture. What little we know about the time must be painted in broad strokes across a vast canvas. Over the background of this picture move slow, massive changes in the physical environment of our planet and the adaptations of plant, animal, and human life to those changes; we have few means of knowing what sharp punctuations might have entered this tale. Two primary dates might give a sample of the scale: *homo erectus* (upright man) is supposed by current guesses to have existed about 2 million years ago; modern human beings are currently believed to have made an appearance only some 40,000–45,000 years ago.

We speak of this whole sweep of time—the stage for one entire act in the human drama—as the Old Stone Age, the Paleolithic Era. It seems by our methods of dating to have extended at least a full million years: to have started before 1,000,000 B.C. with the first creatures we call human, to have begun ending (no simple level of human culture ever quite ends) about 10,000 B.C. Across so vast a stage the human tale made do with very few actors; at any given moment any one of the tiny number of living humans might have walked for days without meeting another. Animal life was everywhere, of course. The solitary human might more likely have been walking (or chasing) after a source of food than searching for another group of his or her own kind. A beast—or a few naturally growing, uncultivated plants—that a person could eat would have meant the difference at any given moment between life and death. Humans were utterly at the mercy of the natural world around them.

Paleolithic people moved constantly, building no permanent homes. In this respect also they could take only what nature was willing to give them—a dry cave, perhaps a wooded glen without too much rain coming through the leaves. They might with a little luck and skill manage to bend tree limbs or pull rocks together to form rude huts. The readiest tools and weapons were of like construction: natural objects—stones, bones, shells, and pieces of wood. Hence the era's name. Human technology centered round the crafting of weapons and tools by chipping and flaking stones into appropriate shapes. Many of the earliest of these are so rude in appearance that they were long thought to have been created naturally. One writer in the sixteenth century looked at such strangely shaped rocks and felt compelled to argue them the product of lightning in combination with exotic types of clouds. He was wrong, and what might have been curiosities for the geologists have instead become for archaeologists the very stuff of history. They are the earliest, simplest products of human hands.

And yet we must always resist the impression that nothing changed across this great span of time. Monumental things can happen by almost imperceptible increments, or they might happen by sudden little punctuations of change (enormously important at the moment of their occurrence) that may always be invisible to our distant eyes. Humans began in this era to speak—to communicate verbally—with one another. We take speech so much for granted that we often forget how great an advantage it gives us over other living creatures. If a Paleolithic man or woman could speak, he or she might pass on knowledge, shout warnings, discuss how wise a plan of action might be, or perhaps be able to make the plan at all. (It may not be possible to think of a plan without the facility of speech.) Some date this new skill rather late in the Old Stone Age—perhaps 35,000 B.C. It might provide one explanation for a leap forward in the quality of life we can observe at about that time. Population increased, the variety of tools improved, life was now made up of more kinds of activities. Though they did not yet live in permanent villages, groups of people tended to return seasonally to the same places. Some place on the coast where they caught fish in the summer was now in some sense "theirs"; or some secluded place in woods where trees might blunt the winter wind. It became a regular "home."

The chief fact is that these ancestors of ours left very few clues about themselves. They wrote nothing. Only the merest flotsam of stones and bones descends intact from their time to ours. Scarcity and simplicity of material remains do not of course lessen their value; they do the opposite. As the importance of each of these earliest objects has been more and more understood, the science of archaeology has become increasingly complex. No longer can it focus almost entirely on the arduous task of excavating things ancient and studying the things found. Students of early times have had, moreover, to understand that monetarily insignificant remains may be worth as much as, sometimes far more than, the obvious treasures. Glitter does not equal gold. If modern archaeologists wish to evaluate their finds they must, like modern detectives, cooperate constantly with scientists in a wide range of ancillary disciplines.

In fact, the methodologies, observations, and philosophies of archaeology have developed so far in the last fifty years that the discipline has blossomed forth a veritable thicket of new branches. They are called, collectively, the "new archaeology"—their adherents endeavoring to examine entire cultures, to follow the processes of change over sweeping spans of time. "Sweeping" is an apt word. The changed archaeology has found its "prime mover" in the rising popularity of the "archaeological survey": a general, interdisciplinary research project that focuses on the human relationship to a particular environment, and does so on a regional scale.

Tied as archaeology is to each particular site and context, it is not easy to choose a beginning example. No single excavation or project can reveal, over its history, the complete range of the discipline, or parallel all the ways in which it has developed over 200 hundred years. But the cave of Lascaux in southern France may give us an excellent start—it demonstrates that both accident and design play their part in discovery. Better yet, it shows just how much the mute record of physical remains may tell us when, after the basic excavation and interpretation of traditional archaeology, a range of auxiliary techniques is brought to bear on a particular site.

LASCAUX

Buried beneath the countryside of the French Dordogne, Lascaux Cave holds within its winding tunnels some of the most famous and overpowering examples of cave painting; their majesty takes the breath away. Their antiquity is awesome as well: more than 20,000 years ago someone painted the moving images of animals and humans, and the sweeping forms of other unidentifiable things, across the walls and ceilings of this spacious cavern. But caves in the vicinity of nearby Les Eyzies were decorated even earlier—5,000 or even 10,000 years before Lascaux. Painters had in fact been at work in other caves before Lascaux. The prints of human hands on the cavern walls tell us something about the artists, but since those hands knew no form of writing, they cannot tell us precisely to whom or to whose culture they belong. They are the signatures of anonymity.

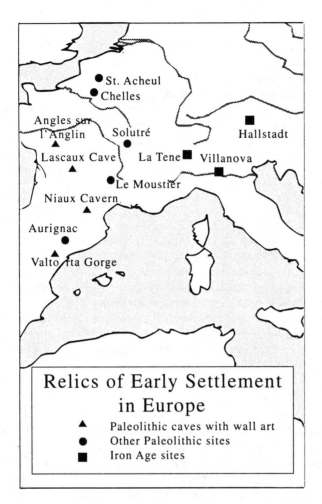

FIGURE 1–1 Relics of Early Settlement in Europe.

Lost in the subterranean darkness for millennia, the drawings were discovered little more than a century ago. A young girl came upon the first site accidentally near Altamira, Spain in 1879. Exploring the entrance to a cave not far from her home, she began to notice paintings on the ceiling. The shapes of great animals strode across the surfaces above her, revealed in the light of her small lantern. She excitedly told her father; he told the world; but the initial amazement soon gave way to doubt as the experts became skeptical. Surely, many of them argued, these paintings must be modern forgeries: no one in the first age of human history had the eye, or hands, or skill to create images so sophisticated or grand as these.

They were wrong. Experts have now demonstrated the authenticity of the Altamira paintings, and of those at more than 200 other ancient locations. Most of these are in France, many south of the Loire River and west of the Rhône; the rest primarily in Spain (especially in the Cantabrian mountains). Some few additional decorated caves occur in Italy; one lies at the foot of the Ural Mountains; and there have been reports of paintings from one cavern in Greece.

These caves vary considerably in their physical form. Some are single; some open into a few large chambers; while other sites are intricate tunnel-systems, where passages stretch and wind for miles. There are miniature caves like the one near Les Eyzies in France—its entrance is smaller than a manhole cover, the figures engraved along its narrow courses stand but 7 or 8 inches high. The Nerja Cave in Spain, by contrast, towers some 120 feet high in one of its galleries. The main cavern at Lascaux reaches about 110 yards long down its major axis, and on the surfaces provided by this ample distance the figures are huge—one looming Lascaux bull ranges almost 18 feet from horns to tail.

People frequented these caves across many centuries. The Old Stone Age—we now place the beginning of that first long chapter to the human story more than a million years in the past—saw humans attempting to come to terms with nature but able to control it very little. Caves would have been ready shelters from the elements. The painted and engraved images in these caves, however, date to a later phase of their use: the earliest examples belong perhaps to around 30,000 B.C.; the latest are almost contemporary with the end of the last ice age (perhaps 10,000 B.C.). We might assign the grand examples at Lascaux to about 18,000 B.C.—they are the end products of a long tradition, incorporating many past techniques into the powerful simplicity of their final form. It goes almost without saying, then, that between the lives of those who painted the first pictures and those who painted the last we must expect profound differences. And yet, since the surviving evidence is so limited, we must be content to delineate those differences, at best, in exceedingly broad strokes. Much of the little evidence that we have must come from the paintings themselves.

The subjects painted are, almost without exception, animals. We should expect this, of course, given the importance of animals in a hunter-gatherer society; such painters will have naturally concentrated upon them because their lives depended upon them. Before they domesticated plants and animals, humans survived largely according to their ability to track and trap animals in the wild. This much is plain sailing, but though the basic value of animals for human existence is obvious, it will not wholly do to explain the meaning of the murals in the caves. To understand completely, it is utterly essential that we get some feel for the context of the artists' lives. Like a crystal, a context has many facets, and the same thing may look a little different viewed through each. Thus, these human artifacts may admit several different, or complementary, explanations.

One point of view claims that in cave art we are glimpsing a magical, as well as a practical, reflection of ancient human life—a way of capturing those beasts by means of "magical sympathies," which the hunters pursued in the real light of day. We witness upon the cave walls, in other words, a symbolic quest for food. Small marks have in fact been distinguished on some of the animal figures and interpreted by this school as wounds and the remains of arrows.

This visible symbolic wounding is not a universal or even a common occurrence, however. As a consequence the great shapes of the animals may have other significances as well, not the least of them aesthetic. To modern eyes much of the art is stunning in its own right; it would require a great historical arrogance to suppose that such majesties did not impress the Paleolithic cave dweller in like manner. It is true that only some of the paintings are of an overpowering presence and quality; others are mere scribbles. It is also true that this variation is likely only in part to stem from the success or failure of an

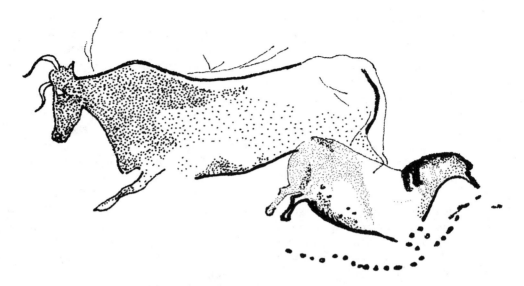

FIGURE 1–2 A small horse passes a large cow along the walls of Axial Gallery in Lascaux Cave. The animals carry the sense of individual presence, not of composed groups. That presence is extraordinarily bold and strong.

individual artist. A variety of functions prompts a variety of images. We cannot suppose that the images were intended simply for their beauties because they were often placed where they could not easily be seen. What was meant for the eye alone would not have been so thoroughly hidden. In many caves the most splendid works of Paleolithic art lie buried in the darkest and remotest depths.

Wherever they are placed, and whatever those lost painters intended, we must keep our own eyes carefully set as we begin upon the simplest, most certain observation: the animal image was the most important element in their art. Thus it is possible that the secret to their meaning lies in their form. Let us look a little closer at the figures that stride the shadows of Lascaux's walls, at their combinations, relations, and settings.

A clue lies perhaps in the compositions themselves. Even where a number of horses, bison, deer, or bulls move forward in a row across the ancient walls, they each move as an individual creature. There is no sense of huge numbers moving or grazing en masse. Although such single figures may be juxtaposed, they are not arranged in hierarchies, nor are their groups or movements patterned. The imaginative reach and skill of the artists—both individually and as a culture—may explain something of this convention: perhaps a carefully composed "group" painting lay beyond their artistic or technical ability. Such things have proved troublesome for far more developed cultures.

Nonetheless, it is possible to regard this "style" as deliberately employed. It need not have been simply forced upon the painters by the level of their culture or their own skill, nor by the kind of materials they had ready to hand. Indeed, we may find the experiment well worth making since it allows, at least in theory, for the ancient artists to impose as much meaning of their own upon their works as we are used to imposing upon them in our modern studies and workshops. What have they left us?

The style or technique of these painted images is first of all extraordinarily bold and vital: the great creatures plunge across the vault of the ceiling, they stride confidently down the walls of the cave. Shapes and textures inherent in the natural rock lend a sense of movement and form to the paintings—one can hardly escape the suggestion that the figures were placed purposely to draw a certain three-dimensional depth from the original features of the rock. There is very little drawn differentiation of bodily forms except for this naturally sculpted use of the cave wall: convex surfaces add bulk, depressions convey texture or movement. Color is perhaps the only exception; several shades are often used to depict a single animal.

We tend, today, to group events, experiences, and objects into categories according to (among other features) their appearance, function, composition, and the skill required to meet or to make them. The kinds of distinctions that seem so customary now were apparently uncommon, even absent. And perhaps also absent in early human history are the means that divide the human, animal, plant, and inanimate facets of life from one another. Many classifications and differentiations—it is not always easy to say precisely which—appear in those human minds we can observe only with the development of literacy. Discrimination of many parts of the world is for the human being an acquired thing.

About literacy itself we shall have more to say or to explore in Chapter Five. It is enough now to note that in a nonliterate culture, such as that of the Lascaux artists, the known sphere of human experience was a single entity providing a single frame of reference: it assimilated into its oneness all features unfamiliar to it. Totemic images, for example, combine in their symbolic immediacy spheres that we should like to separate into distinct groups—animate or inanimate, animal or human or divine. It is possible or even probable that the great beasts of the Lascaux walls embodied a similar range of being. They might well, in other words, combine an intuitive expression of animal power with a more symbolic statement of human power. The grandeur is clear, and the artist exhibits awe, but the grandeur may embody a variety of sentiments. There are after all, as the cavern walls say, more-than-human forces at work in the world.

If this is true, then the figures may have been both painted and looked upon as symbols of the world as Paleolithic people understood it. A noted authority on this art believes that the cave drawings reveal an existence perceived in terms of reciprocal male and female forces. In both the animal and human spheres, life was thought (or rather felt) to consist of the interplay between these—they complemented one another or, depending on how sharply they were distinguished, they "co-inhered." The cave art would then mirror these: the masculine force associated with the lance; the feminine with wounding. Together they symbolize, on one level, sexual union, and on another, death. Man-horse-weapon stands in one place; woman-bison-wounding in another; intermingled they express the order of the world. (Leroi-Gourhan, 1965:119–21). It is well to add that even the proposer of this interpretation himself admitted it was surely a simplistic one, and incomplete. The nature of the evidence allows no certainty. But Paleolithic humans were obviously male and female, and sensed the differing capabilities of each.

By a different interpretation the cave paintings were made and used to preserve the traditional knowledge of their social group. Every culture needs a means to communicate among its individual members; it also has a need almost as basic to communicate with future generations. In fact, a superior ability to communicate in such ways has sometimes been offered as a critical factor in early human development. Some experts maintain that

FIGURE 1–3 An artist's impression of Paleolithic cave dwellers dwarfed by their own artistic creations. The very location and atmosphere of these paintings present clues to their use and meaning.

hominids living as many as three million years ago had sufficiently articulated vocal chords to communicate in a spoken language. We do not yet have evidence that they did. The weight of contemporary scholarship suggests that language recognizable to a modern person is a far more recent thing. It is perhaps what characterizes *homo sapiens* from his predecessors. Such a "modern-speaking" human is associated with the late Paleolithic Era—with those millennia in fact between 40,000 and 10,000 years ago, with the age of the cave paintings. Even though we cannot re-create the texture and sound of the language, we may suspect that the broad language groups—Semitic, Indo-European, Bantu—had already begun their long, particularistic process of breaking up.

If there is no writing, information which a culture feels is vital to its communal survival or happiness must be passed on, judged, and refined orally. Oral tradition is so structured that it can be preserved over many generations, visual images—made by the human hand or called up by the spoken word—coming to the aid of memory. Places and objects often do more than ease the memory of tradition, they create traditions of their own. Stories are embedded in these ancient things, and though we cannot reconstruct them today, we can sense something of the flavor and tone of the tales from the look of the objects themselves.

Thus, John Pfeiffer argues that we cannot understand the art of the caves without understanding group ceremony. Caves are mysterious, and their mystery, as well as the placement of the figures within them, gave a special communal strength to the initiations—the rites of passage—those acts by which an individual was taken into a group of people. He believes that the importance of the art lies in the changes it depicts, changes that were the hinge-pins upon which early life turned: the humble and critical changes in hunting techniques and tool technology.

> There was a new restlessness and wider migrations and exchange networks along with decreasing mobility and somewhat more permanent dwellings, changes above all in age-old egalitarian traditions, the first signs of some people outranking others. All this took place suddenly compared with the slow pace, the almost unimaginable monotony of earlier times. (Pfeiffer, 1982:226)

The caves and their images may present mute testimony to such changes. Their very locations may suggest several clues about the cultures that created them. They are first of all cave paintings—hidden in places naturally formed, not designed or even very much rebuilt by the hands of humans. Caves seem to have had a special status for these cultures. They lay deeply withdrawn from the violent forces of nature. They endured. Animals repainted over other animals speak of how long they retained such a feeling—for generations a culture regarded Lascaux as an important, uncommon place.

Why was this so? We should expect by now that precise answers are difficult to find. The question is after all of the chicken-and-egg variety: did the texture and form of the cave give rise to some singular sort of activities within it, or did the activities hallow the cave? Even if we cannot be very sure of our answer, it is obvious that the paintings were a way of telling something. They spoke.

We might do well to step back and widen our focus for a moment, hoping to learn something from the specific regions in which the cavern art was carried on. Some 80 percent of known examples, by one estimate, originated between 15,000 and 10,000 B.C., and it may be no accident that during that same time many humans in western Europe were beginning to settle in one place for longer periods. Evidence from some sites tells of groups that had once moved constantly coming to a certain place for an entire season. Paleolithic hunters visited sites in the eastern parts of the modern city of Nice, for instance, and their visits were seasonal from as early as 200,000 years ago. As the excavators sift their clues, they speak of eleven consecutive annual visits, probably involving many of the same individuals. And these hunters stayed long enough to produce semipermanent shelters: oval huts measuring from 26 to 49 feet long, 13 to 20 feet wide. Ovals of stone marked each hut's perimeter, branches and twigs may well have made walls and a roof, and a hearth lay in the center of each packed earthen floor.

Round the hearth revolved the activities of the dwellers; here the collected food was cooked. We know from their remains that the visitors hunted small game—birds, turtles, rabbits, rodents—but they seem to have preferred larger quarry: the deer, the elephant, wild boar, ibex, rhinoceros, and wild ox. We are confident that fish, oysters, mussels, and limpets drew them to the seashore, for they left the bones and shells in the earth behind them. Stone tools—both pebble tools and flaked stone implements—assisted in the hunt and in the preparation of the catch. They crafted from their catch other tools, for their special objects were increasingly made of bone.

Social organization also revolved round the hearth. The French historian Camille Jullian has called it

> ...a place for gathering together around a fire that warms, that sheds light and gives comfort. The toolmaker's seat is where one man carefully pursues a work that is useful to many. The men here may well be nomadic hunters, but before the chase begins they need periods of preparation and afterward long moments of repose beside the hearth. The family, the tribe will arise from these customs... (de Lumley, 1969:50)

In the earlier phases of the Paleolithic Age, such groups would have been small, perhaps on the order of twenty or twenty-five people. By a modern estimate it requires some 12 square miles to maintain each person in a hunting-gathering economy, and foraging over 240 to 300 square miles is a possible range for a nomadic group. Rather greater distances are less likely, especially if there is evidence that the community returned seasonally to a specific site. This equation becomes more flexible if the same territory can be exploited more intensively and the range of food resources can be widened. Early farming technology, for example, could manage to support five people on little more than 1/2 square mile, shrinking the landholding necessary for a community's survival dramatically. Whether settled permanently or merely seasonally, longer stays in a particular region would have taught the visitors much about its resources. Greater familiarity with a place and landscape, greater knowledge of the range of food it affords, would in turn have enticed visitors to remain longer.

We may create the broad lines of a picture from this. During the Paleolithic Age a fully sedentary existence—true settlement—was not possible, but it would not be too fanciful if we were to imagine a growing pattern of shuttle-migrations, of trips returning to and from specific, well-known locations. Just as a group might visit the same stretch of seacoast or the banks of the same river during summer months, so they might return regularly to the lands around a cave like Lascaux in the stormier seasons. We should expect, if we are right, that each site over time would then show the effects of longer, more regular occupation. We should anticipate finding evidence of the repetition of practices, of greater concentration upon the shape and refuges and resources of the local countryside. We should posit, in short, greater marks of such a culture's way of life, and even of its members' view of life, for they have begun to interact much longer with a particular place.

This kind of indicator does appear more frequently in the later Paleolithic centuries, since the human communities had by then often developed more complex technologies. Tools grew in number and their quality improved—the final culture of the Old Stone Age excelled in the techniques of working stone. Along with more practical tools (whose history extends far into the past), there were new household items like needles. There began to be luxury items as well. There were moreover a larger number of people making and using tools: between 20,000 and 10,000 B.C. the population of Europe seems to have doubled, estimates ranging from 6,000 to 10,000 inhabitants at the start. By the last centuries of the Paleolithic Era, Europe supported between 12,000 and 20,000 people.

Even though conditions had improved, life as a whole remained difficult. As they gathered rather than produced their food, the folk of the time were still largely at the mercy of their environment, and with this we are returned to our initial impression of the story told on the dim and figured walls of Lascaux. The awe and strength painted there have more context now, as does that artistic acceptance of a given order in the universe (such cultures must either accept such an order, or find life intolerable). There is nevertheless implicit in the art some effort to contain the vital and unruly forces of existence. Significantly, such forces are animal forces; humans are not the focus of the tale of the walls even though they were decorated by and for a human society.

We have now been warned sufficiently that interpreting the evidence in these deep reaches is no easy task. Finding that evidence is even more difficult. A young girl's playful exploration brought about the first discovery of ancient cave art. Luck was the telling factor. We may perhaps be inclined to forgive it in the archaeological work of the nineteenth century, but as recently as 1940 Lascaux Cave itself came to light by pure accident, reputedly when four boys rescued their dog after it had fallen through a hole. It was a cow's plunge through another hole that led to the discovery of evidence in a cave near Bordeaux. We have, of course, more method to our pursuit of evidence in the last years of the twentieth century, but chance is still a major player.

Walking, accompanied by a close scrutiny of the land, is utterly crucial to the systematic exploration of the past. What we now call "survey archaeology" tells a great deal, both as a preliminary tool before excavation, and as an independent method. All sites, even once discovered, cannot be examined by real excavation—we have not enough either of time or examiners—and, since settled life was not typical for humans until the Neolithic Revolution some 8,000 years ago, we should in any case find comparatively little by excavating the sites from the earliest human millennia. Even when excavation is the goal, survey and sampling are now the usual and systematic means by which we discover where the earliest humans lived and recover some few of the artifacts they created and used.

Survey archaeology is the intensive investigation of surface remains—archaeological, geographical, and geomorphic—in a given region. The investigators walk in predetermined (and sometimes seemingly endless) patterns, recording information about the objects found along their strip of the earth's surface. While the data gathered by individual searchers are consolidated onto maps prepared for the project, often only a minimal number of finds are collected. No excavation occurs. The area around a formal "dig" site has of course often been investigated through reconnaissance in the past, but in the last two decades the merits of this less glamorous inspection have become more widely recognized. Survey archaeology has gained an increasing importance of its own. Not only does it present a more manageable problem in logistics than excavation, it is usually cheaper, and a better steward of the data hidden in the land. An excavation by its very nature will tend to erase the upper levels of its site in order to reach the lower; survey archaeology can proceed without destroying its evidence. Because of this, in part, it is often far easier to gain permission for a survey investigation, whereas permits for excavation grow more difficult to obtain with each passing year.

For our own purposes survey holds another, perhaps a greater, value: it provides perspective. Even when excavation is possible, survey's perspective is a broader one. A prominent advocate has defined it in two phrases: "Excavation reveals a lot about a little of one site; survey can tell us a little about a lot of sites...." (Cherry, 1983:387). To gather this "little" body of data, survey teams ask about the settlement patterns and resources of an entire region. What is the relationship of human life to the environment? How do the groups of people in this landscape interact? We may reasonably find such methods especially appropriate for the study of the meager and scattered evidences that survive from the Paleolithic Era.

A survey takes its point of departure when it defines the region it will examine. The units of natural geography are useful ones because geography exerts a powerful influence upon the patterns of settlement. Once launched, a survey team scrutinizes the physical surface of its region, surveying it carefully two or more times. A project in central Greece, for example, used a grid, which it imposed upon part of the area being investigated, the gridded squares of that area then being surveyed by individual crews trudging attentively over a certain amount of land each day. Their purpose was to learn the density of surface artifacts, and to reconstruct from that a plan of settlement and its density. Each person in a crew recorded environmental, topographical, and artifactual information on his or her own plan of that particular ground, and these data were then collected later onto a map of the entire region. A second survey crew investigated the surface area of the entire site. "By the end of this second phase, it was possible to reconstruct a detailed picture of the history of each site, including the main shifts and extensions of the settlement area, as well as gaining an overall picture of its topographical situation" (Bintliff and Snodgrass, 1986:40 *f.*).

The resulting information, ordered and collected in a single place, can truly tell at least a "little" about a broad area. When a team surveyed the Methana Peninsula in the northeast Peloponnese, its members recorded fifty-five sites, only six of which had been known previously. Their dates range from Neolithic into the Bronze Age and onward through the Iron Age, Classical, Hellenistic, Roman, late Roman, and medieval periods.

Scientific equipment can be a great aid in detecting possible surface artifacts. In the early stages of basic exploration, magnetometers and bleepers are the tools of choice—both of them instruments using electric current to measure the intensity and fluctuation of the earth's magnetic field. That field is perturbed by items buried in the earth as well as by those lurking in ditches and pits. These disturbing factors are then much easier to locate even without excavation since the byproduct of this electronic exploration is a terrain map of the contours below the surface of the earth, plotting the shapes of things no human eye could reach.

One might see how fruitful a magnetometer survey can be from the success of the Canadian Archaeological Institute at Athens as it studied Stymphalos in the northern Peloponnese during 1983 and 1984: "Particularly significant," the director reported, "was the discovery of another 80m of the missing N. wall of the city (including a tower) and of a break in the continuity of the N–S streets in the E. area of the city. It was possible to trace the line of five streets for over 400m and to identify a number of peristyle structures along their line" (Williams, 1985:19).

We must return now to our topic of the caves, asking how the newer and older archaeological techniques may have enlarged our understanding. Greece provides a useful case study: a Paleolithic rock shelter in the northwestern region of Epirus. It is less awesome than Lascaux since there are no paintings. A team led by G. Bailey has examined this site in the years since 1983–1984. This site is Klithi—the focus of investigation that has ranged from the cavern itself to its role in the larger local, regional, and even continental surroundings. Geological research there has tried to reconstruct changes in the land, its vegetation, and its water supply, and from that data we now have some insight into the forces that have sculpted its landscape. We also can make some guess about the sort of economy it might have supported.

The very first season of inquiry yielded signs of human habitation. Excavating in trenches to sift for the (sometimes very minute) concrete evidence, the team examined everything, including soil residue, bone, stone artifacts, and carbon specimens. By the fourth season, new drilling techniques allowed even more intensive sampling: the excavators began to investigate deeper levels more rapidly, and with less destruction of deposits. The device was a percussion drill, made up of "hollow steel tubes with a hardened steel cutting edge and window slots cut in the side. The whole assembly is driven into the ground with a motorized hammer and extracted with a mechanical rod puller and ball clamp." After each extraction, "contaminating deposits derived from the side walls of the borehole were cleaned from the window slots, and the column of *in situ* deposit was drawn and photographed. The deposit was then 'excavated' from within the gouge in 5cm units" (Bailey, 1987:30 *f.*).

It is when one thinks of the normal state of cave remains that the value of such cores of material becomes obvious. If a cavern—or any site—has been used over long periods of time the accumulated deposits are likely to be mixed together hodgepodge, every vestige of proper context destroyed. An important cave site on Crete, for example, provides a jumble of remains whose origins range from the Neolithic through the Bronze Age Minoan civilization, right on to the Classical and even Roman periods. A core sample would tell one, in a single pass, something of the order of accumulation.

These remains can then be examined for their individual characteristics. They must be separated carefully from the soil in which they are found and, since such finds are often only tiny fragments, they must still be sought very delicately. The human eye may quite easily miss a bone splinter or a flint chip; consequently sieves are used to catch the fragments as soil is filtered through their holes, and a combination of wet and dry sieving helps to separate the finds. The resulting numbers of items can be staggering: in the 1985–1986 season alone, at Klithi 75,000 flint artifacts and 120,000 animal bones came out of the ground.

Such unglamorous but telltale hoards are not easily discovered, in part, because they are concentrated so densely. At Klithi "an excavation unit 1 meter square by 5 cm deep might yield as many as 400 plotted flint artifacts, 400 plotted bones and 1500 unplotted flint and bone fragments" (Bailey 1985:38). The work of recovery is a laborious one, and since the site had been occupied continuously the team at Klithi found that their "…first step in excavation was to clear the surface layer of goat dung.…For the excavation…each meter square was subdivided into four quadrants, each 50cm by 50cm in thickness. A total of 262 such units was excavated. In 137 of these units individual specimens were accurately plotted to the nearest cm in the horizontal dimension. All flints 2 cm or larger were plotted in this way, and retouched tools less than 2cm. All bone fragments 3cm or larger, and teeth or tooth fragments smaller than 3cm were plotted in the same manner. The deposits were removed with small brushes and plastic trowels. Occasionally small dental picks were used to loosen very hard deposits. This was to ensure minimal damage to fragile bones or the edges of flint artifacts. Soil residues were dry sieved through 1cm and 2mm meshes" (Bailey 1985:38).

Archaeology has seldom sounded less glamorous, and yet these precise drudgeries yield a harvest of real items from humans' distant past which can be studied and compared. A process called *typology* separates the finds by categories: principal function, date, and cultural context. Lest too narrow an attention be focused on the objects themselves, the entire site is scrutinized for its *stratigraphy*—a geological method that attempts to classify the orderly sequence of soil and stone deposits that lie (throughout the neighborhood of the dig) over the earlier material. Archaeologists are sometimes lucky enough to find that the process of accumulation has not been disturbed, meaning that the number and depth of those earthen levels can indicate periods of occupation and use. By excavating the levels in reverse chronological order they can begin producing a guide to the history of the site. It is a sad fact, though, that an undisturbed accumulation is the exception, not the rule. Natural processes and human action have usually at some point (or at many points) in the site's past complicated and muddled the geologist's and archaeologist's work.

An ancient site must be dated. The finds so painstakingly culled from the ground are likely to provide clues both individually and taken as a whole. The natural byproduct of the investigation is a relative dating: objects from lower levels are probably earlier than similar things found in higher levels. If an archaeologist is lucky enough to come upon a truly undisturbed collection of items (the classic example would be the contents of a grave), it is possible to suggest which of them are contemporary. Even in that case, the items obviously may have been manufactured at different times. That one gold antique pin among an otherwise ordinary collection of household valuables may represent a prize heirloom—an exciting find perhaps, but also a dangerous clue upon which to base broad conclusions.

Dates with a rather greater certainty become possible when an archaeologist has access to testing processes that utilize radiocarbon, X-ray fluorescence, X-ray diffraction, and neutron activation. These techniques are perhaps the most vivid illustration of a major development in recent archaeology: its alliance with other disciplines. The most common example is carbon dating, a differential measurement of the two isotopes carbon 12 and carbon 14. Cosmic radiation from nitrogen in the atmosphere impacts upon the ordinary carbon 12, producing the radioactive carbon 14, which acts just the same as its simpler cousin in living matter, but which ceases to exchange with the atmosphere and begins to decay at a known rate when that living matter dies. Determining the level of radioactivity in a substance will reveal in what proportion it contains these two carbons. Barring the disturbance of any outside processes, this proportion can suggest (at least within fixed limits) the time elapsed since the sample died. Most field archaeologists are not trained or equipped to carry out such a scientific analysis of their finds—they may lack the precise scientific training and they very often lack the money. As a good estimate, a laboratory equipped for basic analytical procedures will probably require an initial investment of $250,000, and an operating budget of around $100,000 per year.

The good news is that there are less expensive ways to interpret the material record. Many students of early human existence are convinced, for example, that re-creating the conditions of early human life will shed light on the evidence. We have nothing like a colonial Williamsburg for the Old Stone Age to be sure, but a far-reaching range of experiments has now attempted to reproduce technologies and tools from that era—the chipping and flaking of stone, the production of paint from red ochre and a binder such as saliva. Lamps have been fabricated of a kind that might have given light in the

Paleolithic caves, and a knowledge of the lighting may tell us (as it does for many eras) something about the culture and the art. In every period where our evidence is limited to material remains, it is experiments such as this that may help archaeology across the wilderness of meager data: static evidence can be used to re-create a dynamic, lively picture.

And yet at our end of the twentieth century we still have not built a mechanical aid that can replace the initial investigation of the human hand, eye, and mind in discovering the evidence. Perhaps we may in the not-too-distant future be able to send advanced robots into the narrower, more tortuous tunnel-systems of the caves. Perhaps we can capture through their electronic sensors the locations and contexts of items to be investigated further. Until then, the human eye, aided by a microscope, a magnifying glass, and perhaps a camera containing special film, must blaze each trail of new investigation.

It was the same in the days of the great nineteenth century discoverers; archaeology remains as painstaking and arduous for us as it was in its early years. We have surmounted the labor of its awkward beginnings only to learn the labors that come with precision. At the same time, archaeology has matured into a recognizable discipline. With that maturity have come new alliances, new questions, and even (thankfully) some new answers. While we still have no utterly secure explanation for those great beasts that strike and stride across the rock-walled recesses of Lascaux, we are likely getting closer to a proper sense of them. Across 18,000 years we reach back with newly trained hands, hoping to touch the craftsmanlike fingers (perhaps still stained by pigment and the dust of the cave) of one of our ancestors, and to share his awe.

FURTHER READING

The second edition of *The Idea of Prehistory* by Glyn Daniel and Colin Renfrew (Edinburgh: Edinburgh University Press, 1988) is a fine introduction to the history of archaeology. An excellent application of survey archaeology is T. H. van Andel and C. Runnels, *Beyond the Acropolis: A Rural Greek Past* (Stanford, CA: Stanford University Press, 1987). John Pfeiffer, *The Creative Explosion: An Inquiry into the Origins of Art and Religion* (New York: Harper & Row, 1982) discusses prehistoric art in its larger social and economic contexts. For an assessment of the art, two treasures are Abbé H. Breuil, *Four Hundred Centuries of Cave Art* (Montignac, 1952) and André Leroi-Gourhan, *Treasures of Prehistoric Art* (New York: Abrams, 1967).

Chapter Two

Real Estate Records from Babylonia

For its magnificence the cave at Lascaux may have no rival; as an archaeological site it has many. The aims of those who opened it and have interpreted it are typical. The British archaeologist Glyn Daniel summed them up succinctly: "The purpose of archaeology is to extract history from the monuments and artifacts of the past, to write history from the often inadequate relics that time has spared" (Daniel, 1968:20). Each site is a sort of tenuous hole in time through which modern researchers hope to reach (with patience and long labor) from the present back into the physical stuff of the past, and, if they are lucky, they are able to draw from it a "handful" of its authentic remains.

There is seldom more than a "handful," but those relics allow us to reconstruct a way of life for some particular group of people. We may begin to understand the technology by which they produced things, or the places in which they found them. We may even begin to understand what they used them for. A broadly focused analysis of an entire site tells us the physical spread of a community. If we can compare it with others in its neighborhood, we may begin to see how its region interacted among its communities.

Almost always, though, we must reconstruct this with a very little bit of evidence. Our pictures are always sketches, and large portions of the canvas must (if we do our research honestly) be left tantalizingly blank. Relics survive most often by chance, not design—only an occasional tomb, sturdier than most and hidden somehow for centuries, presents us with a kind of "time capsule." The consequence is that we have more often than not the garbage rather than the heirlooms or even the most useful possessions of antiquity. The views we rebuild from these artifacts are fleeting and seldom connected, hence the "sketches." We draw the glimpses we catch through random tatters in a moving veil; to paint a true picture of the distant past, we should need the magic to part the curtains

The Ancient Near East (3000 - 1000)

Date B.C.	Mesopotamian Events	Around the Mediterranean	Artifacts & Art
3000 -	(c. 3500 - 3000) The earliest real civilizations begin to flourish. Cities appear in Sumer. (c.) Metal-craftsmen regularly begin to make implements of bronze. (c. 2750) Legendary reign of Gilgamesh as King of Uruk, in Sumeria.	(3100) The union of Upper and Lower Egypt under Menes. Foundation of the 1st Dynasty. Settlement of the Canaanites in Palestine. Phoenicians settle along eastern Mediter-ranean coast.	(c. 3500 - 3200) Early pictographs done in cuneiform (Mesopotamia) Egyptian and Assyrian cultures building in brick. (c. 2700) Reign of Khufu in Egypt. The Great Pyramid at Giza.
2500 -	(2450 - 2340) Lagash dominates the lower river valleys. (c. 2350) Sargon the Great of Akkad conquers Sumeria.	(c. 2500) Rise of early Minoan civilization in Crete. A center begins to form at Knossos.	(c. 2500) Royal tombs of the 1st Dynasty at Ur (rich furnishings and evidence of human sacrifice). (c.) "Stele of the Vultures" at Lagash (showing troops in a "phalanx"-like formation).
2000 -	(c. 2150) Sumerian revival; the 3rd Dynasty of Ur. (c. 1900) Idin Lagamal born at Dilbat near Babylon. (c. 1890) The Old Babylonian or Amorite Dynasty at Babylon. Prosperity in Babylonian Sumeria. (c. 1800) Hittites begin arriving in Asia Minor	(c. 2000) Bronze Age culture in northern Europe. (c. 1730) The Hyksos begin to invade Egypt; rule northern Egypt from Tanis until c. 1565. (c.) The eruption of Thera in the Aegean; damage to many mainland and Minoan coastal centers.	(c. 2000) Rise of the Minoan palace culture on Crete. (c. 1600) Early Mycenaean culture: the "Shaft Graves" at Mycenae, heroic weapons such as "tower shields" and boar's tooth helmets.
1500 -	(c. 1792 - 1750) Reign of Hammurabi and publication of his Law Code. Babylonian dominance at its high point. (c. 1600) The Hittites raid and sack Babylon. The city falls to the Kassites soon after. (c. 1366) Beginning of Assyrian rise to power under Assuruballit. (c. 1300) Rise of the Phoenician port Sidon to wealth and power.	(c. 1570) Rise of the New Kingdom in Egypt. (c. 1500) Reign of Queen Hatshepsut in Egypt (XVIII Dynasty). (c.) Evidence of destruction at many palace centers in Crete. (c. 1480) Greatest extent of Egyptian rule (from the Euphrates to the 4th cataract of the Nile). (1480) Hatshepsut succeeded by Thutmose III.	Height of Minoan wealth, culture, and influence. Palace centers like Knossos flourish on Crete. (c. 1470) Work begun on the Egyptian temple to Amon at Karnak. (c. 1400) Construction of the great Egyptian temple complex at Luxor. (c. 1300) Work begun in Egypt on large rockface temples at Abu Simbel.
1000 -			

properly, and to let the folk who lived in that lost world speak for themselves. Archaeology cannot touch so directly the ancient life of the mind, except by inferring from the things it finds. It cannot even infer very specifically—the names, the relationships, the occupations of those who left the relics are usually irrecoverable with physical evidence alone.

Answers to such questions require some further evidence in addition to the material objects: they require the speech, in one form or another, of the people who created and used them. Specific details of even the simplest kind—questions such as What did such people call themselves? or What did they name their children?—cannot be settled without some form of writing. If a written account has been preserved in a relatively complete form, we may even have statements from folk long dead, explanations of themselves and of their thoughts in their own words. We should then be touching minds as well as the random survivals of the physical world. We should then know names.

Humans acquired the art of writing only (relatively) recently. We characterized the Old Stone Age by humans' thorough dependence on the environment, not (as in later eras) by their attempts to manipulate it, or to record facts about it (and therefore to lessen its power to overwhelm them). This dependence did of course become less absolute with time. A number of significant advances mark off what we call the Middle Stone Age (or Mesolithic Era). From somewhere around 10,000 to 6000 B.C., wandering communities of people began settling in certain regions that possessed—at least potentially—an unusual abundance of the resources necessary to sustain life: water, a liveable climate, and wild plants and animals of the sort they could domesticate.

The Near East was an especially easy region into which people could settle and adapt. Deposits of animal bones tell us that humans domesticated sheep and goats there; sickle blades, and mortars and pestles tell of cultivated grain. By 7000 B.C. this more rooted way of life was winning out over the older patterns of migration in the Near East. Not long afterwards, the earliest homesteaders in Europe had also begun to explore farming and the keeping of animals. Overnight, so to speak, the human story grew far more complex. Land on which a handful of humans could once barely gather enough food for survival now supported more than a hundred of them. Population increased, but more important, as people began clustering closer together into permanent villages, they could see for themselves that it had increased. People thrown together in a region began to feel that they were a particular society. Tasks multiplied; folk discovered they had new needs—storage areas, forks for winnowing, ovens for baking, fences to protect the new herds of captive animals. Labor began dividing and specializing, it was no longer enough for a single person to do a little bit of everything the best he or she knew how; folk in a community depended on one another more, but their dependence on nature was far less absolute. If we could define somewhere a moment when this settled way of life became the norm, we would mark it as the opening of the New Stone Age (the Neolithic Era). It dates to approximately 6000–3000 B.C. in the eastern Mediterranean.

Once people produced the necessities of life in communities, under their own control, the pace of change quickened. The earliest real civilizations—appearing about 3000 B.C.—were all erected on a foundation of agriculture. Two parts of the Near East seem to have excelled especially in the arts of complexity that we are really referring to when we use the word "civilization": Mesopotamia and Egypt. In the long descending belt of land between the Tigris and Euphrates Rivers—Mesopotamia (the Greek word means "between the rivers")—and along the narrow, desert-bounded valley of the Nile, farmers found they could use the river waters to create real surpluses of food. The region marked by the arc of these rivers is, in fact, known as the Fertile Crescent. A community could now support members that did not directly engage in agriculture. A few could specialize in things like new technology—metallurgy for example, especially the crafting of bronze from copper and lead. The new tools and weapons from such specialists were superior ones; the productivity and safety of the community increased. Other nonfarmers might now have the time to carry some of the food surplus into the lands beyond the settlement, trading for raw materials or luxuries. A few (for complexity makes it inevitable) supervised the various activities of all the rest, trying to coordinate the interaction of what might easily now be several thousand people. Uruk, settled behind its walls in the southwestern siltlands of lower Mesopotamia, covered some 1,100 acres and was home to about 50,000 people.

One of the things utterly essential in so large and complex a society as this was the ability to record exactly the duties, surpluses, trade receipts, and technological data around which life revolved. Human memory, however brilliantly it might be patterned to store the knowledge of simpler times, could not function precisely enough in a really differentiated culture. So it was that writing emerged. Rock paintings and carvings have, to be sure, sometimes been described as "writing-in-embryo," but it is with the systematic codes of symbol-for-meaning found in the earliest complex cultures of Egypt and Mesopotamia that the tale of writing begins in earnest. Thus one result of the broader changes in human culture was an agreement or convention, struck among the record-keepers of some particular place, that certain symbols should aid human memory by always referring to certain meanings.

Among the Sumerian city-states that nestled themselves into the fertile floodplains at the head of the Persian Gulf, a system sprang up that centered round wedge-shaped signs. We call it *cuneiform* (the Latin word for wedge is *cuneus*), and it is generally credited as the first true writing. The earliest examples of this that we have found date from about 3200 B.C. and are really pictographs—pictures of objects with symbolic meaning done in the cuneiform style. It was only over time that the individual marks and combinations picked up phonetic, syllabic values. Signs making a pictograph for an arrow, by example, were pronounced "T I," since an arrow was called a "T I." If you combined a number of such signs you could say more complex things. The sign for "city" rapidly found itself assimilated into a whole host of words, not the least of them the names of the cities themselves.

Cuneiform had a long life. It managed to remain useful in one form or another (it was easily adaptable to new languages) for some 3,000 years, passing on after the extinction of the cities in which it was born to a variety of other cultures in the ancient Near East. The state that grew like a series of shells round the city of Babylon used this writing to forge an effective control over most of Mesopotamia in the nineteenth and eighteenth centuries B.C. We have an unusual wealth of records from the Babylonian period, both in the amount of material and in the types of information that have survived, because they were written on durable materials. Paper, though it is thriftier to organize and easier to transport, will almost always lose the contest for survival with substances as solid as a clay tablet or a block of stone. Consequently, our earliest complex political document is the famous Law Code of Hammurabi, probably dating between 1792 and 1750 B.C., which compiled and preserved the definition of justice for an entire culture.

We have also, as we would have hoped, accounts by ordinary members of those societies that let us glimpse the forms and share the feel of their lives. One particularly

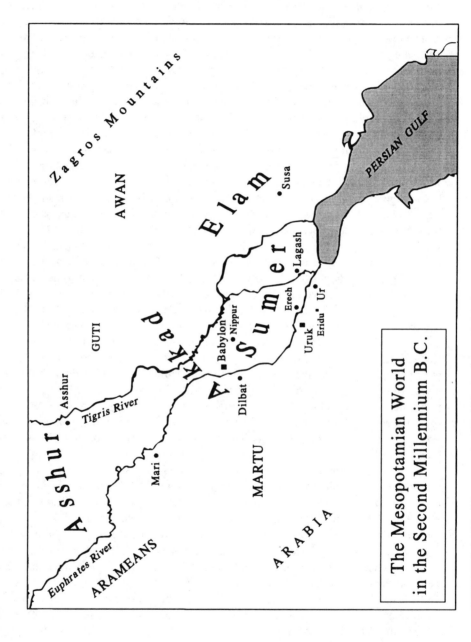

FIGURE 2–1   The Mesopotamian World in the Second Millennium B.C.

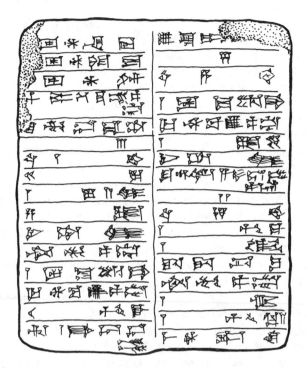

FIGURE 2–2 Sketch of a typical cuneiform record showing use of the wedge-shaped tools to form writing by impression in clay. Idin Lagamal's family would have kept their "books" on similar tablets.

full set contains enough detail and covers enough time to let us trace a family, descendant to descendant, through several generations. The best news is that it was not an especially famous family. Luck has left us a view through the veil of time that lets us focus for once upon average people, both when they were prosperous and when they were not. In the next section, the family of Idin-Lagamal illustrates for us the kind of information we stand to gain by *epigraphy*—the decipherment and study of writing in inscriptions. There are enough surviving records for us to reconstruct the lives and fortunes of four generations in a single family—an authentic slice cut from the history of the kingdom of Babylonia during the reigns of Hammurabi and the kings who preceded him.

But we should not expect our data from such a source to be flawless or exhaustive. Inscriptions are a mixed blessing. Even on a single well-preserved inscription portions are often damaged (if not utterly obliterated) by the wear and wind of the centuries. Evidence that we must have to understand a transaction or an event may simply be gone, even if it were once part of a document now recovered. When we are lucky enough to have an inscription preserved whole and entire, it may be the sole survivor of a larger, interrelated set, all the accounts in which dealt with a process or an event, and none of which told the whole story. However careful we are, we shall still have lost the larger context; and if we are not careful, we might imagine that we understand something on which we have thrown only a tiny and misleading beam of light.

Inscriptional evidence reveals specific and authentic, but also extremely selective, data. What it conveys is focused by the difficulty of writing on the sort of durable materials that make it an inscription. Its limits are tight—tight in the time illuminated, tight in the subject covered, and tight in the descriptive accuracy and numeric detail by which it can reckon. In the following story, for example, we shall find the family vanishes into the darkness of unrecorded history after the fourth generation. We should like to know what happened to them after the curtain has closed again. Even of the four generations whose fortunes we can watch, only a very few individuals fall under the light of surviving inscriptions long enough for a real story to emerge. Were the others only the family ne'er-do-wells? Has the most successful of them fallen through the cracks?

Finally, these accounts pressed and driven into the surfaces of stone and clay show a sharp limitation in delineating the "quality" of any life reconstructed from them: they record no reactions. No one has told us how they felt, and yet these are the long-dead artifacts of human marriages, of purchases, leases, sales, births, and deaths.

A friend and colleague in the study of the ancient world has spent much of his professional career examining the sort of evidence that makes a reconstruction such as this possible. The essay in historical detection that follows is one of his best—certainly the best case study in this vein of inscriptional evidence that we have ever read. With the permission of Tom Bard Jones, let us follow him briefly through the curtain, and look more intimately at one family in the world of Mesopotamia, in the time of the Babylonian kings, in the town of Dilbat on the Euphrates.

"By the Rivers of Babylon Sat We Down" *

Thirty-eight centuries ago in the thriving Babylonian town of Dilbat there lived an obscure little farmer named Idin-Lagamal. Today, Dilbat is almost forgotten,[1] but nearly four-score broken and crumbling clay tablets remain to tell the story of Idin-Lagamal and his descendants.[2] Meager though the evidence may seem and limited in scope, these surviving fragments of the family archives, most of them dated contracts, may be employed to produce something more than an outline of four generations of economic activity.

Idin-Lagamal was born about 1900 B.C.[3] His father's name was Ili-amrâni, and his two brothers were called Bêl-ilum and Ahukinum.[4] Ili-amrâni may have been a native of Dilbat, but it is quite possible that he had drifted into Babylonia about the middle of the twentieth century with the Semitic tribesmen who were to establish their capital at Babylon and found the Amorite or Old Babylonian dynasty there about 1890. At any rate, Ili-amrâni had lived in Dilbat long enough to acquire property in town and some agricultural land as well, and this, according to custom, had been divided among his sons at his death.[5]

Dilbat was the center of a rich farming community. The town itself stood on the banks of the Arahtum, one of the major Babylonian canals, and its fields were watered by several other canals and streams.[6] Within Dilbat were at least four temples: one to Urash, the principal local deity, and others dedicated to Shamash, Sîn, and Lagamal. The records do not give a complete picture of Dilbat, but the town did have a pottery and brick "factory," and among those whose occupations are listed in the tablets are farmers, fishermen, herdsmen, gardeners, weavers, masons, metal workers, and a manufacturer of oil, as well as priests, scribes, and one soothsayer.

---

*©1951 by The Agricultural History Society. Reprinted from Agricultural History by permission of the author and the publishers. The original appeared in Vol. 25, No.1, January 1951, pp. 1–9), by permission.

The eleven contracts in which the name of Idin-Lagamal appears cover a period of perhaps a quarter of a century during the reigns of Sumu-abum and Sumu-la-ilum, the first two kings of the Amorite dynasty. This was an age of expanding agriculture and increasing trade in Babylonia when the construction of new canals fostered the growth of the cultivated area and relatively peaceful conditions promoted an exchange of goods with regions to the north and west.[7] The economic predominance of the temples which had characterized the earlier period was now a thing of the past, just as the increasing use of silver as a medium of exchange was effecting the disintegration of the old barter economy.[8] A brief era of what might be called free enterprise had dawned; or, to put it another way, there had been a secularization of economic activity. As we shall see, Idin-Lagamal and his eldest son, Nâhilum, were able to take advantage of the general prosperity which spread over Babylonia in the nineteenth century B.C. Their foresight and industry laid the foundations for a family fortune that reached its zenith during the reign of Hammurabi.

Idin-Lagamal first appears as a witness in a transaction involving the sale of a field.[9] Awil-Nannar, one of the five sons of Nûr-ilishu, sold three and a half acres[10] of fertile land by the Arahtum canal to Marankina, a neighbor of Idin-Lagamal. Called from his own plot nearby to serve as a witness, Idin-Lagamal undoubtedly had no inkling that some day his family would possess the land held by the sons of Nûr-ilishu. Throughout the succeeding decade, we hear no more of Idin-Lagamal, but we may surmise that he worked hard and prospered for, from the second to the fifteenth years of Sumu-la-ilum, he was affluent enough to be extremely active in the purchase of fields and town property.

Thanks to the Babylonian custom of indicating the boundaries of real estate involved in sales and leases, we can reconstruct (with reference to one another) the locations of the fields mentioned in the Dilbat tablets. In the second year of Sumu-la-ilum, for example, Idin-Lagamal purchased two adjoining parcels of land: one in the second month of the year, and the other four months later.[11] His first acquisition was a fraction of an acre from Urash-bâni, a field bounded on one side by the field of Zâzâ and on the other by the field of Idin-Urash.[12] In the second instance, an acre of land was purchased from Lagamal-emûqi, brother of Urash-bâni; this plot lay between the fields of Idin-Urash and Ili-sulûli on the one side, and the field of Zâzâ on the other (see Figure 11).

In the eighth year of Sumu-la-ilum, Idin-Lagamal acquired more land: five acres from Warad-Sîn, brother of Awil-Nannar, another son of Nûr-ilishu.[13] This field was bounded by the plot of Awil-Nannar on one side and the field of Nannar-asharid, still another son of Nûr-ilishu, on the other; along its front ran the Arahtum canal, and to its rear was the Râkibum, a second canal. After an interval of five years, Idin-Lagamal bought the field of Nannar-asharid, too,[14] and when we find Awil-Nannar being allowed by Idin-Lagamal "to cultivate the field of the sons of Nûr-ilishu," we may assume that most, if not all, of the land of this family belong to Idin-Lagamal (see Figure 12).[15]

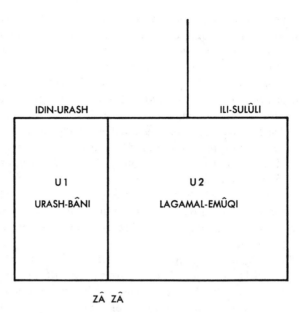

Fig. 11

Still more land was purchased by Idin-Lagamal. Although we have a record of only one field (by the sluices of the Urash canal),[16] the holdings of his sons at a later period[17] show the location of his other acquisitions with relation to the fields enumerated above. Consequently, the land possessed by Idin-Lagamal at his death may be estimated to have been in excess of thirty-five acres.[18]

The real estate operations of Idin-Lagamal within the town itself were conducted upon a much more modest scale. His house, which stood on one side of the marketplace, was probably an inheritance from his father, Ili-amrâni.[19] During the reign of Sumu-la-ilum, Idin-Lagamal twice enlarged his house by small purchases from his neighbors. At the rear, he bought half a *sar* (200 square feet) from Zâzum and Ishtar-rabiat, Aârum's sister.[20] Later, a *sar* and a half bought from Anni-ilum, Idin-Lagamal's next door

Fig. 12. The Sons of Nûr-ilishu

neighbor, extended the original purchase out to the street.[21] We do not know the size of Idin-Lagamal's house, but on the analogy of private houses elsewhere, his purchases would amount to adding another room or two to his dwelling.[22]

After the death of Idin-Lagamal, his property was divided among his three sons, Nâhilum, Shaga-Nannar, and Tutu-nâsir. The eldest son, Nâhilum, was a chip off the old block. A score of contracts, dated in the reigns of Zabium, Abil-Sîn, and Sîn-muballit, provide convincing evidence of his business acumen and even suggest occasionally that his brothers were less talented in this respect.

In contrast to his father, Nâhilum was active in acquiring town property. Most of his purchases were made around the market square; sometimes he bought houses or parts of houses, but he was also interested in small plots not occupied by buildings.

The reconstruction of Nâhilum's activities in town is a complicated process, but it is possible to locate most of his purchases with reference to one another and to the marketplace. The method employed here may be described as follows:

As in the case of the fields, the boundaries of town lots and houses are indicated in the contracts by the inclusion of the names of those who hold adjacent property: "a house (or plot) of such and such an area, bounded on the one side by the house of A and on the other by the house of B, on the front by the house of C, and on the rear by the house of D." In many cases the property bought by Nâhilum fronted on the market square. The names of the witnesses to the contracts are also useful, since the names of certain witnesses reoccur in the sales of tracts or houses which are known to be, or appear to be, adjacent.

A good illustration of the foregoing is provided in the case of two purchases of Idin-Lagamal (PSBA and G4) and one of Nâhilum (G10). The first, part of a house bounded on one side by the house of Anni-ilum and on the other by the house of Idin-Lagamal, was witnessed by Ibku-ishhara, son of Buzija. The second, fronted on the market and bounded by the houses of Manniya and Idin-Lagamal, was witnessed by Urra-gâmil, another son of Buzija. In the case of the third purchase, it appears that the property first acquired by Idin-Lagamal (PSBA) was again involved. Briefly, what had happened was that after Idin-Lagamal died, his house was divided between Nâhilum, Tutu-nâsir, and possibly Shaga-Nannar. At any rate, Tutu-nâsir sold his portion at the rear of the house to Ishgum-Urra (a neighbor), and in G10 we find Nâhilum buying back from Ishgum-Urra one-half sar (the same figure mentioned in PSBA) of the property sold by Tutu-nâsir. This property was founded by the house of Anni-ilum on one side and that of Ishgum-Urra on the other, while at the rear were the houses of Ishgum-Urra and Ishme-Sîn. Among the witnesses were Awîl-ilum and Uratiya who both appear in later sales of property in this area.[23]

During the reign of Abil-Sîn, Nâhilum bought two houses and several small lots up the street above his house. The location of one of these houses is indisputable (G15), and the approximate location of the other house and the plots of land acquired is shown in the accompanying sketch (Figure 13).[24] Another house in the same area, purchased early in the reign of Hammurabi, is less easy to locate.[25]

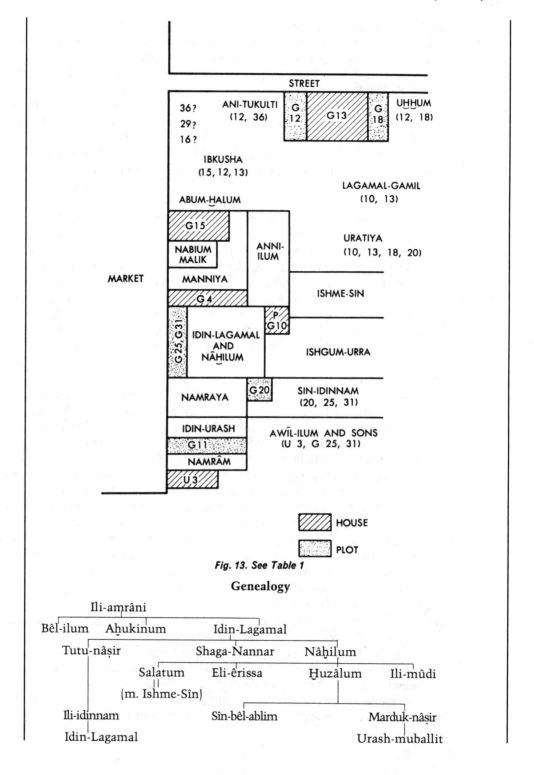

Fig. 13. See Table 1

Genealogy

Chronology

Idin-Lagamal	lived during reign of	Sumu-abum
		Sumu-la-ilum
Nâhilum		Zabium
		Abil Sîn
		Sîn-muballit
		Hammurabi (early)
Huzâlum		Hammurabi (late)
Marduk-nâsir		Samsuiluna (early)
Urash-muballit		Samsuiluna (late)

Down the street, in the opposite direction from the property mentioned above, the various purchases of Nâhilum are not difficult to follow. This property was all acquired during the reign of Sîn-muballit. From G20, 25, and 31 it appears that the houses of Namraya and Sîn-idinnam adjoined that of Nâhilum on the lower side. Then, on the other side of Namraya's house was the property of Ili-zânini, which had been divided among Ili-zânini's three sons, Idin-Urash, Namrâm, and Hunâbum, whose inheritance[26] lay between that of his two brothers, and who had sold his share to Sîn-nâda early in the reign of Zabium (G11). The warehouse (U3) which Nâhilum bought in the first year of Sîn-muballit stood next to the house of Namrâm, while the half-*sar* plot acquired by Nâhilum from Sîn-idinam was in the location indicated on the sketch (G20). Directly in front of the house of Nâhilum was a kind of boulevard, a narrow strip a little over one-third of a *sar* in area. In the eighteenth year of Sîn-muballit this property was in the hands of a man named Marduk-muballit who exchanged it for other property belonging to Adalallum, son of Awîl-anum (G25). Three months later, Nâhilum approached Adalallum, the new owner, regarding the sale of the plot; a deal was made, and the title was transferred to Nâhilum.[27]

Thus, by the beginning of the reign of Hammurabi, Nâhilum owned at least four (and possibly five) houses, a warehouse, and several small plots of land within the town of Dilbat.[28] This property was valuable not only because of its location near the marketplace and because of its potential resale profits, but it could also be rented and so yield an annual income.

Nâhilum did not confine his activities to the town. He was equally busy in acquiring agricultural land. Presumably the fields down by the Arahtum canal had been divided among the sons of Idin-Lagamal, although we hear nothing more about them, but it is clear from the new purchases of Nâhilum that Idin-Lagamal's holdings in the Urash district had been large, too. G19 and G22 show that Nâhilum, Shaga-Nannar, and Tukt-nâasir had divided up their father's holding by the Urash canal (see Figure 14), and then, during the reign of Sîn-muballit, Nâhilum bought 1 1/2 acres from the holder of a neighboring field, Sîn-mushallim (G19); subsequently, Nâhilum also acquired the field of his brother, Tutu-nâsir, a large tract of 6 2/3 acres

Table 1.—Town Property Purchased by Idin-Lagamal and Nāḫilum

Contract and Date	Seller	Buyer	Type	Neighbors	Significant Witnesses
PSBA 6 Sumu-la-ilum	Zâzum and Ish-tar-rabiat	Idin-Lagamal	House	Anni-ilum Idin-Lagamal	Ibku-ishḫara, son Buzija
G 4 13 Sumu-la-ilum	Anni-ilum	Idin-Lagamal	House	Manniya Idin-Lagamal	Urra-gâmil, son Buzija Sîn-rîmêni (see G 16) Idin-Urash (see G 11)
G 10 Zabium	Ishgum-Urra	Nāḫilum	House	Anni-ilum Ishgum-Urra Ishme-Sîn	Lagamal-gâmil (see G 13)
G 11 9 Zabium	Ḫunâbum, son Ili-zânini	Sîn-nâda	Plot	Idin-Urash Namrâm, both sons of Ili-zânini	Uratiya (see G 13, 18, 20)
G 15 7 Abil Sîn	Ibkusha	Nāḫilum	House	Manniya Nabium-malik Abum-ḫalum	Ishme-Sîn (see G 10) Nannar-mâgir (see G 18) Warad-martu (see G 29)
G 12 13 Abil Sîn	Ani-tukulti	Nāḫilum	Plot	Nāḫilum Ani-tukulti	Ibkusha (see G 15) Manniya (see G 4, 15) Aḫuwaqar (see G 13) Uḫḫum (see G 18)
G 13 13 Abil Sîn	Lawsuit over house sold by Awil-ma-tim to Nāḫilum			Appears to be adjacent to G 12	Ibkusha (see G 12, 15) Aḫuwaqar (see G 12) Uratiya (see G 10, 18, 20) Lagamal-gâmil (see G 10)

Table 1. (cont.)

Contract and Date	Seller	Buyer	Type	Neighbors	Significant Witnesses
G 16 Abil Sîn	Sîn-gâmil, son Sîn-rîmêni (see G 4)	Nâḫilum	Plot	Êrishtum	
U 3 1 Sîn-muballit	Abiljatum	Nâḫilum	Warehouse	Namrâm, son Ili-zânini	Sîn-râbi, son Awîl-ilum (see G 25, 31)
G 18 2 Sîn-muballit	Children of Uḫḫum	Nâḫilum	Plot		Uratiya (see G 10, 13, 20) Nannar-magir (see G 15)
G 29 Sîn-muballit	Utetum	Nâḫilum	Plot	Nâḫilum	Son of Warad-martu (see G 15)
G 20 8 Sîn-muballit	Sîn-idinnam	Nâḫilum	Plot	Namraya Nâḫilum Sîn-idinnam	Uratiya (see G 10, 13, 18)
G 25 18 Sîn-muballit	Adalallum and Marduk-muballit exchange property (Adalallum, son of Awîl-ilum)		Plot	Nâḫilum Namraya Anni-ilum	Sîn-idinnam (G 20)
G31 18 Sîn-muballit	Adalallum	Nâḫilum	Plot	Nâḫilum Namraya Anni-ilum	Sîn-idinnam (G 20, 25)
G 36 3 Hammurabi	Marduk-ennam Urra-gâmil	Nâḫilum	Plot	Ippatum ? Nâḫilum	Ani-tukulti (G 12) Nabium-malik (G 15)

Note. In Figure 13, based on data from this table, G 16, 29, and 36 are not located precisely, but it will be seen that the position of the houses of the witnesses suggests their approximate position.

35

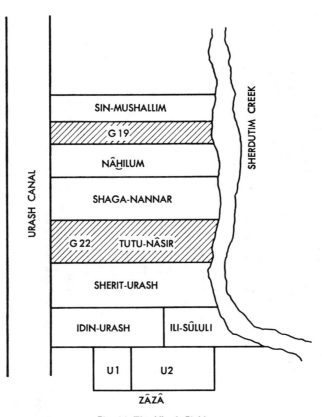

Fig. 14. The Urash Fields

(G22). These contracts are of especial interest because they show that the Urash fields were very close to the property bought by Idin-Lagamal early in the reign of Sumu-la-ilum (U1 and U2).[29] This is clear from the fact that Idin-Urash, whose field was adjacent to the property sold in U1 and U2, appears as a witness in G5, while Sherit-Urash, a witness in U2, was the owner of a field adjacent to the one that Nâhilum bought from Tutu-nâsir (G22).

Moreover, Nâhilum possessed fields in another area: that by the Adad Gate. A badly damaged tablet of the reign of Sîn-muballit mentions a field purchased by Nâhilum from Ibiq-ishhara (G24). The location of this property is clarified by a later tablet (G39) in which Eli-êrissa, daughter of Nâhilum, leased to her brother some 10 acres by the Adad Gate "beside the field of Ibiq-ishhara." In addition, Ili-mûdi, another child of Nâhilum, is known to have bought land in this same district in the eighteenth year of Sîn-muballit.[30] Finally, there is mention of a lawsuit brought by Nâhilum in connection with other property in this area (G35).[31]

The elevated status which Nâhilum must have attained in Dilbat, not only as a wealthy holder of town and agricultural property, but also as a responsible citizen is well illustrated by G32. Awîl-ilum, his neighbor, entrusted the sum of 10 shekels to Nâhilum—for safekeeping, or possibly for investment. This was in turn loaned at interest by Nâhilum to his brother, Shaga-Nannar; presumably both Nâhilum and Awîl-ilum lost nothing by this transaction.

The tablets even reveal a little of the family life of Nâhilum. One of his daughters, Eli-êrissa, became a Shamash-priestess, and we shall meet her again in the role of an accomplished business woman. The other daughter, Salatum, was married during the reign of Apil-Sîn. In the eighth year of that ruler, a marriage contract (G14) was drawn up between her father and a next-door neighbor, Ishme-Sîn.

Two of the four known children of Nâhilum, Ili-mûdi and Salatum, make only brief appearances.[32] Ili-mûdi very likely died young, and we do not know whether Salatum and her husband lived happily ever afterward and were blessed with many children. The other son and daughter of Nâhilum, however, are very much in evidence. Eli-êrissa had property of her own, presumably inherited since it was located in the Adad Gate and Urash canal districts (G39). In the twenty-eighth year of Hammurabi she arranged that her brother, Huzâlum, should cultivate nearly 14 acres of her land planting it in sesame and barley.[33] As we shall see later, Eli-êrissa lived on into the reign of Samsuiluna.

The picture which the contracts give of Huzâlum is one of a very substantial citizen indeed. His lease of Eli-êrissa's fields and his rental of an ox (presumably for draft purposes) in the twenty-fifth year of Hammurabi indicate that he was a farmer like most of the other Dilbat people,[34] but he was more successful than some of his neighbors. His annual tribute of 12 *gur* (about 50 bushels of grain) was large,[35] and he was in a position to loan seed grain to other people.[36] In addition to his wealth in land, Huzâlum had liquid capital and income property. We find him making a cash loan to a lady;[37] and he had property to rent: a house[38] and a barn.[39] We can almost see him comfortably established in Dilbat, sitting back and clipping his coupons (Babylonian style), and cutting quite a figure among the simple townsfolk. His prominent position may be indicated by the fact that often when his neighbors borrowed money to pay their harvest hands, Huzâlum was sought as a witness to their loan contracts.[40]

Eli-êrissa and Huzâlum, the principal representatives of the third generation, were obviously prosperous. It was they who enjoyed the real fruits of the industry of Idin-Lagamal and Nâhilum. The family fortunes were at their peak, and it is noteworthy that these children of Nâhilum were not straining to increase their holdings as their father and grandfather had done. They were well content with what they had.

A score of contracts dated early in the reign of Samsuiluna enable us to follow the family into the next generation after Hu-âlum. Eli-êrissa was still alive. She appeared as a witness to a loan contract in the first year of Samsuiluna,[41] and she continued to rent out her fields and gardens. Her field of nearly 4 acres in the Urash canal district which she had once leased to Huzâlum was not her only property there, for in the sixth year of Samuiluna we find her leasing an 11-acre "garden" to a man named Tarîbum. In the contract it was specified that 1 acre should be planted in sesame, but the plot also contained date palms.[42] In an undated contract Eli-êrissa borrowed nearly 5 bushels of seed grain, presumably to provide one of her renters with seed for the year.[43] This would imply an intention to plant at least 10 acres in barley.[44]

Sîn-bêl-ablim, one of the sons of Huzâlum, was a substantial landholder who possessed more than 24 acres.[45] He also rented out agricultural implements from time to time,[46] as did his brother, Marduk-nâsir.[47] The obvious wealth of Sîn-bêl-ablim points to him as the elder son of Huzâlum, but we are better informed about the activities of Marduk-nâsir. This second son had land of his own,[48] but it does not seem to have been enough to support him. Leases running from the third to the eighth years of Samsuiluna disclose that Marduk-nâsir was tilling other people's fields and also bringing new land under cultivation. He had inherited a portion of his father's holdings near the Gate of Adad,[49] and in the year 3 and year 6 he leased a neighboring field belonging to Samash-magir.[50] In the year 3, however, Marduk-nâsir borrowed about 8 bushels of seed grain;[51] thus, he intended to cultivate at least 16 acres that year—perhaps his own field and the one he had rented. In the year 4, he leased 3 acres from another neighbor,[52] and then, in the year 5, he leased 3 acres of unimproved land which he undertook to bring into full production in three years.[53] This latter contract is particularly significant because it means that, by the year 7, when Marduk-nâsir leased a field of 6 acres in the Misrum area,[54] he was responsible for the cultivation of 9 acres not his own. Apparently satisfied with this program, Marduk-nâsir leased an adjoining field in Misrum in year 8 and also took on a new plot of unimproved land for a 3-year period.[55] Apparently he had discovered a pattern of cultivation which he could follow with profit. His attainment of moderate prosperity is heralded by the fact that he was able to loan seed grain by the year 7,[56] just as his former straitened circumstances are implied by his earlier rental of a house (an indication that he did not have one of his own).[57]

Marduk-nâsir was not alone in his difficulties over land. By the time of Samsuiluna, the land seems to have become concentrated in the hands of large holders. Few sales are recorded in this late period except in the cases of large fields which go to the nobility. Leases, on the other hand, increase in number, and there is a decided effort to bring new land under cultivation. Thus, Marduk-nâsir was like many other younger sons whose inheritance was insufficient for their support.[58]

The fate of the family of Idin-Lagamal is shrouded in mystery after the fourth generation. Ili-idinnam, son of Tutu-nâsir, and Ili-idinnam's son, Idin-Lagamal (named after his great-grandfather), were contemporaries of Marduk-nâsir.[59] Urash-muballit, son of Marduk-nâsir and great-great-grandson of the first Idin-Lagamal, appears as a witness in three contracts of the reign of Samsuiluna,[60] and then the family disappears.

The family founded by Idin-Lagamal is interesting because its story epitomizes the economic history of Babylonia in the Age of Hammurabi. The experience of these four generations was not unique, but one which was shared with their contemporaries. The opportunities for agricultural expansion offered by the early years of the Amorite dynasty were seized by many little farmers, just as their sons were later pinched by the inheritance customs which turned big fields into little ones. The progressive concentration of the land in the hands of a few was virtually inevitable; it is an old story often repeated elsewhere in space and time. We have observed the unfolding of the plot here, and we really do not need the final chapters to guess how it turned out.

Notes

[1]The site of Dilbat bears the modern name of Dêläm, and the place is so unimportant that it does not even appear on ordinance maps. Dilbat was about 17 miles south of Babylon. Hammurabi spoke of the "plantations of Dilbat and the granaries of Urash" there. Rassam dug briefly at Dêläm in the late nineteenth century and brought out the first of the tablets on which this article is based; the others were found by natives and sold to dealers. Hormuzd Rassam, *Asshur and the Land of Nimrod* (New York, 1879), 265.

[2]Autographed texts of the Dilbat contracts may be found in M. J. E. Gautier, *Archives d'une famille de Dilbat* (Cairo, 1908; these texts are henceforth cited as G1, G2, etc.); in Arthur Ungnad, Vol. 7 of *Vorderasiatische Shriftdenkmäler* (Leipzig, 1909; cited henceforth as U1, U2, etc.); one tablet is recorded in the *Proceedings of the Society for Biblical Archaeology*, 29, 275–276 (1907; cited henceforth as PSBA); and there are two contracts in the British Museum series called *Cuneiform Texts from Babylonian Tablets*; one in Vol. 4 (cited here as CTIV46e), and one in Vol. 6 (cited here as CTVI48b). A few Dilbat texts are to be found in Françoise Thureau-Dangin, *Lettres et contrats de l'époque de la première babylonienne* (Musée du Louvre, *Textes cunéiformes*, t. 1, Paris, 1910), but none is applicable here.

In *Orientalistiche Literaturzeitung*, 13: 156–165, 204–210 (1910), Ungnad published a critical review of Gautier in which he corrected many readings. Ungnad also wrote a long commentary on the Dilbat material from VSVII (cited above) entitled "Urkunden aus Dilbat," in *Beiträge zur Asyriologie*, Vol. 6 (1909). Unfortunately, he concentrated his attention on the letters rather than the contracts.

Translations of the Dilbat tablets may be found scattered through Wilhelm Kohler and Arthur Ungnad, *Hammurabi's Gesetz* (Leipzig, 1904–1911), mostly in Vols. 3 and 4. Summaries of the tablets along with transliterations of witnesses' names were published (along with other contracts) in Ernest Lindl, *Das Priester- und Beamtentum der altbabylonischen Kontrakte* (*Studien zur Geschichte und Kultur des Altertums*, Vol. 2, Paderborn, 1913).

Neither the autographs nor the translations of the Dilbat tablets available in these various publications are completely reliable, as occasional comments in this article will show. Finally, three of the contracts (G30, G33, and G41) relating to the affairs of the family discussed here have been omitted because they do not relate to the main story.

[3]The chronological system here employed is that favored by Professor George G. Cameron, University of Michigan. There is now little doubt that Hammurabi reigned in the eighteenth century B.C. The birth of Idin-Lagamal is dated about 1900 B.C. because he was obviously an adult by the fourth year of Sumu-abum (c. 1876 B.C.). See footnote 9.

[4]Bêl-ilum is a witness in PSBA; Ahukinum in G4.

[5]The appearance of Bêl-ilum and Ahukinum as witnesses in PSBA and G4 respectively suggests that the family homestead was involved.

[6]For the topography of Dilbat, see Eckhard Unger, "Topographie der Stadt Dilbat," *Archiv Orientální*, 3: 21 *ff.* (Praha, 1931), and his article, "Dilbat," in *Reallexikon der Assyriologie*, 2: 218–225 (Berlin, 1935).

[7]Many of the date formulae for the age mention the building of canals, as does Hammurabi in his famous code. Archaeological evidence, chiefly the distribution of trade objects, is abundant.

[8]Bruno Meissner, "Warenpreise in Babylonien," *Abhandlungen der preussischen Akademie der Wissenschaften* (1936), 1–40.

[9]G1 dated in year 4 of Sumu-abum.

[10]"Acres" here refers to the Babylonian *ikû*, equal to about 9/10 of our acre.

[11]U1 and U2.

[12]The text of U1 is broken, but the price of 12 shekels paid by Idin-Lagamal for this field strongly suggests that it was smaller than the field in U2, which was an acre in extent, and for which he paid 30 shekels.

[13]G3.

[14]G9.

[15]G6.

[16]G5.

[17]see p. 33.

[18]He had bought at least an acre and a half from the sons of Hilum (U1 and U2), 10 to 20 acres from the sons of Nûr-ilishu, 18 in the Urash district. (When the Urash property was divided among his three sons, each appears to have 6 acres as in G22), and then he had his own fields inherited from Ili-amrâni. In G7 Idin-Lagamal seems to be leasing a field to a cultivator, but his is a little early (reign of Sumu-la-ilum) for a contract of this type; leases are much more common in the reign of Zabium. G8, which is badly broken, is sometimes referred to as a lease, but it could be a loan of seed grain.

[19]See footnote 5.

[20]PSBA dated in year 6 of Sumu-la-ilum.

[21]G4 dated in year 13 of Sumu-la-ilum.

[22]A glance at house plans from excavations at Babylon, Ur, and Nuzi will demonstrate this. The average size of rooms is 1 *sar*, while houses vary in size depending on the circumstances of the owner. Some Babylonian houses in the better district might run over 20 *sar*, while the average size of small houses at Nuzi was 4 *sar*.

[23]Awîl-ilum is a witness in G12, and his sons appear in U3, G25, and G31. Uratiya is a witness in G13, 18, and 20.

[24]Nîhilum became involved in a lawsuit over a house he had bought from Awil-Matim (G13). From the names of witnesses who appear in both G12 and G13, one may conclude that these properties were adjacent, while the fact that the name of Ibkusha appears in G12, 13, and 15 indicates that the first two properties (G12 and 13) were located near G15.

[25]G36.

[26]G11.

[27]Because of the poor transcription of the year date of G31 by Gautier, this contract has been consistently misdated. A comparison of G31 with G25 will show that they are both dated in the same year.

[28]See the sketch and also the accompanying table.

[29]G5. See p. 29. Other fields nearly may be the subject of G17 and 21.

[39]G23.

[31]The Adad district is definitely mentioned, and Ubariya appears as a witness in both G23 and G35.

[32]G23 and G14 respectively.

[33]G39. Three and three-fifths acres in the Urash and 10 in the Adad district.

[34]G45.

[35]G57.

[36]G61 and 64.

[37]U12.

[38]G28.

[39]G52.

[40]G59 and 60. Huzâlum also appears in G43, but the significance of this contract is not clear. This is also true of G54.

[41]CTVl48b.

[42]U27.

[43]CTIV46e.

[44]Bruno Meissner, *Babylonien und Assyrien* (Heidelberg, 1920–1925), 1: 195, gives the formula *30 Sila Saatgut auf 1 Ikû*, or 1/3 bushel of seed grain for 1 acre. Thus, Eli-êrissa may have anticipated planting as much as 15 acres, but 10 is the safer figure.

[45]G48 dated in year 6 of Samsuiluna.

[46]G49 and 50. He also appears as a witness in G55 and U21.

[47]U23.

[48]U26 and U40.

[49]U26.

[50]U17 and U26.

[51]U18.

[52]U19.

[53]U22.

[54]U29.

[55]U31 and 32.

[56]U30.

[57]U36.

[58]It is my intention to discuss these phases of Babylonian agriculture in a subsequent article.

[59]See U17, 22, 26, 29, 30, and 40.

[60]U31, 32, and 37.

FURTHER READING

The Origins of Writing, ed. Wayne Senner (Lincoln and London: University of Nebraska Press, 1989) is a collection of chapters by scholars describing the nature and origin of the major writing systems in the Near East, Far East, Europe, and Central America. Marcus N. Tod, a distinguished student of ancient inscriptions, presented a series of three lectures that remain an excellent introduction to the subject. The lectures, entitled "Sidelights on Greek History," were originally published in Oxford in 1932. They have been reprinted by Ares Publishers in 1974. While the focus is Greek antiquity, the general observations are equally pertinent to other cultures.

Chapter 2 of *Sources for Ancient History*, ed. Michael Crawford (Cambridge; Cambridge University Press, 1983) is a useful survey of epigraphy by Fergus Millar.

Chapter Three

Nestor
and the Decipherment
of Linear B

When we examined Lascaux we saw how the evidence of archaeology allows us to make a picture from the material remains of human activity. We saw the kind of chronology it allows us—a relative one, distinguishing earlier and later stages in a certain activity at a certain site. We found we could suggest the rough and intriguing lines of several narratives from these stages—made up stages determined by combining varying parts from painstaking detective work, anthropology, and sensitive imagination. But we could not settle, using the evidence gathered by these methods, upon a single narrative.

Dilbat on the Euphrates gave us more than physical evidence, since it has also provided written records. Knowing precise dates and specific facts for a past culture, we were able to begin telling a story with some real detail. Best of all, a combination of these telltale clues becomes possible. The Babylonian tablets can show us the form and the importance of property ownership among the ancient cities of Mesopotamia: physical evidence can show us better than any text just how a house was shaped, how it was set into its lot or wedged among others along a street, or how a plot of land was farmed. Together the two evidences, physical and written, say more than either can alone.

But what if we can add yet further sorts of evidence to the mix? Suppose we were able to add to our picture some of the authentic surviving "patterned memory" and metaphor through the poetic clues of an ancient culture. We should then not only know from tablets, inscriptions, and physical items what things were like, but also be able to add some sense of how things were experienced by a people, and how they were recalled.

We now turn to a particularly vivid illustration of what archaeology and inscriptions might show us when we can weave them together with the historical components of stories handed on by a culture down through generations—even over centuries—in poetic form.

The Greek Bronze Age (2000 - 1000)

Date B.C.	Mycenaean, Minoan Events	Around the Mediterranean	Artifacts & Art
2000 -	Advancing Minoan civilization in Crete. Sharp decline in mainland Greece.	(c. 1800) Arrival of Indo-Europeans and the horse in Greece and Asia Minor?	(c. 1600) Mycenaean culture producing early "Cyclopean" walls. The Shaft Graves at Mycenae. "Antique" Mycenaean weapons; boar's tooth helmets and "tower shields." Minoan and Mycenaean cultures producing records in "Linear" scripts (A, and later B).
	(c.) Eruption of the island of Thera in the Aegean; many centers in northern Crete destroyed or damaged (c. 1600). (c. 1600) Rise of Late Bronze Age culture in Greece.	(c. 1570) The Hyksos driven out of Egypt; beginning of the "New Kingdom." (c. 1450) Beginning of the Hittite empire in Anatolia.	
1500 -	(c. 1500) Damage to many palace-centers in Crete. Evidence of Mycenaean culture appears on Cyprus. (- 1425) High point of Minoan influence and wealth; centers like Knossos flourish. (c. 1400 - 1380) Palace-center of Knossos on Crete destroyed by fire.	(c. 1390) The Assyrians emerge as an independent power in Mesopotamia. (c. 1375) Suppiluliumas begins to consolidate Hittite rule across Asia Minor. (c. 1377 - 1358) Reign and monotheistic experiments of Akhnaton (Ahmenhotep IV) in Egypt.	(c. 1425) Use of bronze plate armor in the region of Mycenae (a suit discovered at Dendra). (c. 1400) Bronze helmets in use on Crete (discovery at Knossos).
1250 -	(c. 1250) Legendary era of Nestor's reign in Pylos.	(c. 1300) Phoenician wealth flourishes at port city of Sidon. (c. 1300 - 1250) Destruction of "Troy VI" at Hisarlik in Asia Minor (by earthquake?). (c. 1250) Approximate date of the Israelite exodus under Moses.	(c. 1300 - 1250) The Mycenae "Lion Gate" and true Cyclopean walls constructed. Mycenaean rulers buried in beehive-shaped "tholos" tombs.
	(c. 1200) Destruction of many Mycenaean palaces in Greece. The end of "Nestor's" Pylos. Disastrous poverty and depopulation in Greece.	(c. 1260 - 1225) Destruction of "Troy VII," probably the "Homeric" city (by Mycenaean siege? or marauders?).	(c. 1200) The Mycenaean "Warrior Vase" showing the development of common spear infantry in light, nonmetallic armor.
	(c. 1050) Last evidences of dying Mycenaean culture. (c. 1045) Legendary death of Codrus, last true king of Athens (his family supposed to have been refugees from Pylos).	(c. 1197 - 1165) Rameses III defends Egypt against northern attack (by the "Sea Peoples"). 1112 - 1074 Waning power of Assyria restored under Tiglath-Pileser I.	The Iron Age slowly begins in Greece (after a period from which almost no evidence survives). (c.) Protogeometric pottery in Greece.
1000 -		1006 The reign of David begins at Jerusalem.	

Our attempt will be to see if (like the themes of a fugue) they will make for us a single composition. Historians have indeed had this third sort of evidence for a very long time, much longer than they have had any really scientific archaeology or any sizeable collection of inscriptions. But, they had merely consigned these stories to the realm of entertainment. What might we gain in "exact" data if we gave these tales of war, or love, or adventure—the authentic creative imagination of ancient poets—an intelligent hearing?

Our example comes from a kingdom that throve upon the frontiers of the Bronze Age in Greece. Since their classical era in the fifth century B.C., the Greeks had traced their ancestry to an older, more heroic age. A single man could in those earlier days lift a stone whose weight would make three later Greeks totter and fall. The events that forged the history of those times were wondrous ones, and the most memorable of these was a war, waged somewhere in Asia by the mightiest of men and gods, around the stone-knit walls of the citadel of Troy.

Helen, the most lovely of all women, had been stolen away by Paris, son the Trojan king. Menelaus, the jilted husband, was a prince of the house at Atreus; the head of his clan rose from his throne in the citadel of Mycenae to arm his Achaean allies and bring Helen back. Two long epic poems spun around the tale of this abduction were attributed to a single poet—Homer—recounting the conflict and the wanderings of its aftermath. The *Iliad's* twenty-four books detail some fifty-three days out of the last year in the Greeks' ten-year siege of Troy. Still more odd, they close before the war did: though one can feel in the fiber of the *Iliad* that by its end Troy is doomed, the real defeat is still waiting, off-stage, when the curtain comes down. The *Odyssey* follows the return of a few surviving Greek warriors, most especially the frontiersman Odysseus.

The Greeks had few historical doubts about the reality of Homer's depicted world, though they were aware they knew very little about their remote past. As a consequence, scholars until our own century agreed almost unanimously that Homer had "re-created" a nonexistent way of life. He had himself lived in the eighth century B.C.—some centuries after the collapse of the Bronze Age—and had "projected" his tale into the dim, revered past, magnifying and poetizing the life he knew around him.

It was the archaeologists, as they began poking seriously among the prehistoric remains of the Aegean world, who began to raise doubts among all this smug certainty. The most crucial (and still perhaps the most controversial) contribution came from a German amateur named Heinrich Schliemann, who set out doggedly to hunt the material basis of the world described in the *Iliad* and the *Odyssey*. Taking Homer as his guide to the geography of northwestern Asia Minor (a corner of Turkey still called "the Troad"), he found a hill called Hisarlik set back by a small floodplain from the shores of the Hellespont. When he dug into it, he discovered layers of prehistoric habitation beginning as early as 3000 B.C. and running through the centuries (or up through the strata of the hill) for the entire two millennia of the Bronze Age, and even beyond. Heartened by this success (and ignoring some very loud skeptics), he crossed the Aegean to Greece, searching at the prompting of his well-thumbed Homer for the citadels of the Achaean heroes. There he excavated both Mycenae and Tiryns, unearthing fabulous sites almost as ancient and equally complex as that at Hisarlik.

What Schliemann began a host of excavators continued, though not always with results so rich in treasure and legend. But results can also be rich with suggestion: the Bronze Age archaeology of the Greek world has established that although Mesopotamia

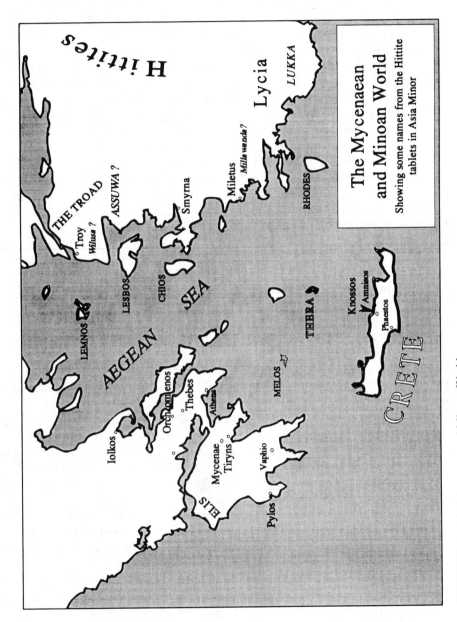

FIGURE 3–1 The Mycenean and Minoan World

and Egypt held the earliest civilizations, they were not the only lands to develop complex and creative cultures over the 2,000-odd years of that era. Indeed, the very richness of the Mesopotamian and Egyptian cultures drew curious travelers from other cultures toward them like magnets. Traders came in peace. Would-be conquerors came in war. Mesopotamians and Egyptians themselves pushed into new areas as their needs for raw materials and their own growing populations moved them. In the rugged lands of Anatolia (modern-day Turkey)—rich in timber and minerals—a network of trading centers sprang up in which the arts of civilization went to work and disseminated further west. In a few places, far from the old river-valley cities, the same forces that had fueled their complex and rising cultures began to create others, each as unique as the locale in which it grew.

In every case, the pattern of life—though it varied each time in detail—included many familiar features. The states that grew largest and fastest were soon coordinated by kings, and the kings drew help from an expanding structure of administrators. Large, diverse populations meant strata: a large peasant base made the bedrock of society, a middle class of specialists busied themselves with the more diverse tasks, and a powerful upper stratum exercised its wealth to employ slaves. Life was still founded upon agriculture and herding (though city folk might see less of it than they once did). Craft production, local trade, and commerce between regions quickened the pace of life in the community. When the competition of cultures grew ugly, they brought their new-found technologies into war. The eastern Mediterranean of the Bronze Age reeled again and again from the clash of growing and ever more sophisticated armies as borders began to clash against one another, and as commercial princes tried to protect their merchants.

A mingling of these processes might explain why a complex civilization began to emerge among the unlikely little islands of the Aegean. The first advances may have come in the south (in the Cyclades), where bronze technology and seafaring had been in active swing since about 3000 B.C. More startling in the longer term was the more durable trading culture that arose on the large island of Crete, where seafaring immigrants from southwestern Anatolia had begun to form communities around 6000 B.C. Farming villages gradually spread from east to west, but the newcomers never forgot their original interest in the sea. Both ends of the Mediterranean soon grew familiar with the sight of the slender Cretan trading ships, and it now seems from the archaeological remains that there was hardly a place in the Bronze Age world to which some Cretan did not sail.

By 3000 B.C., the island was sprinkled thickly with ordered and bustling communities of respectable size. They had reached an economic specialization remarkable even by Mesopotamian standards, and they carried on formal relations with the greatest states that fringed the Mediterranean. Slowly, like stars collapsing into clusters, these seem to have coalesced into kingdoms, and finally into the brilliant and centralized palace-centered realms that mark the island's history after 2000 B.C.

The Greek mainland, where almost every necessity of life had to be wrung with effort from the land and where the land's very ruggedness discouraged interaction, developed slower. Farming and the keeping of animals advanced stubbornly onward, but several bad seasons in such a land could undo years of advances, and around 2000 B.C. the region hit a sharp decline. By 1600 B.C., though, for reasons that are still in part mysterious, the same qualities that mark the other high cultures of the Bronze Age spring suddenly out of the darkness in Greece. We call the Late Bronze Age of Greece the Mycenaean Era because

Mycenae was one of the first and richest Greek sites of that time to have been excavated. As in Crete, though, there were many fortress centers, and the strength and commercial prowess of some became legendary. The time was remembered by later Greeks as the Age of Heroes, so magnificent were the things it accomplished and the heirlooms it left behind.

One of the most rewarding finds began to come to light above the sandy-shored southwest corner of the Peloponnese in 1939. Archaeologists there, slowed by the troubles of the World War II, had uncovered by the early 1950s what must surely be the most aesthetically coherent and impressive building complex produced by the Bronze Age civilization of Greece. Out of the scorched rubble of the site (it had been destroyed by fire), the archaeologists turned up scores of clay tablets imprinted with strange signs and these, with luck and at cost of great effort, were deciphered. They had been mysteries: decipherment made them inscriptions dating to the very years in which the kingdom there had flourished.

The work of archaeologists in the stone and soil of Greece had made it undeniable that sophisticated civilizations had risen and died there long before the classical era. It remained possible to deny, ignoring certain "happy accidents" of location, that Homer's poetry described such a civilization. After all, if an actual Trojan War had been fought in the last part of the second millennium B.C., accounts of it could only have been passed on by word of mouth for the next five centuries. There was no writing in which to preserve them. Now, as anyone might guess who has played the game of passing a sentence round a circle by repeating it person-to-person, a great deal of distortion could have occurred in 500 years. Anything might have happened to the tale.

Our present task is to look more closely at the evidence uncovered for that kingdom in the southwestern Peloponnese, archaeological and inscriptional, and to ask what relation it might bear to a kingdom ascribed in the works of Homer to "Nestor"—a respected and garrulous old statesman in the *Iliad* and *Odyssey,* who sent a large contingent to the war against Troy, and who came along himself to share his wisdom in battle. Do the two make one picture?

NESTOR

> *Nestor,*
> *the fair-spoken rose up, the lucid speaker of Pylos,*
> *from whose lips the stream of words ran sweeter than honey.*
> *In his time two generations of mortal men had perished,*
> *those who had grown up with him and they who had been born to*
> *these in sacred Pylos, and he was king in the third age.*
> (Lattimore, trans. *Iliad* 1.247–52)

Those are the words we have inherited from Homer describing one of the older (and perhaps one of his favorite) Greek warriors fighting at Troy. Nestor was not only an elder among the veterans at the long siege, but also he was unusual because he would survive the war and return to Greece. Not many of his companions would be so lucky. He thus lived on (poetically) to play a part in the second Homeric epic, which picks up a few of the melancholy threads left scattered by the war's end. Telemachos, Odysseus' son, has begun to worry about his father: the war has been some while over and Odysseus has not yet returned. Rounding a cape of the Peloponnese, the son's small ship cuts through the blue water toward the long beaches of the kingdom of Pylos where the king, surrounded by a host of his folk, is making sacrifice on the sand.

The voyagers now lay off Pylos town,
compact stronghold of Neleus. On the shore
black bulls were being offered by the people
to the blue-maned god who makes the islands tremble:
nine congregations, each five hundred strong,
led out nine bulls apiece to sacrifice,
taking the tripes to eat, while on their altars
thighbones in fat lay burning for the god.
                        (Fitzgerald, trans. *Odyssey* 3.4–9)

It was by his age that Nestor had acquired wisdom and authority enough to mediate the quarrel between Agamemnon and Achilles that flares in the first pages of the *Iliad*. By his long life he had accumulated a great store of memories, and Homer seems to love describing his eagerness to share them if only someone will listen. "I remember when..." or "If only I were as young as..." are all we need to warn us that Nestor feels a reminiscence rising within him. And yet Homer, or tradition, has remembered him with more affection than mockery. Though he moves in a world of nobility who swagger and flare at insults, his manners are impeccable in both the *Iliad* and *Odyssey*: he has an easy grace that Agamemnon never learns. In the *Odyssey* he is kindly to family and visitor alike and obviously is much loved. So, too, is he respected for the wealth and grandeur of his kingdom:

Lord Nestor of Gerenia, charioteer,
left his room for a throne of polished stone,
white and gleaming as though with oil, that stood
before the main gate of the palace; Neleus here
had sat before him—masterful in his kingship,
Neleus, long ago a prey to death, gone down
to the night of the underworld.
So Nestor held his throne and scepter now,
lord of the western approaches to Akhaia.
                        (Fitzgerald, trans. *Odyssey* 3.405–12)

This is the image painted by the epic poetry that we call Homer's. We can flesh it out from other "traditional" sources. We learn that Nestor's father, Neleus, was a prince of Thessaly, a land on the northern frontier of Bronze Age Greece, just as Pylos lies on its western frontier. He quarrelled with his brother Pelias, a vicious character with a knack for murder and treachery, who tallied among his victims the parents of that Jason who sailed to find the Golden Fleece. Knowing his brother's way of solving disputes, Neleus thought it safer to settle elsewhere. He married Chloris, daughter of the rich king of Orchomenos, and set off for Pylos on the shore of the western seas, where he defeated an existing king and began a dynasty of his own. Chloris bore twelve sons to Neleus, but they fell under the wrath of Herakles, for the hot-tempered hero had come before their father under blood-guilt of murder, and Neleus refused to absolve him. Only Nestor survived.

For Herakles had come in his strength against us and beaten us
in the years before, and all the bravest among us had been killed.
For we who were sons of lordly Neleus had been twelve, and now
alone was left of these, and all the others had perished.
                        (Lattimore, trans. *Iliad* 11. 689 *ff.*)

Few people have ears dull enough to deny the color and adventure in these stories, but there are many who would dismiss them when the historian begins gathering his proper evidence together. They argue that accounts of the past so filled with the huge forms and footsteps of epic characters exist only because such characters make them lively where they once were dull. History, they say, is the sum of nameless people doing unremarkable things. If it is exciting, you may suspect it is untrue. Adding the grand shapes of heroic men and women to these plodding historical processes may "lift" them in the primitive imagination, but it gets us no closer to real events or objects. Can we seriously expect to forge a chain that would link the tangible facts of archaeology with these tall characters of tradition?

Such arguments are valid. The tales are tall ones. And yet epic tradition is one of the few kinds of information that survives from antiquity; since our data are so limited we should be foolish to cast epic out of our toolkit if we could find any truth embedded in it. Nestor makes an especially fine example of this since archaeology has uncovered the solid remains of the kingdom attributed to him, among them a hoard of clay tablets into which are impressed accounts of the minute details of its operation. It is as we begin to mingle or weave these sources together that we are able to answer the questions about valid evidence. Thus, the oral tradition undeniably gives us a feel for the minds of those Greeks who preserved and retold the tales, but if it is to bear any weight at the real bar of history it must be confirmed by the other sources. Without them, it is fable, even if it is grand or plausible fable.

If, however, we could take archaeological evidence and administrative records from several ancient locations and find upon them names like Nestor, Agamemnon, or Odysseus, those names might become candidates for real people of the Bronze Age. They may conceivably have ruled real kingdoms of ancient Greece even though we do not possess any actual lists of kings. And, in fact, on one of the clay tablets inscribed during the late Bronze Age, there is a name that can be read as "Achilles."

So one way to test the accuracy of the traditional names is by the physical evidence. If we then take those traditional accounts and lay them side by side with archaeological findings, our description of the Bronze Age kings and kingdoms gets a second dimension: location. Archaeology has been able to place many of the sites mentioned in the epics "on the map."

The Homeric poems and old traditions are clear in placing Nestor's kingdom somewhere along the southwestern coasts of the Peloponnese, in a region known as Messenia. The trouble was that during the early decades of investigation no one could find a trace of such a place. Today we have archaeological evidence pointing at a kingdom, slowly unifying over the late Bronze Age, which is regularly attributed to Nestor. We may indeed go into some detail. From the fifteenth and fourteenth centuries B.C. (the early Mycenaean Era), we have physical data showing the region was divided among various small sites. During the fourteenth century B.C., we can see construction commence on the first palace complex at Englianos (fairly certainly identified as Pylos): control is beginning to expand from the palace center and supercede, or at least heavily modify, the authority of the local towns.

We can now tell that the kingdom was a sizeable one. South and west along the peninsula it had, of course, the limit of the seacoast; inland it ran eastward to the ridge of the Taygetos mountain range, and northward (where the Alpheios river valley gave it an easy route of expansion) it pushed as far as the banks of the Nedha. It thus could lay claim to some 1,400 square miles, and within that a person might get around with some ease

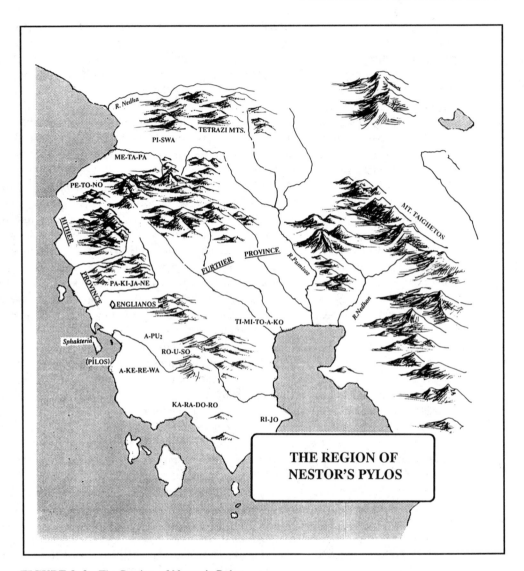

FIGURE 3-2   The Region of Nestor's Pylos

along a network of "roads" or improved trails. These linked the most important towns with one another, and linked them all with Pylos. The best of these (though not, of course, all) were constructed to carry wheeled vehicles.

In the fourteenth century Messenia had a total population of around 16,000 people living in 120 villages. By the thirteenth century there were almost 200 of these villages, and at least 41,000 people. Settlements had been increasing in number and size almost continuously since the early Bronze Age. We may explain some of this growth by noting how secure the region was, both as a place to shelter pioneers and as a defensible kingdom. Villagers felt safe enough, judging by the evidence left behind, to move in groups from more isolated hilltops inland down to more accessible townsites nearer the sea and along the valley trails. Over the 350 years from the early Bronze Age to the kingdom's height the number of coastal towns doubled.

Traveling along the road eastward from Pylos toward the high country, one would have passed through village after village, each supporting around 200 people. As the Pylos district's population grew denser, it pushed out into nearby river valleys, clearing forested land for new village sites. Even more timber fell to create new farmland.

We can tell from the remains of bones that these "Pylian" settlers raised large herds of sheep and goats, along with some horses, oxen, and pigs. Some herds were small—on the scale of a family farm—while other concentrations of animals ran far larger. The villages in which the bulk of the population lived each controlled about 1500 hectares of land (1 hectare equals 2.47 acres), and of this, the best and nearest land went under heavy cultivation for grain—most of it (judging from the preserved pollen) being barley and some wheat. On less fertile land, tree crops (like the olive) and vines were the rule. Flax, which was rather less usual for Greece, grew in the well-watered (and probably closely watched) land that lay around the capital of the kingdom.

Flax means linen, of course—for clothing, light armor, and perhaps household use—but there were other specialized crafts. In many of the villages one could have found a furnace, for baking clay or for the melting of copper and tin ingots imported from other regions. These last are significant: Greece (then as now) was poor in metal resources, meaning that making any extensive use of them required traveling out of the country—sometimes great distances—to obtain them. The investment required shows that Pylos was obviously a kingdom of some means.

Archaeologists have followed the movement of these economic resources (aided by the account books preserved among the clay tablets) enough to see that activities like farming, the crafting of objects, and their sale were largely directed by authorities in central locations. Orders went out from the "center"; things were grown, or made, or processed; products were brought back to the "center." By the thirteenth century, these "centers" were palaces which owed much of their shape and design to architectural techniques borrowed from Minoan Crete. Most Mycenaean Greek palaces were fortified almost like bunkers: Pylos seems to have been without a wall. It is true that the fairly steep hill, together with the heavy exterior walls of the buildings, may have provided some reasonable defense. In any case, the largest structure atop the Englianos hill was a large mud-brick and timber-walled complex of two stories, rather geometric in its style, with several smaller buildings scattered around it.

The grand entrance was on the south. One passed a guardhouse and then plunged through a columned walkway into one of the palace courtyards. Directly ahead rose the tall nucleus of the palace: the *megaron*. This was a big, oblong decorated "hall" (in the same sense, almost, that medieval castles had "halls") with a fine, circular hearth in the center. Four columns rose from around the hearth to a skylight in the roof. Down each side of the *megaron* ranged a long corridor, doorways leading out from each into a multitude of chambers and storerooms. Stairways rose also from each side toward the second story, where the living quarters were. Its walls were decorated, enlivened by a profusion of bright, stylized frescoes. Floors were decorated, too. Baths, fed by running water connected to an elaborate drainage system, cooled (and cleared) the atmosphere of Pylos.

FIGURE 3–3   A reconstruction of the spacious nucleus or *megaron* of "Nestor's" palace (following Piet De Jong), giving some hint of the vivid decoration. A myriad of bright patterns must have brightened the political and ritual uses of the room. Smoke rose and light fell through the columnal opening in the roof.

Around this sunlit edifice stood a wine-storehouse, a palace workshop, and the "old palace" built a generation before the building we just examined. It still had its uses: the kitchens were there, themselves probably much expanded by wealthy times. The quantity and quality of goods throughout the complex convince us eloquently that this is more than a residence: it governs the creation of goods, the ebb and flow of raw materials and crafted products as they collect and are disbursed through the kingdom of Pylos, and into the outside world. Archaeologists have found, for example, one cupboard that contained more than 6,000 undecorated cups, drinking goblets, and bowls. The storage area for olive oil was crowded, row upon row, with great, elongated vessels known as *pithoi*.

This kind of archaeological evidence gives a sort of concrete, bustling color to our picture of a Mycenaean kingdom that we should never have had from the legendary sources. We can reconstruct from it, at least in general outline, the way in which people lived during the second millennium B.C. We would still, of course, not know names. But we have yet a third category of evidence to add to the mix: the written records which were preserved during the last days of the palace, preserved in fact by the disaster which destroyed it. Pylos is, to put it plainly, the source of the greatest single quantity of written evidence found at any mainland Bronze Age site. We have now unearthed on the mainland of Greece approximately 1,200 clay tablets that bear inscriptions in the writing system known as Linear B, and 1,070 of those have come from Pylos.

The existence of all this written evidence is not really, by the standards of modern archaeology, very recent news. Sir Arthur Evans was discovering inscribed clay tablets as he excavated Knossos at the beginning of this century. Carl Blegen found some Linear B tablets on the mainland in the very first trench he dug at Pylos in 1939, though it was not until 1952 that the numbers there were truly appreciated. Pylos began to be completely excavated in that year, and it proved to be full of tablets—so full that they helped by their very numbers to push open another door.

So much has been made of their decipherment that we should first acknowledge those things which the tablets told us about the Bronze Age world immediately, before their inscriptions could be read. We could associate them with palaces, and that meant administration. Administration at such sites (as opposed to mere military force) meant, in turn, the sort of complex organized structure for Bronze Age kingdoms that we had already begun to suspect from the archaeological record. The script, moreover, was the same on the mainland as it was on several places in Crete, making us look for some relationship between them. What we did not know were the details: the meaning and specifics of each administration or their relationship to each other would have to wait for decipherment.

Efforts had been made to unlock the secrets of the inscriptions since their discovery, but none made much progress during the first half of the century. The Mycenaean tablets had no Rosetta Stone—no convenient text on which the undeciphered characters or hieroglyphics could lie parallel with some known language like classical Greek. As if this were not bad enough, most of the clay tablets are in very poor condition, there have never been very many to work with, and very few of those contain the long combinations of symbols one would want for determining syntax. On top of this, the material from Knossos (about which everyone had heard) was kept from publication for many years. The surprising thing is that despite all this some initial hurdles were cleared anyway.

One place to start was simply classifying the material. There were three main kinds of symbols on the tablets: some were recognizable pictures of objects, others were obviously a method of counting—vertical and horizontal bars, circles, circles with rays. The third group were the signs that were neither pictograms nor numerals: with any luck they would represent sounds (they would, that is, be phonemes). Once collected and counted there turned out to be about ninety different forms in this last category. The good news was that scholars were not dealing with a kind of hieroglyphics—ninety forms are too few for a sign to represent a word; the bad news was that it also could not be a manageable alphabet—ninety forms are too many to reasonably represent the consonants and vowels utterable by the human mouth. This left scholars with the likelihood that they had a syllabary, each sign representing either a pure vowel or a consonant plus a vowel. The actual decipherment proved this true.

The next logical probability was that the three types of symbols were related to one another, the numbers perhaps indicating how many of the objects shown in the pictogram an ancient scribe had just counted. Granting this possibility for a moment, and adding the fact that all the tablets seemed to be turning up in palaces, it became reasonable to suppose that they were inventories.

An American scholar named Alice Kober cleared the next obstacle in the 1940s. She detected patterns in the groups of symbols, especially at the beginnings and ends of groups, and concluded that she was dealing with an inflected language. Root words, that is, were being modified by prefixes and suffixes to indicate such things as gender, number, tense, case, person, and mood. Not all languages vary in such predictable ways, of course, and so Kober had placed an encouraging limit on the range of possibilities.

The actual "cracker" of the code was a British architect named Michael Ventris. He had been intrigued since his boyhood by cryptography, and had served his apprenticeship as a decoder during World War II. In 1951, Ventris was able to lay his hands upon newly published descriptions of the Pylos tablets prepared by an American named Emmett Bennett. He also had the help of the British philologist John Chadwick. Building upon the earlier probabilities, he tried assigning values to the individual signs to see what sort of results he got, taking care to build a grid as the likelihood of his identifications increased. This process may sound random, but it was not. One important clue is always the general frequency of certain sounds in any language— pure vowels, for example, occur very often at the beginnings of words but very seldom in the middle. He took it as probable that two signs on the Linear B tablets might be "a" and "e." He found another hint on Cyprus, where a syllabic form of writing had continued in use right down into the classical period. Seven of the symbols in that script looked a lot like symbols in Linear B. One could always suppose a direct Bronze Age link between the scripts because archaeologists knew that the Mycenaeans had first traded with, and later settled on Cyprus.

All this was of some help, but Ventris had a better clue in Kober's guess that the language was inflected. If she were right, he ought to find a repeating pattern in certain of the syllabic forms used to alter tense, or person, or number in the various root words.

As Ventris worked, and his series of grids became increasingly complex, he developed the habit of circulating a series of "working notes" on his research among a dozen or so sympathetic scholars. When he began these unorganized "roundtables" he was working on the belief (encouraged by the script) that the language of Linear B was related to Etruscan. By "Work Note Twenty," he had begun to suspect that he was on the trail not of Etruscan, but of Greek. Interviewed on a BBC program in June of 1952, he said, "During the last few weeks I have come to the conclusion that the Knossos and Pylos tablets must, after all, be written in Greek—a difficult and archaic Greek, seeing that it is 500 years older than Homer and written in a rather abbreviated form, but Greek nonetheless."

Ventris did not persuade everyone with this conclusion, and he shocked some. The attacks were swift in coming. "Critics," wrote Sterling Dow, "worked themselves up into a truly Baconian frame of mind, making charges which in the realm of truth (not to mention that of decency) were a hundred times more improbable than anything they could find to attack" (1968:135). But evidence, a tiny piece here and a tiny piece there, began

FIGURE 3–4   The "Tripod Tablet" inscribed with the curvilinear characters of Linear B gave Michael Ventris strong evidence that he was on the right track to cracking the code. Note the number of legs and handles on the objects in the top row particularly. (The accountant was making sure his employer knew precisely the sort of objects being inventoried.)

to weigh in on the side of Ventris. Carl Blegen wrote to Ventris from his ongoing excavations at Pylos in May of 1953 about a particular Linear B tablet:

> "It obviously deals with pots, some on three legs, some with four handles, some with three, and others without handles. The first word by your system seems to be *ti-ri-po-de* and it recurs twice as *ti-ri-po* (singular?). The four-handled pot is preceded by *qe-to-ro-we* [four-eared or four-handled], the three-handled *ti ri-o-we* or *ti-ri-jo-we* [three-eared or three-handled]. The handleless pot by a-no-we [without ears or handles]. All this seems too good to be true. Is coincidence excluded?" (quoted by Chadwick, 1958 and 1967:25)

The complaints of the critics have diminished (though they have not quite gone away), so that at last, more than forty years after Ventris announced it, we may accept with most scholars the essential correctness of his identification. Linear B is Greek.

And so we may at last add the information of the tablets to our picture of the Bronze Age kingdoms, giving it a richness impossible with only the legends, or with only the archaeology, or even with both. We can say with certainty that the "world of Nestor" (if so specific a king actually lived to see it from the porches of Pylos) was a world of Greek-speaking peoples, whose culture was complex enough to require their keeping constant records. That they participated in both economic and military affairs with other contemporary cultures will have given further intricacies to their lives, and they may have taken from those civilizations' models upon which they developed their own, Greek, administrative records.

These records were inventories after all, rather like those painstaking lists we compile as tax reports for the Internal Revenue Service. They seem to compile everything: people, livestock, agricultural produce, ownership and use of the land, tribute, ritual offerings, textiles, vessels, furniture, metals, military equipment. The list begins to seem both exhaustive and exhausting. One tablet can be extremely specific—a single wheel together with three pairs of wheels made of willow. Others detail chariots without wheels, adding sometimes that they are painted, or inlaid, or dismantled, or assembled, or even assembled in part! A great many tablets distinguish different kinds of cloth, ticking off the amount, color, and quality, or perhaps the fact that it has been made into a certain kind of garment. There is a particular category of tablet that informs us about offerings to the gods, for the gods are jealous and far-seeing, and expect good value in their gifts. We suspect that every year, in a certain month, a specific quantity of honey was offered in a good jar to the Earth-shaker, and once it was offered someone made a note on a tablet.

All this detail may lend new depth to our knowledge of the material culture, but it is the longer texts, dealing as they can with more complex topics, that are truly intriguing. An important tablet from Pylos lists the landholdings of certain primary officials, and in doing so it casts an offhand light on its society. A landholding is a *te-me-no*. *Temenos* in classical Greek indicated a special cut of land. At the top of the landholding list is the *wanax*, his allotment calculated at 3,600 liters of wheat. Next comes the *temenos* of the *lawagetas*, who gets 1,200 liters. Below the blank line which follows are three *telestai*, who may divide 3,600 liters among them. Finally there is a rather difficult kind of landholding—Ventris and Chadwick guess at a cult association—which is allowed 720 liters. Luckily these words persisted into the classical period, and (allowing for the sharp changes time can force upon common usage) we can supply a meaning for each: *wanax* is likely to be "king"; *lawagetas* "war leader"; *telestai*, perhaps "service men" (either in the religious sense as Chadwick originally thought or in one of the secular functions which he later favored).

This suggests a great deal. We can first of all confirm an impression first made upon us by the archaeology that these were truly palaces—centers of kingdoms ruled by kings and their subsidiary officials. To the military sound of these officials we can add another long Pylos tablet detailing guardsmen and lookouts along the coast. Individuals are listed in military groups, under the command of specific persons at specific locations. Ampelitawon, Orestas, Etewas, and Kokkion, for example, belong at *O-wi-to-no* and should be following the orders of Maleus. According to the next line they should be able to make use of 50 *su-we-ro-wi-jo* men, and though we are not sure what kind of men those were, we have no doubt about where they belonged. The military clerks and nobles of Pylos ran a tight ship.

Even when we do not know the details, we can weave together information from a number of tablets and begin to sketch out the organization of the kingdom. The holders of titles such as *wanax*, *lawagetas*, and *telestai* all appear to have been connected with the palaces, which is only to say that their duties seem to have applied to the kingdom as a whole, and not merely to some small part of it. There were of course lesser officials who exercised authority only in outlying regions. Again the tablets help us with details.

The kingdom had two "provinces": a "Hither" (meaning the western one, nearer the capital), and a "Further" (probably to the east, around the Gulf of Messenia). The Hither Province had in it nine districts (each noted by the name of its principal town), and the Further Province had seven. An official called a *ko-ro-te* seems to have been something like a provincial governor, with a *po-ro-ko-re-te* as an assistant. Interestingly, it is an official even lower than these whose name strikes the deepest chord among scholars of the later Greek world. Far down the hierarchy, pressing his tiny authority in his minor and very local position was the *pa2-si-re-u* or *basileus*, ruling his little retinue, or household. Later in Greek times, when the common wisdom "knew" that the arrogance of ancient men who called themselves *wanax* had brought down the wrath of Zeus upon the Mycenaean world, it was considered too chancy to use the old royal title any longer. A man who wished to be king played it safe and called himself "basileus."

The common thread that runs through these officials from top of the ladder to bottom is the fact that they all were responsible for managing their part of the economy of the kingdom. A Mycenaean principality was in a sense almost perilously like the modern one a "business." The tablets are full of central controllers governing the use of land, of natural resources, of labor, and of finished products. Slaves would seem to have been numerous (mention of them appears constantly), and they were assigned to a wide variety of specialized tasks. The report that over 500 slave women and their children were attached to the palace center at Pylos might raise an eyebrow or two. Having learned of them, it is rather less surprising to find their daily rations of grain and figs noted with precision on the tablets.

The primary crafts appear to have engaged both free and slave workers at the same time, an indication perhaps that production and markets for Pylos were constantly outgrowing the available labor, and that its officials made up the difference in impromptu ways. These crafts included the production of textiles—especially woolens and linens— the production and trade of specialized olive oils, weapon-making, other metalworking, carpentry, shipbuilding, and the manufacture of jewelry, pottery, inlaid furniture, and perfumes. We have traveled a long way from the subsistence economies of Lascaux. To grasp the scale of industry at Pylos we must catch glimpses of the "big picture"—19,000 sheep are inventoried on one single tablet. And as with quantity, so with quality: a tablet has survived keeping track of "one ebony footstool inlaid with figures of men and lions in ivory." If we worked from their broad outlines, the economic, social, and political environment we can sketch from the Linear B tablets is remarkably like that of the far larger and equally centralized kingdoms of the Near East.

Even when we have sensed the texture of the little Mycenaean states we have not exhausted the value in those crumbling clay tablets. People, like places, have names. We have already met the four men (lieutenants?) assigned under the command of Maleus: a wealth of such personal names seems to crowd forward for attention from many categories of tablet. We even know that during the last days of the palace its *wanax* was probably named *E-ke-ra2-wo* (something like "Enkhelyawon"?) since, though he is not called the king, his name appears where the king's should in another list of landholdings. He was obviously very rich, and forty of his own men served as rowers in a Pylian fleet. John Chadwick thought it safe to put two and two together: "It is hard to see how such an important person could be fitted into Pylian society, unless he stands at its head" (1976:71).

We might thus reasonably identify Enkhelyawon as "*wanax* of *Pu-ro*" or "King of Pylos." The data in the tablets allows us to picture him supervising the business of the kingdom. His authority rested in part on centralized resources, particularly on his control of land. He also directed the use of labor in some detail, using a system that gives hints of a contractual, feudal-style system. Important trade connections beyond the immediate kingdom seem to have been a major concern: Pylos was the hub and depot to such trade, and the *wanax* took care to preserve his authority in it. If we are right in making Enkhelyawon the last *wanax* we can also see something of his direct role in military affairs. Much of the inventory of Pylos deals with the equipment of war and raiding, as Mycenaean physical remains would have led us to expect: the world of Mycenae, Tiryns, and Pylos was particularly caught up in its own military prowess.

About judicial matters we have, oddly, almost no clue in the records, but they do tie the *wanax* to the sphere of religion. It seems that the palace deity of the wealthy little realm was Potnia, "The Mistress," a very important deity. Four references to "the King" in these tablets could intend divinity as one of his attributes. Is another deity shrouded in the language here, or has the king divine status because of a link to Potnia, or has he simply a king's share of sacral responsibilities? The evidence is very slim, though a lack of clear talk about a god-king might be negative evidence for the humbler conclusion.

Areas of doubt such as these make it hard to reconstruct a full calendar of duties for *Wanax* Enkhelyawon, though we can sketch some parts of it. He will have spent his time making decisions about resources, talking with other officials, leading his forces upon the more important raids or campaigns, transacting his religious duties and enjoying himself (he was after all very rich). It is even possible to read the results of bone analyses, and to examine the frescoes painted on the walls of Pylos, and to imagine some plausible likeness for the man. But where is Nestor, king of "sandy Pylos"? Is there any link with *Wanax* Enkhelyawon?

It is not possible to really anchor a connection based on the various ways of dating: archaeological data can establish a fairly likely date, and textual materials sometimes a nearly exact one, but poetry at its heart can be as nearly timeless as anything human can. (We shall examine oral narrative as it faces that problem in the next chapter.) We would be on firmer ground if Nestor, the voluble old emeritus of the Homeric epics, could somehow appear in the Linear B tablets. Is such a thing possible?

Let us begin with the obvious: there is likely only one royal name given in the records and there certainly must have been many kings. We cannot even be certain that a man who appears in the last records of a kingdom's destruction is typical of the royalty who have gone before him. It could easily be that, by the random chances of survival, no tablets of Nestor's reign were preserved: we know only that we have a good many from the end of Enkhelyawon's rule. Alternatively, were no records kept during Nestor's reign? Both the names in question are Greek, and since the tablets prove that Mycenaeans "kept their books" in Greek, the name Nestor is not improbable for a Greek living in the thirteenth century B.C. A genealogy of Pylian kings as we now have it is so sparse as to afford plenty of room for both a Nestor and an Enkhelyawon, or more than one of either. And, since we have asked, the tantalizing name *Ne-qe-u* does occur on the Pylos tablets; it would transliterate roughly as "Neteus." It is interesting to remember that the name of Nestor's father was Neleus.

It is not likely we shall ever have a full list of kings for Pylos. We would be exceedingly grateful to have even a partial one, and, since written records are the only means of providing this sort of information, we seem to be limited to Linear B tablets that existed on the occasions when palaces were burned. The accident of the fire curing the unbaked clay is what has preserved them for us in the first place. Use of the rather cumbersome script involved seems also to have been the reserved craft of only a tiny part of the population. Written records were confined to palaces, just as we should expect if literacy served the palaces and only the palaces fostered literacy. As a consequence, the habits of literacy had not dug themselves deeply into Mycenaean society when the administrative centers were destroyed. As the centers vanish, so vanish the records, and all that flavor of the old society that so depended upon them. It would seem that if we go on searching for fuller, later written evidence for Bronze Age Pylos, we shall only be sifting the wind.

And we cannot expect any more help from archaeological data: though it be the primary evidence for prehistory, it will not tell us if Nestor were ever king there. As Glyn Daniel warned so eloquently:

> all prehistory is anonymous. We do not know the name of the architect of Stonehenge, or of the man whose body was recovered from the Tollund peat-bog in Jutland and whose noble features look calmly at us across twenty centuries. We do not know the names of the communities or societies whose material culture we study and classify as cultures. This is why prehistory reads with such difficulty to so many people, with its Beaker people and its Long Barrow men not to say its pieces of archaeological algebra like Iron Age 1 (a) i. (1988:119–20)

An archaeological history of Mycenaean Greece is every bit as anonymous. It is also, to many people, every bit as boring. One leading scholar's authoritative conclusions about the collapse of Mycenaean power will do nicely to show how dry the tree of history can wither when it has only the baked rock of the material record in which to root. Would we like to date the fall of Pylos? We have only to date the pottery. "We can date the fire to a time when the style of Mycenaean IIIB was nearing its end, but had not yet been superseded by that of Mycenaean IIIC since only about a dozen out of 8,000 vases have LHIIIC characteristics." (Blegen: 1961:133). We need such technical information to understand the clues properly, but it is a kind of history without faces or names, the kind of history that tastes like sand.

FIGURE 3–5 A "chariot fresco" from the walls of Pylos evokes the adventurous image of royal warcraft and raiding-lore familiar from the tales of Homer. (Following Piet De Jong. The dotted lines indicate damage to the original walls.)

And so we come back with a new appreciation to the epic stories. They at least are full of names, but are the names ones that historians can make any honest use of? If so, how?

One of the central habits of oral tradition is to focus itself upon the most noteworthy and memorable people and events it can find. The Nestor who found himself a home in the oral tradition was undeniably memorable. Consequently it is not an accident (much less a disqualification) that he should attract to his figure a body of saga. Historians so fastidious that they must eject every morsel that comes to their plate with a bit of story attached to it cannot complain if they go hungry in the end, or if they are forced to make do with a meal of sand. The Linear B records, in any case, show that Nestor's name is very like one used in the Bronze Age. The archaeologists have now excavated a palace and explored an entire kingdom in the countryside associated with Nestor by the epic tradition. Homer has not fared so very badly after all. Heinrich Schliemann was unembarrassed enough to take his "fiction" as a guide, and he discovered lost worlds behind the gate at Mycenae, and under the hill of Troy.

So it is the weaving together of three strands of evidence that tips the balance toward faith in the old poet, and his oral sources, even though we cannot yet make the characters of the epics exactly equal the material evidence of the sites and accounting tablets. A Bronze Age king of Pylos may well have won such renown in his chariots and council chambers that the generations remembered him, and swelled the accumulation of tales round his name. Oral tradition does that. It is the modern literary tradition that finds it easy to make tales of nothing, and nothing of tales.

It is not impossible that such a king might have participated in some short or long campaign before a citadel that then passed into tradition under the name of Troy (even that maligned story has had new evidence, and begun to look plausible again). A citadel is there, and archaeologists now say it was destroyed at least very near the time when Pylos was center of an extensive kingdom. We should not have to stretch belief very far, by historical standards, to picture Nestor marshalling his regimented men from their appointed labors in the Hither and Further provinces, to see them putting wheels and yokes to his dismantled chariots as his scribes ticked them off their figured pads of clay, his officers bundling together weapons from the bronzesmiths of those compact and bustling workshops, and to find Nestor himself joining the other quarrelling *wanaktes* before the clifftop walls of Troy, ready with a wise look and a long word of advice to help clear the honor of the house of Atreus.

FURTHER READING

The Mycenaean World by John Chadwick (Cambridge: Cambridge University Press, 1976) is an account of Mycenaean Greece as it "begins to emerge from the tablets." Pylos, the kingdom of Nestor, is a primary focus of his attention. Dr. Chadwick has also contributed *Linear B and Related Scripts* (London and Berkeley/Los Angeles: British Museum and University of California Press, 1987) to the series undertaken by the British Museum called "Reading the Past." That series includes accounts of related interest on cuneiform, Greek inscriptions, Egyptian hieroglyphics, and runes.

The Minnesota Messenia Expedition was the first large-scale project in the region with field work continuing from 1959 to 1969. Their findings were published in 1972 as *The Minnesota Messenia Expedition* edited by William McDonald and George Rapp, Jr. (Minneapolis: University of Minnesota Press).

Chapter Four

David
and Legend

Our search for Nestor's kingdom portrayed how rich the rewards may be when we can combine evidence from both archaeology and inscriptions. It also began to suggest the added richness possible when there are traditional stories available that might bear reliably on this evidence—might flesh it out, or suggest a plotline to join together the various objects and records we have been able to recover. Nestor figured in accounts that survived through countless years of storytelling, and in Chapter Three we explored the ways in which stories of such historical persistence can be used along with the other sorts of data. But there are many cases in which those stories are the only information we possess about a certain historical event or person. How valuable can they be to the honest historian when they stand alone?

Tradition comes in several forms, and its validity varies with each. Some types of tradition survive longer than others, especially when the cultures that founded the accounts decline or go through deep-seated changes. One of the most prevalent forms in which ancient tradition survives for modern scholarship is legend: the casting of a tradition as an account of grand or deeply important events believed to be based upon fact, but without any other evidence to verify those events. It would be wise to keep this definition firmly in mind. We are inclined to use the word legend rather loosely, to apply it offhand to accounts which antiquity itself knew were fictions, or to accounts which seem too colorful or too grandiose for our historical palates.

Nestor, for instance, is a figure of legend proper, and we may never be entirely sure of his own existence even though the accumulating evidence of archaeology has been surprisingly kind to the body of traditions collected around his name. We shall try to see now whether the David who is portrayed in the Old Testament belongs in this same

Israel & The Dark Age (1100 - 850)

Date B.C.	Events Around Palestine	Around the Mediterranean	Artifacts & Art
1100 -	Assyrian influence over Palestine. (c. 1050) Philistines conquer Israel. (c. 1040) Career of the legendary judge Samuel in Israel. (c. 1030 - 1010) Reign of the Israelite king Saul (dies in defeat vs. Philistines at Gilboa).	Assyria in decline. (1065) End of New Kingdom in Egypt (death of Rameses XI).	"Sub-Mycenaean" and "Protogeometric" pottery in Greece (very few artifacts remain from the immediate post-Mycenaean Dark Age).
1000 -	(c. 1006 - 1002) David consolidates the Israelite kingdom in southern Palestine. (c. 1000) David takes and establishes his capital at the hill-fortress of Jerusalem.	(c.) Rise of Philistine power in central Palestine. (c. 970 - 940) Reign of Hiram, King of Tyre.	(c.) Iron implements beginning to appear in Israel. (c.) "Solomon's Temple" built at Jerusalem.
950 --	(c. 970 - 931) Reign of Solomon in Israel; dynastic connections to Egypt. (c.) Solomon builds the Great Temple in Jerusalem (dedicated 953?).	(c. 945) Beginning of the XXII (Libyan) dynasty in Egypt; capital at Bubastis. (c. 935) Resurgence of Assyria under Assurdan II.	(c. 950) Est. of Solomon's cavalry stables (now excavated) at Megiddo. (c. 927) Stele commemorating the Pharaoh Sheshonk's campaign in Palestine (found at Megiddo).
900 --	(c. 931) Th;e kingdom of Israel splits under Solomon's son Rehoboam (Judah, the south) and the rebel Jeroboam (Israel, the north). (c. 927) Pharaoh Sheshonk I (Shishak) invades Palestine; pillages the temple in Jerusalem.	(883 - 859) Assyrians conquer Phoenicia under Ashurbanipal II. (c. 860) Assyria again controls most of its old empire. (858 - 824) Shalmaneser III rules Assyria. Egypt weak through early 700's.	(c. 900) Geometric pottery in Greece, painted with increasingly complex linear patterns (meanders, semicircles, polygons). (c.) The "Seal of Jezebel," with name engraved in Phoenician script (Hebrew University, Jerusalem).
850 --	(854) An allied Palestinian army (Ahab of Israel, Ben Hadad of Damascus, and Irkhuleni of Hamath, supported by Judah and Egypt) attempts to halt Shalmaneser III's invasion. Defeated at Kharkar.	(853) Battle of Kharkar: Shalmaneser defeats the armies of Palestine on the Orontes River.	(c. 852) Pictorial bronze palace gates at Balawat (N. Syria) commemorate the victory of Shalmaneser III in Palestine.

category. The story of David is regularly regarded as having a uniform style and theme, features that make it an appealing case study. It recounts the life of a truly extraordinary person, a life studded with extraordinary feats, which we will investigate in order to learn how to disentangle fact from fiction. The careful ancient historian can find many uses for legendary accounts; they are a major element in the mix of one's available evidence, and tools for interpreting and applying them should always be ready in one's historical kit.

Other evidence for David's era in history is quite limited because of the great events which shaped the late Bronze Age—the later 1200s and 1100s B.C. Complex states, landmark civilizations which flourished in the thirteenth century came almost simultaneously to an abrupt end. Causes as diverse and interrelated as drought, economic collapse, civil strife, and the migration of peoples combined to destroy the rich, interactive life of the Mediterranean and Mesopotamian regions for several hundred years. Trade routes became dangerous and disused, or simply worthless because the markets merchants had once sought at the far end had vanished. Droughts attacked the agricultural mainstay of life and—whether the droughts themselves were worse or some other cause made the culture working the land more brittle—the resulting disasters seem to have been worse than usual. Famine and plague may well have followed. Neighbor fought neighbor, and in the havoc, relations among the old power-centers fell into pieces. Discontented elements in the turbulent, embattled kingdoms may have seized the chance to throw off their overlords.

From Anatolia in the north to Egypt in the south hardly an institution characteristic of the Bronze Age survived. From Greece and the islands of the Aegean in the west to Mesopotamia in the east, the brilliant, vibrant cultures of some three or four centuries' development crumbled, and their survivors hunkered down among their ruins into a dull, shrunken village existence. This was the time, when shadows came back from the corners of human existence and closed again over the lights of the high civilizations, that we may truly call the Dark Age. Those who lived at its end actually thought it a slight improvement when they could call it the Age of Iron. It was a harsh time, almost as if the human clock had been turned back to the early years of the New Stone Age, forcing humans to make a fresh beginning. We treat that concept too lightly in our own luxurious culture. For the survivors of the Dark Age it must have seemed that every comfort, every convenience and advance, the whole artistry that had once made life seem a rich thing had to be invented anew.

Conditions were, as always, more devastated in some areas than in others. Greece, which always lived near the margin of its agricultural resources, proved especially brittle. The population plummeted by 90 percent. Even where the situation was a little less grim, small city-states or locally confined kingdoms replaced the sweeping Bronze Age empires—the Egyptian or the Hittite showpieces of the second millennium. In Egypt, the union collapsed; the Hittites who had held Anatolia under an iron sway found themselves shattered and running, forced in the end to try and scrape a new homeland out of northern Palestine. Whatever was left of the confident old Mesopotamian culture hid nervously among the shards and rubble of its old citadels; the stern Assyrians took in booty and slaves—the only profit that could be made any longer in that land.

In the power vacuum left by these collapses rose up scattered congeries of little city-states, usually independent even of each other. They might cooperate under great threat of war. The relations between states, both of friendly trade and of militant aggression,

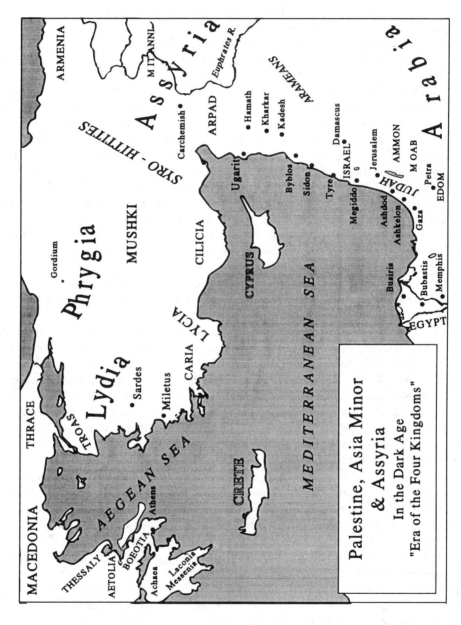

FIGURE 4-1 Palestine, Asia Minor & Assyria. In the Dark Age "Era of the Four Kingdoms"

withered away to a barely recorded minimum. For most people the nature and extent of the experienced world was once more defined by the agriculture or pastoralism of their own village life. The 300 years (roughly) between 1150 and 850 B.C.—and even later along some coasts of the eastern Mediterranean—are what we very justifiably call the Dark Age.

Along the eastern fringe of the Mediterranean, small Phoenician states like Byblos and Tyre stepped into the role of carriers and traders both by land and by sea. South of them, several related tribal groups conquered and then gradually settled into the farmlands between the Jordan River and the coast. They formed, for a time, the single kingdom known as Israel. The splintering was perhaps greatest in Greece. Thousands of tiny groups—each of them isolated from the others—struggled to stay alive under overwhelmingly adverse conditions. The archaeologists tell us that a successful community might have boasted fifteen or twenty people! And yet, beaten down as they were, they were independent. They could make their own futures, if there were to be any futures at all for them to make. In the desperation of their struggle, the survivors blazed a myriad of new paths through the labyrinth of human existence. Every institution rebuilt, every intellectual hurdle cleared was a new victory.

But archaeological remains of such a time are by consequence both few and rather poor in quality. Communal life is a simple life. Record keeping is less necessary to such a life, even if a culture retains a means to do so, and some of the Dark Age peoples, including the Greeks, became for all we can tell totally nonliterate—that is, no one could read or write. Since only the slimmest communication (if there were any at all) remained between regions, the accounts of people who could still read and write contain few mentions of their neighbors.

And yet all communities, even nonliterate ones, need to remember certain fundamental things from one day, or one year, to the next. With no writing to fasten them in the world of accessible fact, those things must be preserved by word of mouth. Then, in some cases, a written script developed later can catch and save those orally transmitted accounts, solidifying them before its culture changes enough to make radical alterations in them, or (in the worst cases) before the culture begins to find them unnecessary and they fall into oblivion.

The legendary events, individuals, and peoples in Dark Age Israel may be just such a case. Though writing remained a practiced skill in Dark Age Palestine, the Hebraic tradition transmitted itself commonly by oral accounts. Told from one generation to another, the stories were in time written down on durable materials, and preserved with an unusual intensity. They have survived for posterity in the Old Testament.

DAVID

Once upon a time there lived a giant of a man known as Goliath of Gath; he was the mightiest warrior of a people called the Philistines. Raiding and trading, they had carved themselves a strip of good farmland along the southern seacoast of Palestine, and dotted it with mercantile strongholds. Now, so long as Goliath was their champion, the Philistines were unbeatable, and they used their good fortune to spread their power into the lands around about them.

Several tribes who shared a common history and way of life dwelt in the hill country east and north of the Philistines. These folk, who would in coming days form the kingdom of Israel, felt the full weight of the Philistine expansion pressing in upon them. They armed themselves and went to defend their hard-won countryside, but each time that the two hosts met and aligned themselves for battle, Goliath would step forth from his ranks and call for an Israelite warrior to meet him in single combat. He demanded a champion of the Israelites. It was a heroic age, and the custom had long been for a duel, if offered, to settle the issue of battle as though the two armies had fought.

But Goliath was a man "six cubits and one span tall" (about 9 1/2 feet), clad in the unmatchable bronze armor of the sea-traders. He carried a spear of such size and heft that it looked like a beam from a weaver's loom. The Israelites could find no man big enough or hardy enough or courageous enough to face him. As often as he called for an opponent, he went back unanswered, and laughed.

This could not go on forever; the time for some sort of reckoning drew closer. The two forces had eyed one another warily from camps on the opposite sides of a valley for forty days and nights, when David, the unremarkable young son of Jesse, led his pack animals into camp from Bethlehem carrying cheeses and loaves of bread from his father to the captain under whom his three older brothers had gone to fight. David himself was too young for soldiering—his father kept him at home to herd the sheep—but while he stayed in the camp, he heard Goliath bellow his contemptuous summons across the valley. He then told the Israelite commander that he would go himself, and accept combat with Goliath.

Men brought him armor and weapons but he refused them all, taking only his staff, his familiar sling, and five stones he chose for smoothness from the brook. Goliath watched the unarmed boy walk resolutely onto the field of combat and taunted him as he came: "Am I a dog, that you come at me with sticks?" He cursed the boy by his own gods, and told him, with the laughter of death in his voice, "Come to me, and I will give your flesh to the birds of the air and to the beasts of the field" (1 Sam. 17:43–44).

David was undaunted. "You come against me with sword and spear and javelin," he replied, "but I come against you in the name of the Lord of Hosts, the God of the armies of Israel that you have dared to insult" (1 Sam. 17:45). He fitted one stone into his sling, spun the sling above his head, and hurled it straight and true at the giant. It struck Goliath full in the forehead. He fell forward like a tree, unconscious. David ran up to the great, fallen man, drew out his own sword, and slew him with a single mighty cut.

It would not have been hard to tell this story in straightforward narrative rather than in the manner of a folktale, but the traditional form and language is a living part of all such tales. For our purposes it is useful, perhaps even essential, to keep its native character.

Beyond its color (to which we will return shortly), the tale contains the fact (which other sources confirm) that David was a historical figure—the first ruler over a united kingdom of Israel from 1000 to 961 B.C. Goliath may have been an actual person as well:

FIGURE 4–2 David and Goliath: A folk hero slays a national enemy against impossible odds. All the smaller civilizations that managed to persist under the harsh conditions of the Dark Age must have felt something of this giant-killer confidence and initiative. The success and unity of David's own kingdom was to be short-lived and the memory of him all the more piquant because of it.

a victim named Goliath appears in 2 Sam. 21:19, and the report of a man's death in 1 Chronicles 20:5 makes him "the brother of Goliath of Gath." Because they carry such weight in the early history of Israel, both David and the Philistines figure prominently in later sources. Nonetheless, the major contemporary source for both Philistines and Israelites is historical legend.

The account of David's life and reign extends across several books of the Old Testament. The short book of Ruth begins it by telling of the birth of Obed, David's grandfather (4:13–17). David's own story runs through both books of Samuel (beginning at 1 Sam. 16) and on into the first chapters of 1 Kings. A condensed version also appears in 1 Chronicles. The story stands out because of the king's accomplishments: Under David the many quarrelling tribes of Israelites were gathered together into a united state for the first time in their history:

> So all the elders came to the king at Hebron, and King David made a pact with them at Hebron in the presence of the Lord, and they anointed David king of Israel. David was thirty years old when he became king, and he reigned for forty years. (2 Sam. 5:3–4)

The wonder that hung around that time held even more awe for the Israelites of later years: The unity of Israel was short-lived, and coming events in the Near East would bring them severe hardships. David's era would wear the aura of a golden age in later memory.

Unravelling the principal threads of the tale is not difficult. David was the eighth son of Jesse, who belonged to the tribe of Judah, lived in the town of Bethlehem, and held grazing land in the countryside of Ephrath around about it (1 Sam. 17:12). Jesse kept sheep, and David was herding his father's flocks on the occasion when the Israelites first encountered Goliath. The Philistines fled upon the death of their champion, and Saul, the Israelite leader, recognized that David had won a larger success than the killing of a single man. "Saul kept him by him from that day forward and would not let him go back to his father's house" (1 Sam. 18:2).

David lived with Saul and his family, becoming the true friend of Saul's son Jonathan. In time, he even won the hand of Michal, Saul's daughter, in marriage. He was given a command, and did frequent battle with the Philistine princes "but every time they went out to battle, David was more successful than all Saul's officers, and his name held in great honor" (1 Sam. 18:30). Such successes were dangerous, however: they kindled Saul's jealousy. The older warlord determined to kill his young prodigy, and would have succeeded had not Jonathan and Michal intervened. David escaped.

For some while a fugitive, David gradually drew a body of followers around him—"all Israel and Judah loved David" (1 Sam. 18:16). As his band became too conspicuous for safety he took refuge in the lands of Israel's enemy, the Philistines. Achish, son of Maoch, king of Gath, set him up with his 600 men in the town of Ziklag, and during the next year and four months David and his men used it as a base, raiding the Philistines' (non-Israelite) opponents. "Achish trusted David. 'He has made himself hated by his own people Israel,' he thought, 'and so will be my servant forever.'" (1 Sam. 27:12)

Hostility intensified between the Israelites and Philistines until, while David was still living among them, the Philistines "mustered all their forces at Aphek while the Israelites were encamped near the spring which is in Jezreel" (1 Sam. 29:1). At this time David and his force marched with the Philistines, but certain of the Philistine commanders began to be uneasy about this renegade force lurking in the rear of their column. They demanded that their king send David back, lest "he turns on us once battle is joined. Would there be a better way for the man to regain his master's favor?" (1 Sam. 29:4). David turned his troop and headed back into Philistine country; Achish went on to a pitched battle at Jezreel, where the Israelite force fell in defeat with three of Saul's sons among the slain. Saul himself, badly wounded, ended his life by falling on his sword.

When word came to David of Saul's death and the Israelite defeat, he returned to Judah. He had had no part in killing the king, and he was now the land's most famous champion. In the towns round Hebron he was recognized as king over the southern tribes, ruling from Hebron for seven years and six months. A day came, however, when representatives of all the tribes came to the little citadel and made David king over all Israel and Judah. He reigned for thirty-three years.

Some time around 1002 B.C., David, pressed by serious Philistine attacks, took the almost impregnable hill-fortress of Jerusalem from the Jebusites and made it into the center of his united and expanding kingdom. The union of Israel and Judah remained a fragile and fractious partnership (Jerusalem conveniently occupied neutral clifftops between the two regions), but somehow it persisted. David was able to hand it on at his death to his son Solomon. "So Solomon sat upon the throne of David his father; and his kingdom was firmly established" (1 Kings 2:12).

There are few enough elements of "wonder" in this account (especially in our bare outline of it). The trouble comes when a student of history must deal with the nature of this evidence, and with the intent of its creators. Some scholars take this story of David's rise to power as one of the oldest of genuine historical writings; others are just as certain that it is a later pastiche—a reconstructing of varied elements, many of them fabricated, by overly clever scribes. J. H. Hexter defines a position located between the two camps:

> Like the tradition of many similar peoples, transmitted by word of mouth, generation after generation for many centuries, the tradition of the tenth-century Israelites was an extremely intricate mixture of myths, legends, tales of folk-heroes, and historical fact. (1966: 8)

The Old Testament seems to have so intricately entwined these several elements that we now find it unusually difficult, if not impossible, to disentangle them one from another.

What we are presented with is a final fabric in which all these strands are finely and organically woven, an anthology written down over the course of nearly 1,000 years. In it are a broad variety of literary genres: hymns (the Psalms), adages (Proverbs), romances (Ruth and Esther), love lyrics (the Song of Solomon), a religious dialogue (Job), a witty essay (Ecclesiastes), the deeds and utterances of various prophets (Isaiah, Jeremiah, Ezekiel, and others), laws (Leviticus), folk legends (Joshua), genealogy (1 Chronicles), and even some recorded civil documents. We need add no example of a purely historical book since the matter and narration of history are mixed throughout the Old Testament books. Very few of the ancients were inclined to separate history from its context.

So thorough is the mix that it is no easy matter to isolate historical data from everything else; deciding what is intended as precise information by solely scientific means consequently poses a serious dilemma. Even if we could do so, we should have torn the "facts," thus garnered, from the soil in which they were planted, and out of which they grew, making us wonder whether we had killed the meaning in them. Hexter's (not very helpful) conclusion for a person demanding a clear rule of thumb is that

> In this situation, to tell the real story of the Israelites up to the tenth century is out of the question, since no one is sure what the real story is. (9)

Hexter believes, for instance, that the story of the primitive Hebrews from the days of Abraham through the years spent in Egypt into the earliest settlements in Palestine is entwined into a narrative that is not rooted firmly to either time or place. Many scholars would not agree with this assertion: those who have examined the narrative itself (it is a veritable rabbit's warren of references that embarrass precisely because they seem so specific), and those who are familiar with the way in which oral tradition drives and anchors itself into particular landscapes (the abstract tale of wanderings is a relatively modern thing). Still, if there is any truth in Hexter's view, it points up a fundamental problem. Since chronology and geography are two of the elemental concerns in the writing of history, any medium of transmission that is intrinsically vague about both poses a danger for a would-be user.

It is true that in the Old Testament the character of the narrative undergoes a change by the time we reach the so-called historical books: Joshua, Judges, Samuel, Kings, Chronicles. The information set down in these books may have been set down sooner after the events described than in the earlier Old Testament writings. It would not be surprising, in fact, if it were the new needs of the politically unified state that produced the change; David would in that case have forged not only the kingdom but also the revolution in the kingdom's means of preserving its past.

Written records are just the sort of telltale mark left by a sudden increase in the complexity of a culture; they would fit the way of life we can otherwise see developing among the Hebrews of the tenth century. Oral bards may have prodigious and patterned memories, but in most observed cultures traditions drift irresistibly toward subtle changes after about two or three generations. Written records are far more permanent, and allow a much greater precision of memory over longer periods of time. A unified kingdom will have needed all sorts of new administrative abilities, new ways to manage the internal complications of the various coexisting tribes, new means of interacting with foreign neighbors: all of which would have called for the precision of writing.

Beyond its use in administration, the revolution will likely have provoked intellectual changes. Writing, as Jack Goody once said, preserves the past in the present. Walter Ong, another of the great scholars of oral and literary culture, has countered that writing actually separates the past from the present. This conclusion is a reasonable one since writing is also likely to change mentalities and ways of seeing the world. As they are frozen in permanent form, written accounts allow reflection upon a thing over time. They allow comparison of one account with another; later readers may question both the accuracy and meaning of things written before. Unlike the winged and fleeting word of oral tradition, the word inscribed on some durable material can be carefully studied. When the mind can at last consult several different sources on a topic, it might begin for the first time to perceive patterns, to develop hierarchies and categories of classification. Writing "sharpens the outlines of the categories...furthermore it encourages the hierarchization of the classificatory system. At the same time, it leads to questions about the nature of the classes through the very fact of placing them together" (Goody 1977:102). Early literacy is quite often marked by a tendency to classify and arrange things in the form of lists and tables.

Another and more striking habit of the literate mind is the tendency to think in abstract terms. The ground under this argument is a soft one, and though the true trail is vital for our journey into the past, the false trails are many; let us tread carefully. All our conceptual thinking is done by abstracting things; oral cultures are certainly able to conceptualize. The difference is that in these cultures each concept tends to be linked to an actual situation; an abstract thing is understood as it refers to some solid activity or object in the human world. The anthropologist Goody once described watching a nonliterate person being asked to count. The response was, "What do you want me to count?" Obviously different objects are counted in very different ways (Goody, 1977:12–13). There is no such thing as "five," but we have very often seen such a thing as "five trees." The making of purely abstract concepts and purely absolute standards begins to emerge when information stands "before the mind" with an existence of its own. This, in turn, very often occurs when the information is written, when it stands alone and need no longer lean upon concrete beings and objects. Wishing we had a more elegant term, we might say that words become "decontextualized," that they exist whether their old surroundings of ongoing human life are there or not. One can count at last without counting sheep or pebbles or trees.

These are the characteristics we might expect to develop as writing gained more importance among the Israelites, flourishing under the central government that David and, later, Solomon were beginning to forge. Side by side with it, the habits of the old oral tradition will have persisted. It provided, in the matter patterned into its recollected tales, the first raw material to be studied and recorded in the new manner of literacy. Thus, the traditional tales were inlaid into the new record of the past as it was built, and changed as they passed from a vision and a word to become permanent things, engraved into an edifice that could begin to be called "history." It is precisely the point of that transition that may give us the clue to our broader dilemma: *Legend* might be viewed best as the thing produced just as tales are transforming into historical, permanent records of the past.

Webster's Unabridged Dictionary defines *legend* as:

> a story of some wonderful event, handed down for generations among a people and popularly believed to have a historical basis, although not verifiable.

Legend is often coupled with *myth*, which again according to *Webster's Unabridged Dictionary* is:

> a traditional story of unknown authorship, ostensibly with a historical basis, but serving usually to explain some phenomenon of nature, the origin of man, or the customs, institutions, religious rites, etc. of a people; myths usually involve the exploits of gods and heroes.

The definitions share a close kinship; we associate them by long custom. Both are born of Greek words: *mythos* carries the sense of word or speech and, by extension, of a thing said, of a tale or story. The Greek verb *lego* (or *legein*) means both "to say" and "to gather"—some ancient poets spoke of "stringing words" almost like beads. We may connect both myth and legend, therefore, to the original realm of the spoken, not the written, word.

But can we distinguish the two, and if we can, by what measure? Scholars have never agreed upon an answer, and only the very bold or foolish would pretend to untie a knot in a moment that has resisted the hands of experts for so long. Let us merely suggest one feature that might differentiate usefully between the two: In every sort of folktale, that is, legend, supernatural elements seem to lie in the background. Though deities and divine forces play their roles, it is the human beings who hold center stage. To do the supernatural work of a *legend*, the gods send servants, or the servants send a holy man. Premier billing goes to the humblest creature, a human.

In addition, the importance of human beings affects the setting of the tale. Since both myth and legend are preserved by spoken tradition, their information will be vague about places unless the places attached to the tales still lie ready to the eye and ear. The travel of a population can make all the places in its older tales dim and magical in a moment. Information about dates will almost always be vague. Oral cultures do not easily distinguish abstract times or places by the mental measures familiar to literate societies. Measurements are inexact unless the thing measured is a present object and they are expressed from the perspective of the folk remembering them.

There is more to a distinction between myth and folktale; we must consider the element of time. Because a *myth* may often be associated with creation or the beginning of some human institution, it will be set in the timeless past. A *legend*, on the other hand, is set in time. It does not belong to an ageless present, but (since it relates the acts of specific humans) it presses closer to the real present.

Finally, we may find help by leaning upon one sense of the Greek verb *legein* to which *legend* owes a particular debt. The implication of "gathering" is important. In many of the great and memorable legends, numerous individual tales have been collected and attached to some one person who enjoys a special prominence in that people's past. Continued recounting of those legendary exploits, in turn, ensures that his prominence will continue. Now it is at least safe to say that such a character was originally prominent, or he would not have attracted such a cluster of stories around him; we may expect, in other words, that the central figure of a legend was a historical person.

That is only to say that legend gets us rather near the historical accounts. The two cannot, however, be equated. The historian who wants precise data must tread upon the precincts of legend with a special caution, for while such accounts are seductive, they can also deceive. All sorts of things may be woven into the apparently seamless cloth of legendary tales. It is possible to see both negative and positive examples of this sort of evidence in the legend of David.

Elements traditional in all forms of folktale come readily to the eye. David is, unsurprisingly, the youngest son, and prevails over a pack of hostile relatives. When he took provisions to his three brothers fighting in the army against the Philistines "Eliab his elder brother heard him talking to the men, and his anger flared up against David. 'Why have you come down here?' he said. 'Whom have you left in charge of those few sheep out there in the wilderness? I know your insolence and your wicked heart; you have come to watch the battle'" (1 Sam. 17:28).

As he is the youngest, the hero David often starts out weak and inexperienced. Goliath spurned David, because he "was only a youth, a boy of fresh complexion and pleasant bearing" (1 Sam. 17:42). He taunted him about his meager weapons. But David prevailed nonetheless, overcoming not only Goliath but a succession of other enormous obstacles before he rose to an unprecedented position in the history of his people. In some of the tales his means of succeeding also betray the traditional style of the narrative. He used his personal talents, acted vigorously and directly, heroically. David was before all else a warrior, and it was his skill in battle that enraged Saul when he heard the women sing,

> *Saul has slain his thousands,*
> *And David his tens of thousands.*
>   (1 Sam. 18:7)

But David assumed other, plainer duties as a result of his military prowess. By uniting the people of Israel, he found he had become their principal judge (2 Sam. 15:6). To manage the new administration, he found it necessary to hold a census. "Go," he said to his commanders, "throughout the tribes of Israel from Dan to Beersheba and take a census of the people; I wish to know the size of the population" (2 Sam. 24:2). He was also responsible for the proper enactment of religious rites: "David appointed certain Levites as ministers before the ark of the Lord, to commemorate, glorify and praise the Lord, the God of Israel" (1 Chron. 16:4). Yet none of these civil achievements, however deeply they might ring in the structure of the new kingdom, ever overshadowed his success in battle.

There was another side to all this; David owed much of his accomplishment to the constant meddling of the holy man Samuel. The Lord (a plain English translation for *Jehovah* or *Yahweh*) had commanded his spokesman to call Jesse (David's father) and his children to make a sacrifice with Samuel in attendance. When David was brought in to the Presence of the Lord, "the Lord said 'Come, anoint him, for this is the one.' At this Samuel took the horn of oil and anointed him where he stood with his brothers; and the spirit of the Lord seized on David and stayed with him from that day on" (1 Sam. 16:12–13). The central figures of legends may be human beings, but they regularly receive the special favor of their god, or gods.

Divine favor and a hero's own talents can tend to "gather" heroic feats and tales into a single person. In 2 Samuel we learn that "Elhanan son of Jair from Bethlehem killed Goliath of Gath" (21:19), while we have already seen David slaying Goliath in 1 Samuel. We may be dealing with one of several things here. "Elhanan" may be another name for David, specific to some local legend (and so "Jair" for "Jesse")—the dialect is not always the same in the last chapters of Samuel. We may be dealing with another Goliath: It is a common enough occurrence in heroic cultures for a variety of ambitious men to take the name of a dead champion (there were a number of both "Beowulfs" and "Arthurs" in the first years after the legend of each began to circulate). But this may also be one instance when, in Jan Vansina's words, "a central figure is the magnet that attracts anecdotal scrap metal from everywhere" (1985:165 *f.*). As oral traditions are formed, bits of recent information are collected and "sorted." Any pieces remarkable enough to be kept in memory must be fitted to the larger tradition, bringing in just as much specific complication with them as the skill of the particular culture or bard can bear. Each new layer of tradition tends to center on a heroic individual; it must join, holding its own or assimilating, existing layers older than it is. These also, if they are pliable enough, will tend to cluster around important figures. The final product is a tidy one, thrifty in the memory and organization it requires, cohering with a minimum of loose ends.

It is only when we attempt to do serious history that the tidiness can become a disaster. "Temporal transpositions are frequent, fusion prevents one from disentangling the original elements that were fused, selection discards data, and secondary causes are eliminated," as Vansina writes of oral history (1985:172). Dates and numbers can be particularly affected. Precise reckonings for large numbers are abstractions and fare badly in oral cultures since the present concrete objects necessary for oral counting are absent or hard to take in at one glance. Jack Goody, for example, describes the speed with which the Lodaaga of northern Ghana counted cowrie shell money before him. Multiples of five stood for whatever number the counter could check as he extended his hand for another group of shells. (Goody, 1977:12–13.) One cannot of course reckon animals by these same means. Counting ceases to be a single abstract action, and becomes any number of specific activities, each depending upon particular objects.

Imprecise numbers can also occur because oral cultures often use a set quantity to indicate "a few" or "many" or "a huge quantity." Numbers in accounts remembered and passed on by word of mouth are often "round figures." The Philistines slew "about four thousand men on the field of battle" (1 Sam. 4:2); Saul "took three thousand chosen men" to seek David (1 Sam. 24:2); "six hundred men" joined David in Philistine territory (1 Sam. 27:2). These numbers are not by necessity inaccurate—transactions or choices in an oral culture may involve round figures as easily as reckoning, and for the same reasons—but they are dangerous: An impression of size rather than a precise amount may be lurking beneath the exactness.

Reckoning time presents a similar problem. Reading through an account yields a feeling of sequence: first this happened, later that, and then the other. Mnemonic verses to help retain a sequence of names (of rulers, perhaps, or ancestors) are common enough, and vary according to the quality of a particular oral tradition, but these have only a relative value. Events in legend have been structured to make a coherent tale, but no absolute chronology anchors them at certain distances from one another.

Occasionally the reader is lucky enough to learn a "total duration": "David the son of Jesse reigned over the whole of Israel. His reign over Israel had lasted forty years; he had reigned in Hebron for seven years, and in Jerusalem for thirty-three" (1 Chron. 29:26–27), or "After the death of Saul, David returned from his rout of the Amalekites and spent two days in Ziklag" (2 Sam. 1:1). The account seems precise. Is it factually precise, or are past and present flowing together to create the sort of continuous stream that gives a tale immediacy for its listeners? The individual elements, being only duration and not references to some outside, datable thing, have a value only inside their context.

The result is rather like the relative dating we could get several chapters back when we had only the objects found in a core sample taken from an ancient cave. Nothing gives us an absolute date, but many things are clearly "before" or "after" other things. Sometimes we might even guess how far before or after they belong—we lack only a real reference point by which to anchor them in time. But these durations do quite well in the stories themselves. Because of them we can even isolate little vignettes of legend, as it were, and enjoy them in isolation, since their compact dating and organization make them self-contained, the sequence of each comprehensible in itself.

Beside the pitfalls, such accounts hoard up a wealth of information for the historian. It is of course "oral" information. Communication by the spoken word is immediate: it must be instantly understandable to its hearers, as very few of them will have the mental talent to ponder the meaning of long phrases or whole sentences. It must also be intelligible, and it must recall familiar knowledge and values. The backdrop is the world of its audience, reflecting the structure of its society, the problems it perceives, and the strengths that make it endure. Oral tradition often preserves a few heirlooms, memories of the most precious of objects that are no longer used, but the great percentage of material in it will be constantly "modernizing" itself, conforming to the social, political, ethical, and economic shape of the world around it. Speaking of the *Iliad* (another grand product of oral transmission), James Redfield said:

> ...song is for an audience and in this sense is located in history. In reconstructing the heroic world, we implicitly reconstruct the audience which understood it, the audience for whom the

Iliad was not...problematic. In this sense, and really only in this sense, the *Iliad* is a direct source for its own period. (1975:23)

So, even allowing for these difficulties, the traditional account of David can tell us a great deal about the world in which he lived. It was evidently an age of conflict at many levels. The Israelites were not in firm possession of the territory in which they had settled—a fact we might have been inclined to forget if our minds were too quickly focused on the coming (and archaeologically better known) unified kingdom under David and Solomon. The Philistines lived close upon their doorstep, forcing them to fight for their homes just as they fought with "the Geshurites, the Girzites, and the Amalekites; for these were the inhabitants of the land from of old, as far as Shur, to the land of Egypt" (1 Sam. 27:8). To make matters worse, many of the Israelites' enemies were settled farmers such as the Jebusites around their fortress of Jerusalem; much of Israel's population were shepherds. When Saul came hunting to kill David, he went "in front of the Wildgoats' Rocks. And he came to the sheepfolds by the way, where there was a cave" (1 Sam. 24:2–3).

The Israelites were a nomadic people, joined to one another by ties of blood rather than territory. By their own account, local tribes had played a major role in the settlement of Palestine, each having generated something of its own "history" in the traditions, since no one tribe had had quite the same pattern of success or acclimating to the land as any other. "And in those days the tribe of the Danites was seeking for itself an inheritance to dwell in; for until then no inheritance among the tribes of Israel had fallen to them. So the Danites sent five able men...and they came to the hill country of Ephraim, to the house of Micah, and lodged there" (Judg. 18:1–2).

It was as leader of a tribe that a person achieved his success. If he became powerful enough he might hope (and only hope) to gain the allegiance of other tribes. David managed to get recognition as king only from the southern tribes at first. Winning allegiance from the north took him another seven years. Almost as often as the tribes cooperated, they fought as rivals. The twentieth chapter of Judges describes with shocking matter-of-factness how the tribe of Benjamin was once nearly exterminated by "the men of Israel [apart from Benjamin],...four hundred thousand men that drew sword" (Judg. 20:17). The division that recurred most often seems to have pitted the tribes in northern Palestine (in the mountains along the Jordan valley and around the Sea of Galilee) against those in the south (the mountains around the Dead Sea and the gentler hill-country that ran west toward the Philistine coasts). It was to remain a sharp division, healed temporarily by a pair of charismatic kings, but destined to destroy the unity of the little realm in the years after Solomon's death.

Not one but a number of lines ran through the people of ancient Israel along which they might very easily split if pressure were applied. Early in the story, religion was a prominent line of fracture—Yahweh prevailed only with difficulty as the sole god of his chosen people. The native inhabitants of the land when the Israelites had arrived to settle had worshipped gods of their own, and the temptation to adopt these perhaps less demanding deities—already tied to the luck of the land—must have been a great one to the simpler folk. As the people of Israel homesteaded among the "Canaanites," they "took their daughters to themselves for wives, and their own daughters they gave to their sons; and they served their gods" (Judg. 3:6).

Yahweh was not only a jealous god, he also insisted upon certain attitudes and behaviors among his people that must have seemed foreign, even incomprehensible, to the prevailing cultures of the region. As early as the time of Samuel, a question had begun to hang in the utterances of the Lord through his human spokesmen, cutting some of the ground from under the old, traditional, and easy magical view of sacrifice.

> *And Samuel said, 'Has the Lord as great delight in burnt offerings and sacrifices,*
> *as in obeying the voice of the Lord?*
> *Behold, to obey is better than sacrifice,*
> *and to hearken than the fat of rams.'*
>   (1 Sam. 15:22)

Even among those who kept faith in their commitment to Yahweh there ran a recurrent, nagging disagreement: how should one learn of the Lord's commands? Priests holding recognized positions can be found offering regular sacrifice throughout the Old Testament, but there are other individuals like Samuel, called into service directly by the divine voice, who could not be so easily mortised into an official hierarchy. "And Samuel grew, and the Lord was with him and let none of his words fall to the ground. And all Israel from Dan to Beer-sheba knew that Samuel was established as a prophet of the Lord" (1 Sam. 3:19–20). These patternings of belief and ways of life may have been intended to co-exist or complement one another, but they could swing into opposition very easily.

Unfortunately, in an oral culture one could not very readily hold such things at "arm's length"—belief in (and life according to) one or the other of these permeated the collective approach each of the tribes of Israel took to its day-to-day existence. Unravelling a ritual belief to understand its rightness or its real meaning could easily have had a catastrophic feel—as though one were picking apart the very bonds that reassuringly held the universe together simply to squint a little closer at them. Questions like that found in 1 Samuel 15 were indeed radical and disturbing ones.

As they needed priests to pattern and smooth their relations with their God, so they needed human leaders to direct them in battle against their enemies. But what if earthly kingship conflicted with the ultimate commands of the Lord? The men of Israel said to Gideon, "Rule over us, you and your son and your grandson also; for you have delivered us out of the hand of Midian." Gideon told them, "I will not rule over you, and my son will not rule over you; the Lord will rule over you" (Judg. 8:22–23). Not every successor to Gideon (as judge and war-leader) would have such scruples.

Although Israel could not resist enemies as powerful as the Philistines unless it were unified, such unity had a cost. It hemmed in like a fence against the old autonomy of each individual tribe, making new demands and changing the structures of life. Settled village life meant new trade, and trade pushed Israel closer to neighbors it had once ignored. Foreign kings came into focus suddenly on the outskirts of its world, like Hiram of the great trading emporium at Tyre, who "sent messengers to David, and cedar trees, also carpenters and masons" (2 Sam. 5:11). Israel assimilated the new wealth, and began developing the craftsmen to work it. The short days of its greatest political glory were about to begin; the shadow of Solomon filled its immediate future. These were heady times, but all such bright new complexity would ring the death knell for the old nomadic

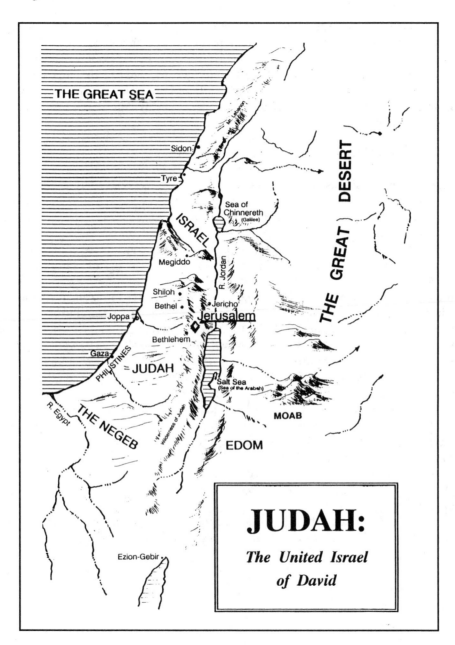

FIGURE 4–3 Judah: The United Israel of David

days of herding. The culture that had fostered Israel retreated to the rural hills until hard times would make it vital again. In the new palace and temple of the king, within heavy stone walls upon the crag of Jerusalem, the scribes began to set things down in written form, freezing the old memories on their charactered scrolls.

   This is the material of history, or at least some of the material. It is not statistical data; the reckonings remain stubbornly imprecise. Rather it describes the feel and weight of a period that recorded its story in legendary form. In the story of David, epic deeds have been assimilated into current, life-sized events, and out of this melting pot the historian can take things that allow him to write both social and cultural history. The historian who demands mathematics must content himself with other times, and with other sorts of evidence.

FURTHER READING

   The essential reading is the Old Testament, especially the books of Ruth, 1 and 2 Samuel, 1 Kings, and 1 Chronicles. Various definitions of folklore are to be found in the *Standard Dictionary of Folklore, Mythology, and Legend*, ed. Maria Leach (New York: Funk and Wagnalls Co., 1949–50).

   For a view of Hebrew historiography in a larger context, see John van Seters' *In Search of History: Historiography in the Ancient World and the Origins of Biblical History* (New Haven: Yale University Press, 1983). Chapter 7 of van Seters' book presents the views of a number of scholars on the distinctive narrative forms and their connections. Chapters 8 and 9 treat the process of weaving that resulted in the unified books of Samuel and Kings. Pages 264*ff.* deal specifically with the David tradition. Another valuable and focused case study is R. A. Carlson's *David, the Chosen King: A Traditional-Historical Approach to the Second Book of Samuel* (Stockholm: Almquist and Wiksell, 1964). Eugene Maly's *The World of David and Solomon* (Englewood Cliffs: Prentice-Hall, 1964) sets our present problem within its regional context.

   For the archaeological sidelights, which become increasingly rich over the course of David's reign, two older but still very useful standard texts are M. Unger's *Archaeology and the Old Testament* (Grand Rapids: Zandervan, 1954) and G. E. Wright's *Biblical Archaeology* (Philadelphia: Westminster Press, 1957). Even earlier, but especially complete, is W. F. Albright's *The Archaeology of Palestine and the Bible* (New York: Fleming H. Revell Co., 1932). The journal *Biblical Archaeology Review* regularly covers new discoveries in this field.

   James G. Frazer, of *Golden Bough* renown, used a comparative anthropological approach in *Folklore in the Old Testament* (London: Macmillan, 1918).

Chapter Five

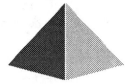

The Proto-Literate World

We have explored legend now, on our voyage into the distant eras and special methods of ancient history, but we have not yet exhausted the worlds contained in the phrase "oral tradition." The reader must stay aboard ship a little longer and touch in at a few more ports, for one cannot survive as a scholar on the seas of the distant human past without learning all the tools of this discipline. Reefs are everywhere, especially for the researcher who cannot see beyond the thought-patterns of his own insistently literate world.

There are the treasures, too. The rewards for an intelligent and careful handling of oral accounts may not be real gems or gold, but they are riches nonetheless. Our new understanding of oral history has restored to us characters like Nestor of Pylos and David of Israel, suggesting the historicity of one and enriching that of the other, and surrounding each with a wealth of cultural color and detail we would otherwise have dismissed or misunderstood.

When cultures are not literate cultures they must use oral accounts to preserve and to transmit to their descendants every kind of information they will need if their community is to continue. Classical Greek civilization, which we are so quick to associate with certain famous and polished masterpieces of writing, sprang from a soil of complete nonliteracy. During the Dark Age and even into the Classical period itself, rules of behavior, tales to lighten the drudgery of subsistence farming in a depopulated and unforgiving land, even the instructions for hitching a plow or building a little boat, were passed from one generation to the next solely by word of mouth. Because the Homeric *Iliad* and *Odyssey* were created in this kind of age, they served as "encyclopedias of life"; people continued to sing and treasure them not just because they were about Troy, but because they were about everything.

Homer is for us (as for the classical Greeks) the best known example of an oral bard. We have only tantalizing snatches of information about other—perhaps less gifted—bards

The Early Archaic Age (850 - 700)

Date B.C.	Greek & Ionian Events	Around the Mediterranean	Artifacts & Art
850 --	(850 - 700) The Greeks at some point begin to adapt the Phoenician alphabet, though it is long before they make any extensive use of it.	(854) The Battle of Kharkar. Shalmaneser III of Assyria defeats in the kings of Palestine (including Ahab of Israel).	(c. 850 onward) "Geometric" pottery is a flourishing style in the Greek world (e.g., vases and large jars --
	(c. 825-750) Homer (or perhaps some Ionian poets using his name) refine, collect, and eventually write down the *Iliad* and the *Odyssey*. The Trojan War becomes fixed as the central catastrophe of the lost	(814) The Phoenicians, who already have a few colonies in N. Africa, found Carthage (which means "New Town").	*amphorae* -- decorated with patterns of geometric line, sometimes representing stylized figures).
800 --	world.	(c. 800) A few rustic Italian settlements on the Palatine Hill (at the future site of Rome.	(c. 850) Athens: date of the small bulb-topped clay geometric shrines in the Agora Museum,
	(c. 800) Greeks at sea again; beginning to use the Phoenician sea routes.	(783-745) Assyria weak; prosperity in Phoenicia, and in Israel under Jeroboam.	Athens.
	(c. 800) The Oracle at Delphi rises to prominence, providing a god's answers to the hard questions of Archaic life.	(753) Traditional date of the founding of Rome (a Latin outpost town on the river-	
	(776) Traditional date of the first Olympic Games.	border of Etruscan country) by Romulus and Remus.	(c. 750?) Greeks producing small "geometric" (very
750 --	(c. 750) The first "Messenian War" in the Peloponnese (won by Sparta, about 716).	(c. 750) First Greek colony at Cumae in western Italy.	abstract) bronze animal figures like the horse statuette in the
	(c. 750) The Greeks begin colonizing outside the Aegean.	(745) Tiglath Pileser III becomes King of Assyria. (c. 740) The Assyrians begin reducing their conquered lands	Metropolitan Museum, New York.
	(c. 740-700) Hesiod, a Boeotian farmer, writes the *Works and Days* and the *Theogony*.	to provinces, sometimes deporting large populations.	
	(c. 700-600) The Greeks colonize	(735) The Greeks begin to plant colonies in Sicily.	
700 --	north toward Chalcidice, the shores of the Hellespont and the Black Sea. Information about possible sites is collected and exchanged at	(734) Corinth plants its Sicilian colony at Syracuse. (722) Sargon II of Assyria	Archilochus fl. (the first major Greek lyric poet).
	Delphi. They also begin to spread across the "boot-sole" of the Italian peninsula, which comes to be called "Magna Graecia" (or "Greater Greece").	conquers Israel. Ethiopian kings rule Egypt until 682 (the 25th dynasty). (c. 704) The height of	(c. 700) the Greeks begin to produce monumental stone sculptures. (c. 700) Israel: date of builder's inscriptions in the tunnel of Siloam (cut
	(c. 700) At least a few Greeks are now literate.	Assyrian power. (c. 700) The fledgling city of Rome begins to develop its own culture and religion.	into the rock beneath Jerusalem to safeguard a water supply against the threat of Assyria).

in early Greece, but we know that they existed. They often were not famous enough to be remembered as individuals, but their world could not have survived without them. The experience of anthropologists among a variety of nonliterate peoples today tells us that a "bard" is necessary in every community. The nature of oral communication requires a man or woman to master the craft; it is one of the "survival skills" for human society.

One singer of this kind was Hesiod, who lived in a little farming village, in a valley near the center of the Greek mainland, around 700 B.C. The two major poems attributed to him are probably better examples of the practical use of song and verse than the *Iliad* and *Odyssey*, since Hesiod kept them firmly grounded in the "feel" and values of his own community. They cast much of their glance not backward at an age of heroes but at the plows and goats, the rock and dust-ridden world around them. For the historian this is exciting: any insights we can glean from the verses will be contemporary with (actually will be about) the world of the singer himself.

Something dynamic and pioneering had begun to happen throughout Greece by the end of the eighth century B.C.: the seeds of what would become the classical Greek era had begun to push their way out of the soil. They had lain buried for a long time, crushed under the rubble strewn by the crash of the Mycenaean kingdoms in the twelfth century B.C. The next 400 years were a Dark Age that really deserved the name, in Greece even more than around the rest of the eastern Mediterranean. Depopulation was almost unbelievably harsh: as many as 90 percent of the human inhabitants of Greece vanished; communities became tiny, desperate things, cut off and remote from one another as the mountain passes and foothills became wild again. They retreated further and further from the seacoast where unruly bands of marauders (themselves dwindling) burned everything they could not carry away. The larger Mediterranean world became half a rumor, brought by an infrequent tramp trading boat from the Levant, whose merchandise seldom penetrated very far inland. Villages or individuals scraped their subsistence from the dry land, or migrated from pasture to pasture in the way of long-forgotten eras. Craft and technology shrank to the barest, simplest levels. The lost Mycenaean Age must indeed have seemed an Age of Heroes.

Since the ninth century B.C., however, conditions had begun to bounce back with increasing speed and energy. By Hesiod's day, though one might not always guess it from his mood, the rate of transformation was truly revolutionary. Population exploded in the 800s. Communities mushroomed, spreading quickly out onto nearby land and creating new occupations. Many rapidly outgrew their old village-family organization and improvised newer, tighter means of control. Communities began to contact each other again, hesitantly at first. As roads through passes or down the coast reopened, and as growing communities began to demand new and more resources, trade became regular again. Contact and the flowering of specialized skills in the little towns acted like mutual catalysts to one another, and the recivilizing of Greece pushed forward at an accelerated speed.

We have hinted that Hesiod's poems do not reflect much joy in this bustling new world. His life remained a farmer's, keeping him harnessed to the stern soil of Greece, and keeping the focus of his poetry close to home. But for all that, we learn a great deal about how revolutionary the Archaic Age felt from its agricultural underside. Land had

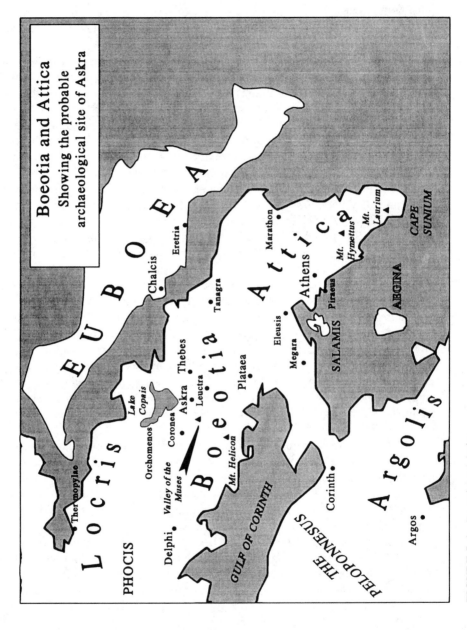

FIGURE 5–1 Boeotia and Attica

become a precious commodity; men fought over it now, even if there were ties of blood between them. Many were turning to strange crafts and pursuits, even (to Hesiod's endless disgust) toward "foolish commerce by sea." No longer content with merely managing the details of community life, there were persons now in the nearby village that claimed special governing powers. Hesiod, who could (by oral tradition) remember the equality and communal simplicity of the old days, did not stomach that development well at all.

We do not possess a strictly "historical" account of these monumental years. Herodotus owns the title "Father of History," but he lived and composed his prose account of the Persian Wars during the mid-fifth century B.C. What we can glean from Hesiod's poetry is historical information of another sort: varied, moving images of a historical era frozen in a dark and rather personal sort of mirror. The student must have a very clear understanding of the mirror itself, but if it is used with care he may find himself confronting the authentic acts and beliefs of an age 2,700 years ago.

HESIOD'S WINGED WORDS

> *Then drag your swift ship down to the sea...*
> *As did my father and yours too, O Perses,*
> * you great fool,*
> *who used to sail in ships, for he wanted to live*
> * like a noble,*
> *and once on a time, leaving Kyme of Aiolis,*
> * he came here*
> *in his black ship, having crossed over*
> * a vast amount of water;*
> *and it was not comfort he was fleeing, nor wealth*
> * nor prosperity,*
> *but that evil poverty that Zeus gives men*
> * for a present;*
> *and settled here near Helikon in a hole of a village,*
> * Askra....*
>
> (*Works and Days*: 633–40, Lattimore trans.; the other translations
> in this chapter are also taken from Lattimore's edition.)

This is Hesiod of Askra in Boeotia acidly reminding his brother Perses not to "put on airs." One can almost hear him spit out the line about the "hole of a village" in which he must live, a place he can only call "bad in winter, tiresome in summer, good at no season" (*Works and Days*:640). He was, in fact, unhappy with life in general. Only a fool expects much good in the world, says he, "For here now is the age of iron. Never by daytime will there be an end to hard work and pain, nor in the night to weariness, when the gods will send anxieties to trouble us" (*Works and Days*:176–77).

Hesiod poured his complaints into song around 700 B.C., the very end of what is known as the Dark Age of Greek history. As he reminded his brother, their father had come to the mainland of Greece from the family's home in Asia Minor. He had been poor and starving (that was the sort of gift men could expect from Zeus), and he had "gone west" looking for a new life. We have evidence that many Greeks around him were doing just the same; rising population was making land scarce and expen-

FIGURE 5–2 This late classical (4th century A.D.) mosaic by Monnus is the only certain portrait of Hesiod remaining to us. The sharp canny eye and the wry mouth are remarkable—just what we might expect from the dour poet-farmer.

sive, driving the smallest farmers further from the towns or deeper into poverty unless they could start over somewhere else. Between 750 and 550 B.C., Greek colonies spread outward like a thicket of ivy across the northern Mediterranean and Black Seas' coasts.

Hesiod's own words have come down to us in the form of two long poems, *Theogony* and *Works and Days*, though there are several shorter works which claim (debatably) to be his as well. Like Homer, Hesiod became famous enough to attract a whole cycle of poems around his memory, genuine work growing so tightly interwoven with the poetry of others that now they are exceedingly difficult to separate. Readers who have come with us through the chapters on Nestor and David should by now find this natural. Even though Hesiod himself was able to read and write, the overwhelming majority of cultural information—both in tiny villages like Askra and thriving cities like Corinth—was still transmitted by human speech. Writing had reappeared in Greece, but its spread was very slow. A few curious Greeks could learn the craft of writing; their world, by and large, did not. Even in its Golden Age, the culture of Greece was still fundamentally an oral one.

We shall concentrate on Hesiod's long poems later in this chapter, but before we turn to them it might be wise to get a surer grounding in the character and texture of the oral Archaic Greek world. It is likely to transform the questions we ask about Hesiod and give fresh meaning to our answers.

During the Bronze Age, Greeks of the Mycenaean palace cultures were able to read and write but they used this skill in surprisingly limited ways. They put into writing their account-books, but almost nothing of their personalities, loves, wars, myths, or the lore of their farms and crafts. Perhaps because of this limitation, their curiously hedged-in form of literacy disappeared when their culture did during the Dark Age. After the palace-centers collapsed into fire and ruin, it would be some 400 years before another kind of Greek writing appeared to take its place. Even more remarkably, as the Archaic world began to bustle again, as improvisation and creativity began so to fill the air that Anthony Snodgrass has called that era the "Age of Experiment," Greeks as a whole returned to writing at what now seems like a snail's pace. Three hundred more years lie between the mid-eighth century B.C., when Greece seems to have been completely non-literate, and the mid-fifth century, when literacy began to penetrate more aspects of life. Only fifty of those years had passed by 700 B.C. Hesiod and a very few other Greeks were literate; he was one of a select group.

No society that hopes to continue can afford to lose the really important information from its past. This presents no real problem for a literate culture: its written records allow it to fix its data more or less permanently, to store it and to go back to it easily when it is needed. A culture without writing must take another tack with the problem, and that tack is almost always a patterning of human speech and memory, usually by a transformation of both into some form of poetry. The reasons have to do with human nature. Poetic patterns of speech are easier to recall and more readily betray errors. Words can be combined into various fixed, interchangeable units which function almost like generic puzzle pieces, because they describe a particular thing with economy and grace and because they fit into a convenient metrical rhythm. These puzzle pieces of poetized speech are called "formulas," and they form the preserved core of the bard's craft, for while he may individually make up a number of new formulas and forget others, he will preserve all the best and most necessary ones. They are the tools by which he first learned and constantly reweaves his apparently seamless songs.

The word *seamless* is often used by those lucky enough to have watched this craft in practice. As with garments, the making of something seamless appears simple but is really a matter of great intricacy and skill. Once a singer begins his song or tale, the well-learned formulas must well up from somewhere within him, attaching themselves in their right places to the thread of narrative as it passes through his mind. If he is making a new song they must rise naturally as the rhythm flows into new patterns. In either case, the patterns carry the utterance forward almost like a boat upon a stream. The old song stays the same because the bard knows the patterns; even the audience will recall long stretches as the bard sings and will catch him if he slips. New song melds organically out of old, reborn phrases.

It is not easy to imagine the power of purely verbal, cadenced utterance when poetry does not play any important part in the mainstream life of a culture. In America today only subcultures react very intuitively to patterned speech. The best current exception to offer might be the lyrics of popular songs, for though they often sound like rhythmic nonsense to the unsympathetic (and so untrained) ear, any particular form of music has a subculture of "fans" who can recall them from beginning to end. A friend of one of the authors can sing without interruption for as many as five hours, but when asked to repeat the words without the aid of his guitar, he finds them slipping away.

It is not just the music that makes the words memorable; poetry unsung goes far to aid the memory. Americans may no longer resort readily to limericks but they once did, and the comparison to poetic speech is apt: words will not fit comfortably into a limerick unless they fit the pattern, but if they do fit, they become fixed in the reader's mind. John Luce once ended a scholarly symposium on Minoan palaces in impromptu meter:

> *King Minos now judges the dead.*
> *Let us hope that he'll judge what we've said*
>   *with candour, not malice;*
>   *But as for his palace...*
> *God knows where the argument led!* (1987:333)

He could of course have ended in elegant prose and looked much more the serious scholar, but many readers are likely to find his limerick more memorable than even the best prose. If such a "quirk" is true even of us, we must evaluate nonliterate individuals and their cultures with care. By comparison with us they must absolutely rely on the poetic form.

Consider the nature of communication, at the most basic level, in oral societies. Whoever depends totally on the spoken word is conditioned by sound. And since you cannot capture sound without electronic or at least a rather fancy mechanical technology, it will always be impermanent. Sound is tied to the immediate, the present. There is an advantage: sound is accessible to everyone in the group except the physically impaired. Sound, in that sense, is "universal." The more members of a culture who can participate in its vital knowledge the better, especially if the culture is a small one and struggling for its survival. Let us suggest then one of the "rules" that govern such societies: an oral tradition cannot function well unless it is fixed in the collective memory.

The consequence of that rule is that in such societies traditions are created by and for the entire culture. We should not be surprised if the identities of individual singers are submerged, if even some of the greatest songs are rendered anonymous. Although there are specialists in the crafting and preservation of oral tradition, the substance of the tradition is communal knowledge. The eccentricities of individual bards will drop away; it is the central things about which the culture cares most that it will wish to preserve. The truth caught in an oral tradition is even more than usually specific to the life of its particular people.

So, how do you create a tradition? How can a culture make so lasting a mold from the tools of its oral bards that the truth cast within it emerges in nearly permanent form?

First, it must be decided whether a certain piece of information needs remembering. The community as a whole decides—not an individual poet (or even an individual ruler)—though it may not do so consciously. The winning or losing of a battle, the ancestry of chiefs or kings, the proper occasions for ritual offerings to the gods could all promote the making of traditional accounts to preserve them. Raw material is collected—also quite unconsciously—from individual anecdotes or the knowledge of specialists like priests, seers, judges; it then blends these pieces through the skilled tongues of the bards into a fuller account that is likely to persist as long as the culture needs it. Individual memories or anecdotes that are not fitted into a larger context probably disappear. This process is likely to happen fairly fast: any tradition gets its basic structuring in the first or second generation of being handed down. After that, the uncertain details are likely to have become too vague to be recalled properly.

Most oral societies find they need specialists to create and preserve the traditions. These specialists must be both "authors" and performers: bards, minstrels, praise singers in some royal courts, genealogists, clan historians, *rawi* (official performers of the Arabic world) all combine the "making" and the "showing" of their themes. Anthropologists tell us that the more specialized a society grows, the more its bards begin to specialize. In a simple culture, one celebrated singer may be able to fill all the functions required, though he may spend long hours traveling from village to village. A more complex society can usually afford and requires the skills of several specialists, perhaps even a guild of specialists, who preserve the remembered tradition in a range of different styles.

It goes almost without saying that a tradition is unlikely to be preserved unless both narrator and audience find it memorable. So the center of a tale stays very close to concrete events and remarkable persons. The "plot" of a story should be easy to grasp, the people at least as large as life (larger, if possible), and episodes full of suspense. All these devices provide tonic for the human memory and carry the story forward, catching and holding the attention of the audience.

Some readers object that the repertoire of oral accounts seems limited: situations recur again and again, resolutions are predictable far in advance even when you have not heard the tales before. Everyone knows what will happen and, if all has been structured by a good bard, there are no loose ends. Past and present may overlap through anachronisms or split apart through floating gaps—telltale holes in the tale, which have few remembered details, passed off with only a stock phrase to cover them. These "defects" may provide endless worry to the cold-eyed and detached observer, but they do not trouble an oral audience. Listeners are there to hear the story of Troy, or Arthur, of the ancestral lore of farming, or of chivalry, not to nit-pick with a critic who cannot enter the tale as he listens. Nevertheless we ought to learn something from these tendencies when we can. Studies of more recent oral traditions show that accounts tend to take on an "hour-glass effect": the remote past and immediate present get the fullest telling because they are the two most significant periods. Events and people in between wither by the wayside. It is equally important to be aware of the linear nature of the narrative: since a bard must recount his tale in sequence, figures and events that may once have been contemporary soon begin to appear one after the other. Brothers have a habit of becoming father and son. Traditions are not static; they tend to change shape as the needs of a culture change.

Several particular clues will almost always mark an oral tradition. The fine distinctions between one kind of character or event are often minimal when they are present at all. Images, grand themes, heroes, conflicts will tend in a tale to be single, predictable, and "essential."It is more important to know something's essence—that Homer's "wine-dark Sea" *is* the sea, that "Shaker of Earth" *is* Poseidon, that in *Beowulf* "sundwudu" (which means "swimming-timber") *is* a ship—and those things are all one really needs to know.

A prominent trait is the human-centered nature of oral traditions. Humans have decided what they wish to remember; it is only natural that the tale should, in turn, center on humans. Other forms of life often relate more closely to humans than they ever do in our more "scientific" experience. Plants may "talk," birds may carry the founders of historical kingdoms on their backs, horses may shed tears for their masters slaughtered in battle, even the weather or the rocks in a landscape may do things or show feelings we expect only from a human. Even space is viewed as inhabited, filled as it is with "winged words." In most traditions, the interaction between spheres of life has a vivid and miraculous, but also disquieting tone. Seldom neutral or passive, life is filled with action.

There is no agreement among scholars about the fundamental reason for these tendencies. It could be that oral cultures have a tendency toward anthropomorphism: the bard and his culture are familiar with human reactions and ascribe similar reactions to all other creatures around them. Another clue may be at hand in the hierarchy of beings within the tales. While all the "spheres" of the world are alive in these traditions, rocks and thunderstorms and the sea as much as humans, it is some great human character important to the culture with whom they, the bard and the listeners, communicate at the high point of an oral tale. Everything included in almost every tale of a truly oral culture will either argue for, ally with, or fight against, the human heroes who represent the audience. Everything must take a side in the conflict or it has no place.

Hesiod's poetry is a beautifully thorough example of all these tendencies. Conflict pervades both the *Works and Days* and the *Theogony*. Conflict, according to Hesiod, evoked the first poem. He was locked in a struggle with his own brother and, while some struggles are good, theirs was of the wrong kind. Hesiod, blessed with a bard's insight, tried to tell his brother about the distinction.

> *It was never true that there was only one kind*
> *of strife. There have always*
> *been two on earth. There is one*
> *you could like when you understand her.*
> *The other is hateful. The two Strifes*
> *have separate natures.*
> *There is one Strife who builds up evil war,*
> *and slaughter....*
> *But the other one was born*
> *the elder daughter of black Night.*
> *The son of Kronos, who sits on high and*
> *dwells in the bright air,*
> *set her in the roots of the earth and among men;*
> *she is far kinder.*
> *She pushes the shiftless man to work,*
> *for all his laziness.*
>
> (*Works and Days*:11–20)

As far as Hesiod can tell, Strife is the ruler and mover of life at every level: among gods, between gods and mortals, among mortals, in the animal realm (as the nightingale learned from the hawk), and even in what we would call the sphere of abstractions. "There is an outcry when Justice is dragged perforce, when bribe-eating men pull her about, and judge their cases with crooked decisions" (*Works and Days*:220–21).

The early lines of the *Theogony* seem to imply a much gentler sort of account, full of kinder gods. The Muses seem kind, though they drop a hint that they can lie to human bards (ll:27–29). Hesiod begins by singing of the Helikonian Muses,

> *who possess the great and holy mountain of Helikon and dance there on soft feet by the dark blue water of the spring, and by the altar of the powerful son of Kronos* (*Theogony*:2–5).

But soon he turns to other divine beings—to Artemis of the showering arrows and to Poseidon, who encircles the earth in his arms and shakes it—and recounts how the present generation of gods came to be. The story is not a gentle one, and we almost sense again the dark satisfaction Hesiod takes in describing injustice and violence. Kronos ruled because he had seized and mutilated his father Ouranos (*Theogony*:179–81). In the next generation of the gods, Kronos' son Zeus (from whom Hesiod hoped to get justice, if it could be found anywhere) would also fight against his own father, for Kronos had heard the law "that it had been ordained for him, for all his great strength, to be beaten by his son, and through the designs of great "Zeus" (*Theogony*:463–64).

Preoccupation with this polemical nature of the world is closely woven into the genealogies of heaven, and mortals are well advised by Hesiod to pay attention since it is not so much the intention but (what is almost worse) the accidental byproduct of the gods' own violence to one another that causes all the intolerable suffering of life on earth. Look, for example, at a list of the offspring of Night, who is known as destructive Night: Nemesis, "who gives much pain to mortals," "cheating" Deception, "malignant" Old Age, and "overbearing" Discord. The list of their births reads, in Hesiod, like a tale of torture. Discord bore "painful" Hardship, Forgetfulness, Starvation, and "the Pains, full of weeping, the Battles, and the Quarrels, the Murders, and the Manslaughters, the Grievances, the lying Stories, the Disputations, and Lawlessness and Ruin, who share one another's nature, and Oath, who does more damage than any other to earthly men, when anyone, of his knowledge, swears to a false oath" (*Theogony*:223–32).

This catalogue of "children" demonstrates another quality of Hesiod's poetry: the way in which every corner of its universe breathes with anthropomorphic life. The *Theogony* especially resounds with the hum and activity of nature:

> *From Chaos was born Erebos, the dark,*
>   *and black Night,*
> *And from Night again Aither and Hemera,*
>   *the day were begotten,*
> *for she lay in love with Erebos*
>   *and conceived and bore these two.*
> *But Gaia's first born was one*
>   *who matched her every dimension,*
> *Ouranos, the starry sky,...*
> *Then she brought forth tall hills...* (123–28, 129)

The same life breathes irrepressibly in the *Works and Days*. Nightingales converse with Hawks, the Polis weeps, and Hope, trapped by the lid of a great jar, is unable to fly away and so remains "in the unbreakable closure" (96).

We might call such language figurative. But if we do, we should first have to undo in our minds all the modern and artificial meanings with which we normally associate the word. The human mind naturally thinks in figures; we make abstractions only by taking figures and removing most of the meaning from them. In an oral culture this process has barely begun. All things in tales are concrete objects—birds, beasts, deeds, conflicts—and they are seen from a concrete human perspective. When something like a concept manifests itself, it does so as something very solid and often very human. The physical entity called "Gaia" (Earth) conceives and bears children, such as Heaven and hills. These are all solid things. Yet they also do carry an abstract meaning. The difference from our modern manner of speaking is that these ancient words carried their "figurative"—abstract or metaphorical—meaning and their "plain" one simultaneously. Night was both a material object and a state of being—a presence—at one and the same time. Ralph Waldo Emerson wrote in the fourth chapter of *Nature*, that there is a "radical correspondence between visible things and human thoughts." Just so.

We have by now gone far enough into the psychological borderlands of "oral theory" that our historical purpose may be fading. There is a more practical side to the use of poetic speech in the spoken and patterned memory of a culture.

Form as well as subject aids memory: oral tradition uses a language whose patterns fall into phrases that often fit the needs of a particular poetic meter. Milman Parry, the groundbreaking student of Greek epic, defined these units as "formulae" that evolve over time. A proper formula expresses a specific idea in a way that is beautiful or memorable or poetically useful. A good formula does all three. Combinations that are both easily understood and sound well in the ear will survive; murky, awkward, and aesthetically jarring combinations tend to be replaced. In Homeric epic, for instance, rhythmic blocks of words were adapted to a six-footed line in which syllables had to fit a pattern of:

$$- \quad u \quad u \quad - \quad u \quad u \quad - \quad - \quad - \quad u \quad u \quad - \quad u \quad u \quad - \quad -$$
long short short, long short short, long long, long short short, long short short, long long

Obviously, one would not want to alter an elaborate sequence of syllables that already "worked" well, especially if there were no other words that could convey the same meaning in the same metric pattern. Oral traditions come to possess a stock of well-established words and phrases precisely because they need a "box of tools" large and varied enough to suit the task. If a new and fancier "tool" can do a particular job better, perhaps it might replace an old tool, but the business of oral composition would grow impossible for the average bard if this happened very often. Adherence to the stock phrases, not innovation, is the hallmark of the oral performance. Parry claimed that:

> Without writing, the poet can make his verses only if he has a formulaic diction which will give him his phrases all made, and made in such a way that, at the slightest bidding of the poet, they will link themselves in an unbroken pattern that will fill his verses and make his sentences. (1930:138)

The pattern is supported by the rhythm of the meter and, indeed, the rhythm in music is an important aid to memory. Bards often sang their woven words to the accompanying melody of a stringed instrument, or drums, or even to the movements of a company of dancers.

These were the most typically Greek ways to shore up the human memory under the strain of long recitation, but there are several other such supports. Inca remembrancers used objects called *quipu*, knotted ropes made of different colors of cord in different lengths to jog recall of specific words. Notable landmarks at fixed and known places may serve the same purpose when the matter to be recalled is something as tricky as a route across the wilderness. In *The Songlines*, Bruce Chatwin described the way in which the

Australian aborigines use their own countryside as a means of communication and the preservation of knowledge. Ancestors, remembered by the totems associated with them, once passed through the wild country of the Outback, scattering trails of music and words behind them. These trails persist as paths between places and the dwellings of people. Chatwin was told that a song would serve as both map and direction-finder. The one who knew a song, could "always find his way across the country." "Anywhere in the bush" his teacher told him, "you can point to some feature of the landscape and ask the Aboriginal with you, 'What's the story there?' or 'Who's that?' The chances are he'll answer 'Kangaroo' or 'Buderigar' or 'Jew Lizard,' depending on which Ancestor walked that way." (1987:esp. 12–15). A "stretch" of song is the measure of distance between two of these monumental landmarks. The paths of songs grew almost organically out of the natural shapes of the land. They are recalled generation after generation as new travelers come upon the same places, the rhythmic words rising afresh to their minds as a guide.

Pictorial images made and held before the mind's eye can also hold things powerfully in a human memory. An extraordinary case of retentive ability was documented by the Russian psychologist A. R. Luria in *The Mind of a Mnemonist: A Little Book about a Vast Memory*. Luria was studying a subject who was able to retain phenomenal amounts of data simply by recollection. He set a text in 1934 that involved a convoluted and meaningless mathematical formula.

The Mind of a Mnemonist
by
A.R. Luria

$$N. \sqrt{d^2 x \frac{85}{vx}} \cdot \sqrt[3]{\frac{276^2 \cdot 86x}{n^2 v \cdot 264}} \; n^2 b = sv \frac{1624}{32^2} \cdot r^2 s$$

S. examined the formula closely, lifting the paper up several times to get a closer look at it. Then he put it down, shut his eyes for a moment, paused as he "looked the material over" in his mind, and in seven minutes came through with an exact reproduction of the formula. The following account of his indicates the devices he used to aid him in recall:

Neiman (N) came out and jabbed at the ground with his cane (.). He looked up at a tall tree which resembled the square-root sign ($\sqrt{\ }$), and thought to himself: "No wonder the tree has withered and begun to expose its roots. After all, it was here when I built these two houses" (d^2). Once again he poked with his cane (.). Then he said: "The houses are old, I'll have to get rid of them (x);* the sale will bring in far more money." [The Russian expression literally means to cross out in the sense of "get rid of," to "cross something off one's list." trans.] He had originally invested 85,000 in them (85). Then I see the roof of the house detached (———), while down below on the street I see a man playing the Termenvox (vx). He's

---

standing near a mailbox, and on the corner there's a large stone (.) which has been put there to keep carts from crashing up against the houses. Here, then, is the square, over there the large tree ($\sqrt{}$) with three jackdaws on it (^{3}). I simply put the figure 276 here, and a square box containing cigarettes in the "square" (^{2}). The number 86 is written on the box. (This number was also written on the other side of the box, but since I couldn't see it from where I stood I omitted it when I recalled the formula.) As for the x, this is a stranger in a black mantle. He is walking toward a fence beyond which is a women's gymnasia. He wants to find some way of getting over the fence (———); he has a rendez-vous with one of the women students (n), an elegant young thing who's wearing a gray dress. He's talking as he tries to kick down the boards in the fence with one foot, while with the other (^{2})—oh, the girl he runs into turns out to be a different one. She's ugly—phooey! (v)... At this point I'm carried back to Rezhitsa, to my classroom with the big blackboard... I see a cord swinging back and forth there and I put a stop to that (.). On the board I see the figure 264, and I write after it n^2b.

Here I'm back in school. My wife has given me a ruler (=). I myself, Solomon-Veniaminovick (sv), am sitting there in the class. I see that a friend of mine has written down the figure 1624. I'm trying to see what else he's written, but behind me are two students, girls (r^2), who are also copying and making noise so that he won't notice them. "Sh", I say. "Quiet!" (s)

Thus S. managed to reproduce the formula spontaneously, with no errors. Fifteen years later, in 1949, he was still able to trace his pattern of recall in precise detail even though he had had no warning from us that he would be tested on this (1969:48–51).

Although powers of memory so great, rapid, and detailed as this must be unusual in any culture and at any time, we should expect to find something a little like them far more often in an oral than in a literary era. Without writing there is no alternative to the collective memory so that great pains are taken to train the memory, to stretch its capabilities and guard against its weaknesses. What might only seem a curiosity to a twentieth-century psychologist might easily be a matter of survival to a society for whom the very preservation of its collective knowledge was at stake.

Once a tradition has been sufficiently crafted, it becomes, as much as any building or weapon or painting, an artifact of that culture to be passed on from one generation to the next. Since the components in a tradition come together as the whole culture decides what knowledge it wishes to preserve, it is not unreasonable to speak of traditions as the "records" of particular, nonliterate people. Eric Havelock has described the products we have inherited from the Greek oral bards as the "encyclopedias" of the Dark Age. We mean, of course, to use the word *encyclopedia* only in its most general sense; Homer and Hesiod had no intention of rattling together compendia containing all the knowledge they could recall, even if they had the time or the memory or an irresistible power to keep their audiences endlessly still as they heard it all. Nor do we mean that such composers have left us "histories" in the modern sense. Rather we mean to say that they are encyclopedic in type. The actions, objects, and values portrayed in the tales were conditioned by the society for which the poet or bard recited them. And, in turn, the way in which they crafted what they sang acted to affect—condition—their listeners.

It is high time to return to Hesiod, to see what his poems, now that we have a fresh perspective on them, tell us about his world.

T. A. Sinclair, an editor of the *Works and Days*, makes a rather curmudgeonly observation in his introduction, almost acid enough to be worthy of Hesiod himself:

> The author began to write a series of admonitions, and such was his enthusiasm for his subject that he almost succeeded in writing a fine poem. That he did not quite succeed in a task which he had never really set himself must not be counted a great fault. (1932:xi)

Does Hesiod deserve this? Hesiod's position on the spectrum of orality and literacy does much to explain the nature of his poems. If we can picture Hesiod's position along this spectrum, we might go far toward understanding his predicament, toward knowing what he set out to do and what he was capable of accomplishing, and whether he came close to achieving his goal.

In the first place, there is a high proportion of lists or "catalogues" in both poems. The *Theogony*, in fact, is little more than a mosaic of lists of the gods. When he wants us to understand the earliest, most primeval state of the earth, Hesiod strings his facts neatly:

> *Without any sweet act of love*
> *she [Earth] produced the barren*
> *sea, Pontos, seething in his fury of waves,*
> *and after this*
> *she lay with Ouranos, and bore him*
> *deep-swirling Okeanos*
> *the ocean-stream; and Koios, Krios,*
> *Hyperion, Iapetos,*
> *and Theia too and Rheia, and Themis,*
> *and Mnemosyne,*
> *Phoibe of the wreath of gold,*
> *and Tethys the lovely.* (131–36)

In the *Works and Days*, on the other hand, there are many things to compete with the lists. Hesiod has homespun, hard-edged things close to his heart on which he means to have his say—things like goat-herding and lawsuits, and those bribe-devouring new magistrates in town for whom the vengeance of Zeus had better be waiting—but the lists are still there. Often they appear in the form of maxims which are, after all, only lists of the little wisdoms other men have gained. Here Hesiod takes up the agricultural year:

> *First of all, the first, fourth, and seventh*
> *of the month are holy;*
> *it was on this last that Leto gave birth to Apollo*
> *of the golden sword. Then the eighth and ninth,*
> *two days in each month*
> *as it waxes, are excellent for mortal labors.*
> *The eleventh day, and the twelfth too,*
> *are both very good days*
> *either for shearing sheep or for reaping*
> *the good harvest* . (770–75)

The information was probably invaluable to many of the new colonists who set out from the overcrowded towns of the late eighth century to stake themselves a new life in the wild country of Greece and the west. The form, by contrast, is not likely to provoke long applause from a town-bred audience. These two facts tell us something important. Jack Goody, who has made intensive studies into the differing forms of the literate and oral mentalities, argues that the appearance of writing in a culture leads very quickly to a lot of list-making. Writing not only aids in preserving data, it also allows new uses of data. Once individual facts are frozen in script, they can be sorted and rearranged, criticized and compared. Lists in an oral society are seldom long; in cultures that have recently learned to write, they flourish like pines, stretching further and further until they satisfy the intense new hunger to know not just enough about something but all about it.

Even the smaller "literary revolutions," which punctuate the rural histories of the higher cultures, can be tracked by this feature. As the fortunes of more developed civilizations fluctuate, their agricultural hinterlands and frontiers tend repeatedly to rise a little above, and then fall back below, the level of functional literacy. Each time they rise to this watermark they tend to produce their own (often little) new literature of lists. When literacy crept briefly out into the Roman countryside in the first century B.C., it very quickly produced Cato the Elder's little handbook *De Re Rustica*. When the English countryside became more literate in the sixteenth century A.D., it produced Thomas Tusser's *Five Hundred Points of [Animal] Husbandrie*, with verse that could (except for an occasional outbreak of gruff optimism) have come from Hesiod's own speech. Even the "anthropomorphic" life in the very land is there: a bad farmer "defrauds the land," a good one gives Earth her way—"let seede have her longing, let soile have her lust."

Thus the unattractive lists in Hesiod's poems provide more than a handy catalogue for his rural audience; they reveal important historical processes in the eighth-century mind. By Hesiod's day it had just become possible to group and order information in new ways, and the culture—pressed by a burgeoning population in a land with little fertile soil to spare—was ready to see what it could make of the newly compiled data. It needed the sort of thing that Hesiod could do. He was a man "working with disjunct bits and pieces of verse drawn from his oral reservoir which he [was] trying to put together in a new way" (Havelock, 1982:213).

If we may make our own list, the importance of Hesiod's information becomes much clearer.

1. The *Theogony* traces the history of the universe through the genealogy of the gods. A healthy culture should know where it began, and how it should relate (conduct its diplomacy, if you will) to the greater beings that sometimes take notice of it. Remember that, as we saw earlier in Hesiod and Homer, these beings are both humanlike and utterly other than humans; the great suffering and benefit they cause to crops and lives on earth is often a mere byproduct of their own business among themselves. Hesiod's information may help men avoid offending them, but if it does not, understanding may at least ease the pain a little.

2. An agrarian society must care for its land and its products if it is to survive. Lines 383 to 617 of the *Works and Days* are a compendium of the farmer's year, urging hard work and honest treatment of others.

3. The second major thrust of the *Works and Days* is a bitter but reasoned plea for justice. Hesiod knows that there are two kinds of strife—good and evil; he himself has been the victim of evil strife at the hands of his brother:

Now once before we divided our inheritance,
  but you seized
the greater part and made off with it,
  gratifying those barons
who eat bribes, who are willing
  to give out such a decision. (37–39)

In several short tales, Hesiod repeats, "The road to justice is the better way." The importance of justice in any community needs no explanation, but we have evidence that it was an overpowering concern in Hesiod's day. As we have seen, most of what is called "The Greek Dark Age" appears to have been totally nonliterate. In writing's absence, the elaborate system of oral tradition developed. Just how rich it became we can see from its end products: the Homeric epics. The system which worked to create these epics tried to preserve all the information needed for the well-being of the Dark Age communities: it was "a body of invisible writing imprinted upon the brain of the community" (Havelock, 1963:141).

Hesiod lived at a time that the economy of Greece was growing in new directions and the old mechanisms for justice were not functioning adequately. Hesiod's bursts of preaching and invective against the bad old and the bad new "justice" around him are a very compelling historical signal about his times.

About the middle of the eighth century, Greece learned a new form of writing, more flexible both for learning and for setting down language in poetic meter. While this "alphabet" did not replace orality, it did become increasingly popular for the keeping of communal and individual records. And as writing became an alternative meaning of remembering information, the system of the oral tradition began to weaken. Even though they sponsored contests (like the *rhapsode* competitions) to preserve the old skills, it soon grew necessary for communities to entrust their most essential and treasured rules, laws, and songs to the fixed certainties of written script. Hesiod's attempt to find a communal definition of right and wrong must surely belong in the category of essential and treasured material.

So it is that the poems of Hesiod allow us an intimate look into the mind of the late Dark Age, even though they carry few hard historical facts. That is both the good and the bad news. Without him we should hardly have known about life on the land in the pioneering years of the Archaic Age. On the other hand, from his description alone we could never be sure where Askra was. (Interestingly, recent survey archaeology has given us a location.)

The lesson is that the literate, modern student of history must not go to oral or predominantly oral sources expecting to get the same kind of data available in the publications of a predominantly literate society. The method of a poetic compiler like Hesiod is what the French scholar F. Hartog calls "mirroring." Such accounts reflect and elaborate the world in which the compiler lived; they do not analyze and they almost never compare. The fuller the work of such a person, the more we will know what about the things his or her culture truly cared for. We will have a chance to replace, temporarily, our own mental furniture with that of the poet, to see that other culture through some of its own values, and so perhaps to really understand it rather than simply knowing things about it. The setting may become a vivid picture for us, as it did with such immediacy long ago in the ears of its listeners.

Hesiod's Askra was an agrarian village. The productivity of the soil around it was a matter of life, death, and prosperity to the sour old poet and the neighbors with whom he quarrelled and without whom he could not have survived. There were a few specialists among them, but more often than not

> *A man looks at his neighbor, who is rich:*
> *then he too*
> *wants work; for the rich man presses on with*
> *his plowing and planting*
> *and the ordering of his state.*
> *So the neighbor envies the neighbor*
> *who presses on toward wealth. (Works and Days:21–24)*

The evidence reveals minimal stratification based on wealth and also differentiation of standing between most people and the "gift-devouring lords" whose role it is to settle disputes. Often, according to Hesiod, the lords make "crooked" judgments, as they did in his own situation. Thus, accounts like the *Works and Days* reveal values, standards of proper and improper behavior.

> *If any man by force of hands wins him*
> *a great fortune,*
> *or steals it by the cleverness of his tongue,*
> *as so often*
> *happens among people when the intelligence*
> *is blinded*
> *by greed, a man's shameless spirit tramples*
> *his sense of honor;*
> *lightly the gods wipe out that man, and diminish*
> *the household*
> *of such a one, and his wealth stays with him*
> *for only a short time. (321–26)*

We cannot see much hierarchy in the evidence left us by Hesiod: a little by wealth and a little by social rank. What we can see is that above everyone else strutted a little group of "gift-devouring lords" whose role it was, by tradition or their own assertion, to settle disputes. About the quality of their judgments Hesiod means to leave no doubt: crooked, every man of them, and he himself had been one of the victims. These are the real historic values pushing forward to assert their presence in the *Works and Days*.

Modern historians who turn their eye on Archaic Greece are quite adept at telling you what you will not learn from Hesiod. Many of them are on the trail of exact dates, events, locations. For the exact placement of an uncertain date or place, oral tradition will prove a clumsy tool. But if we are after priceless insights into the shared mentality of an era, if we really want to find the everyday lore of the anonymous singers, to feel the values and knowledge of the men and women who molded their cultures as they sat and listened, we can hardly ask for any better tool.

Pope, who was often himself on the side of the wiseacres, may serve to finish for once on the side of the farmers and the bards:

A perfect judge will read each work of wit
With the same spirit that its author writ.

FURTHER READING

Richmond Lattimore has translated *Works and Days*, the *Theogony*, and *The Shield of Herakles* in *Hesiod* (Ann Arbor: University of Michigan Press, 1959). There is also a translation of the *Theogony* and *Works and Days* by Dorothea Wender (Harmondsworth: Penguin Books, 1973).

A useful introduction to the nature of orality is by Walter J. Ong, *Orality and Literacy: The Technologizing of the Word* (London and New York: Methuen, 1982). For Greece, the foundations of study in orality and literacy were laid by Eric A. Havelock. A collection of his essays is entitled *The Literate Revolution in Greece and Its Cultural Consequences* (Princeton: Princeton University Press, 1982); it includes a discussion of "Thoughtful Hesiod."

Chapter Six

Croesus
and Coinage

They laid the coins before the council.
Kay, the king's steward, wise in economics, said:
'Good; these cover the years and the miles
and talk one style's dialects to London and Omsk.
Traffic can hold now and treasure be held,
streams are bridged and mountains of ridged space tunnelled;
gold dances deftly across frontiers.
The poor have choice of purchase, the rich of rents,
and events move now in a smoother control
than the swords of the lords or the orisons on nuns.
Money is the medium of exchange.'

—Charles Williams,
"Bors to Elayne; on the King's Coins"

Just as the slow half-felt pressures of time may distort one person's perceived memory of an event, so the collective perception of a people may change, consciously or unconsciously. When a man like Hesiod begins to record the conditions and landmark deeds of his world, he describes things as he sees them—largely as his culture has taught him the worth and meaning of values and institutions. How far can a modern historian (who aims at the truth but inherits his own, very different, collection of mental furniture) trust the earlier person's description? Must we always be boxing at shadows?

However reliable we may decide an ancient source is, a little corroborative evidence is always a welcome thing. What merely seemed trustworthy before, always begins to assume a solid, objective texture when two different historical disciplines can confirm its trustworthiness, each from its own direction. Two witnesses looking from two vantage points are unlikely to see the same illusion.

The Late Archaic Era (700 - 500)

Date B.C.	Greek & Ionian Events	Around the Mediterranean	Artifacts & Art
700 --	(c.) Pheidon of Argos allied with Aegina and Miletus (a port in Asia Minor)?	(689) The Assyrians destroy Babylon.	(c. 700) 1st gold and silver coins struck in Lydia (early date).
	(c. 685) Gyges reigns in Lydia; takes the Greek center of Smyrna. (c. 683) Athens ends rule by its board of hereditary "kings"; nine *archons* now chosen yearly from nobility. (c. 680) Rise of Pheidon, King of Argos; armies of heavy infantry (hoplites) in "phalanx" formation appearing in Greece.	(682) The kingdom of Judah surrenders to Assyria. (675) Sidon destroyed in Phoenicia. (663) Assyrians sack Thebes in Egypt. (612) Nineveh taken by an army of Medes, Babylonians, and Scythians.	(c. 670 - 660) Late date for the invention of coinage. (c. 660) Simonides of Samos fl. (somber lyric poet). (c. 650) Tyrtaeus (Spartan warrior-poet) fl.
650 --	(c. 655) Cypselus (tyrant at Corinth) fl., promotes trade, culture, colonization. (c. 650) beginning of Spartan social and military system. (c. 650) Social and political unrest in Ionian cities leads to decline of hereditary nobility, rise of merchant class and "tyrants." (c. 621) The law code of Draco in Athens. (c. 620) Pheidon, tyrant of Argos, dead.	(609) End of the Assyrian Empire. (605) Battle of Carchemish: Nebuchadnezzar II defeats Egypt. (c. 600) Massilia (Marseilles) in southern Gaul colonized by Greeks from Phocaea. (587) Nebuchadnezzar captures Jerusalem. (574) Nebuchadnezzar takes and destroys Tyre after siege.	(c. 610 - 600) Early coins and metal pieces from the Temple of Artemis in Ephesus. (c. 600) Sappho (lyric poetess) and Alcaeus (poet) fl. on Lesbos. (c. 600) Early mud and brick temple at Delphi. (c. 580) Nebuchadnezzar begins building the "Hanging Gardens of Babylon."
600 --			
	(c. 594) Solon becomes archon at Athens. (c. 560) Croesus, King of Lydia, friendly to the Greek city-states; but begins to subjugate Ionia.	(559) The Persian Empire established by Cyrus the Great (rules to 530). (c. 550) Celtic peoples of Gaul begin to import Greek pottery. (c.) Zoroastrianism begins to spread in Persia.	(c. 560) Black figure vase painting in Atica.
550 --	(546) Battle of Sardis: Cyrus of Persia defeats Croesus. Lydia reduced to the status of a Persian province. Persian rule spreads across Asia Minor; Greek world shaken by fall of Ionian cities. (546 - 528) Peisistratus rules as tyrant of Athens; establishment of Athenian drama.	(539) Cyrus reduces Judah and Phoenicia to Persian subjects. (530) Cambyses rules Persia, conquers Egypt in 525. (c.) Greeks and Etruscans clash in central Italy. (521) Darius I becomes King of Persia (to 486); the empire is divided in 20 provincial *satrapies*. (Trad. 509) Last king expelled at Rome; beginning of the Republic.	(Trad. 550) Fables of Aesop at court of Croesus (Lydia). (c. 530) Height of "red figure" pottery in Greece. (c. 530 - 510) Great Archaic temple of Apollo built at Delphi. (c. 520) Pindar (poet) born in Boeotia.
500 --	(508) Democratic reforms of Cleisthenes in Athens.		

We saw in an earlier chapter how archaeology might lend this sort of "stereo" sharpness to oral history, but as we work nearer the times called "classical antiquity," another kind of evidence becomes available—an evidence that can give solidity to those parts of the past that were occasionally touched by the economic action of people. This is coinage, the use of small, inscribed metal units as symbols of value—as a medium to ease the exchanges that cultures make among their own members, and between one another, as they trade and organize goods and labor. Coinage allows the trading of value-symbols rather than the plain barter of bulky commodities. It even allows the trading of intangible things—a certain value for the work of an artist, perhaps—and so the coming of coinage stands in the economic sphere a little like the coming of literacy in the sphere of the mind. Coinage shows the tradable values of a culture as written down on a durable (and compact) material.

Coinage appeared in the Mediterranean world during the seventh or sixth century B.C. Before this, wealth had been measured in the amount of some specific (and widespread) commodity: a slave, for example, might have been worth six cows; a shield worth half a cow. In the third and second millennia, metals do seem to have served as a medium of exchange (one would expect it in an era called "the Bronze Age"), but they were not shaped as coins. Traders and expert craftsmen whose lives were tied to the metal itself used ingots or similar large chunks of material, and a number of these have been found in the wreckage of a Bronze Age merchant ship. But the ordinary person had no convenient small metallic means of counting poverty or wealth. More important for historians, these ingots bore no real writing or artwork; compared to true coins. They tell few tales.

That last point is critical. Beyond anything they might say archaeologically, coins often carry inscriptions; they function both as artifacts and as documents. They are thus a sort of physical evidence that can make declarations about their own use—about the actual day-to-day working of economies like the one Hesiod described. When the old poet advises a tenderfoot settler to "get first a house, a woman, and an ox for ploughing" (*Works and Days*:404), he does not bother to say how or where such things are available. Would the young farmers in his audience expect to barter for them? Is there some standard of values or prices?

Finding or not finding coins in the archaeological record of his culture might tell us the things we still do not know when the poet has finished speaking. If coins were being used for trading in Greece as early as 700 B.C., we might conclude that the purchases in the poem were a business of money. If coins did not exist, Hesiod's listeners would have expected to barter for those things they first needed when they began to farm. Lastly, when a coin carries an inscription, it can tell us things of its own: a coin marked "Askra" would say much about the capabilities of the town which made it.

Coined money joins the stream of recorded evidences for ancient Greek history, though it probably begins a little after (not during) Hesiod's lifetime. It is especially interesting that the Greeks, who loved to take credit for their inventions, did not take credit for this one. They said coins had come to them from a people known as the Lydians, one of the first foreign peoples they met as they began to venture out of their Dark Age isolation.

As the Dark Ages ended, the Greeks made their first enduring contacts with non-Greeks in the inland valleys of Asia Minor (modern western Turkey). Since about 1000 B.C., Greek settlers had been building tiny foothold communities along the Aegean coast of that country, while larger Dark Age states began to rise in the interior. The first of these was Phrygia, which began to sprout after the Bronze Age collapse around a

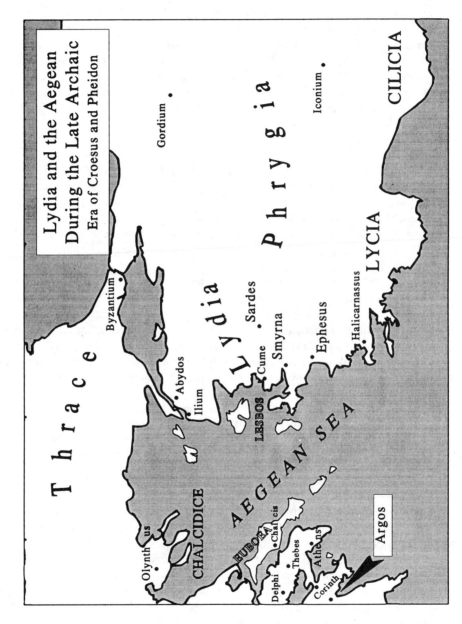

FIGURE 6–1 Lydia and the Aegean During the Late Archaic Era of Croesus and Pheidon

capital far inland at Gordion, but the Asian Greeks (who remained rooted to the seacoast) caught only sporadic glimpses of the Phrygians. They contacted the second important kingdom far more frequently and intensively: Lydia spread through the western interior of Asia Minor, very near the Greeks' own lands. From the early seventh century onward, they traded with the Lydians, exchanged ideas, and (inevitably) defended themselves in battle as their rapidly developing neighbor made one troubling and historically exciting advance after another. The Greeks' very survival depended on how quickly they could assimilate and improve upon what they saw across the Lydian frontier. From this turbulent, fruitful interaction many new things began to pass into the Greek west, and the idea of coinage was among them.

CROESUS

It is still possible sometimes to hear an extremely wealthy person called "rich as Croesus." The phrase is disappearing, but it deserves to be saved from oblivion, especially since we can now be virtually certain that Croesus was once an actual person, not merely some invented personification of wealth. Evidence for the richness of his Lydian kingdom takes several forms, each one showing how the straw of the material record and the magic of oral tradition may, for the historian who can combine the best of each method, spin some true and solid gold.

Lydia was a comparatively small but prosperous kingdom in Asia Minor when Croesus became the last of its hereditary kings. The time was somewhere around the middle of the sixth century. Since the Lydians were near neighbors to the Asian Greeks, the affairs of each people often intersected those of the other (the result sometimes sparking into high drama or even violence), and so we learn much of what we know about Lydia from Greek sources. As the fifth-century Greek historian Herodotus told the tale of the Lydians' first dealings with Greece "proper" (on the mainland), he calls Croesus:

> the first foreigner so far as we know to come into direct contact with the Greeks, both in the way of conquest and alliance, forcing tribute from Ionians, Aeolians, and Asiatic Dorians, and forming a pact of friendship with the Lacedaemonians. (*Histories*:I.6, in the de Sélincourt translation, which we shall use throughout this chapter)

Croesus' relationship with the Greeks had many facets to it, and not every exchange between the cultures ran from Lydia toward Greece. The Greek world had oracles, and Croesus needed advice from a source greater than human wisdom. He ruled in a day when the uncertain new shapes of a huge and shadowy power had begun to move beyond his eastern horizon. Persia was growing, gathering power like a slow and irresistible storm in the river valleys of Mesopotamia, the plausible and bureaucratic themes of its complex empire eating up the old independent Dark Age states one after another. The shadow of its clouds had pushed recently across many of the borders of the Mediterranean world. "This gave Croesus food for thought," Herodotus said, "and he wondered if he might be able to check Persian expansion before it had gone too far. With this purpose in view, he at once prepared to try his luck with the oracles, and sent to Delphi, to Abae in Phocis, to Dodona, to the oracles of Amphiaraus and Trophonius, and to Branchidae in Milesia" (I.47). Croesus, who knew the jealousy of the gods often cut against a rich person's luck, prepared lavishly to win their favor. His treasure-houses were by Greek standards inexhaustible, and to soften the heart of the Apollo who spoke at Delphi alone, he brought out an almost mythological wealth of gifts:

> Of every kind of appropriate animal he slaughtered three thousand; he burnt in a huge pile a number of precious objects—couches overlaid with gold or silver, golden cups, tunics, and other richly coloured garments...he melted down an enormous quantity of gold into one hundred and seventeen ingots about eighteen inches long, nine inches wide, and three inches thick.... He also caused the image of a lion to be made of refined gold, in weight some five hundred and seventy pounds. There were also two huge mixing bowls, one of gold which was placed on the right-hand side of the entrance to the temple, the other of silver, on the left.... In addition Croesus sent four silver casks...and two sprinklers for lustral water, one of gold, the other of silver. There were many other gifts of no great importance, including round silver basins...a figure of a woman, in gold, four and a half feet high...and his own wife's necklaces and girdles. (I.50–51)

It was for the most eloquent reasons, then, that men could not recall the name of Croesus without recalling at the same time a vision of fabulous wealth. The irony is that the wealth (while believable) is not among the greatest of the landmark developments we can now attach to ancient Lydia. What actually amounted to more in the long run was the form in which some of that wealth was stored. Herodotus takes up the tale again: "The Lydians were the first people we know of to use a gold and silver coinage and to introduce retail trade" (I.94). The notice sounds drab and matter-of-fact after the splendor of Croesus' offerings, but the inventing of coins set a chain of events into motion that would one day change almost every part of life for Lydia, the cultures around her, and all the civilizations that have been her heirs from the sixth century to the present. It also created a new source of data for historians; we call it numismatics.

A coin is an easy enough thing to define. For the purposes of this chapter let us call it "a piece of metal of definite shape and fixed weight, bearing the mark or seal of an issuing authority as a guarantee of its purity and weight, and employed as a circulating medium (money)" (Jones, 1967:175). Although metals had been an item used in exchange during much of the previous human past, their value was not distilled or symbolized into coins until civilization had developed in the eastern Mediterranean for more than 2,000 years. Once the change came, its after effects spun off like sparks in uncounted directions. History is full of such sudden, unexpected, punctuations.

A time came, probably during the seventh or very early sixth century B.C. (though perhaps as soon as the later eighth century), when shaped pieces of metal came to be appreciated as truly useful. Suddenly metals of varying kinds began to be cast in molds or struck from dies, treated as (and before long inscribed with) symbols of "understood" value. The metals most common at first were gold and silver, along with an alloy of both together called *electrum*. As a whole range of weights and values came into use, people began to make coins representing the lesser values out of copper and bronze.

Where did all this start? Herodotus, as we have seen, gave the credit to the Lydians, and a "pre-Socratic" philosopher named Xenophanes (who admired advances of every kind) had about a century earlier been of the same opinion. This view has always

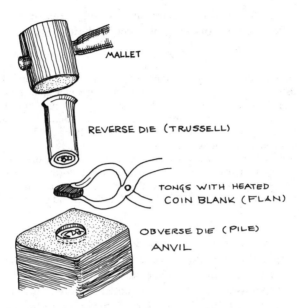

MALLET

REVERSE DIE (TRUSSELL)

TONGS WITH HEATED
COIN BLANK (FLAN)

OBVERSE DIE (PILE)
ANVIL

FIGURE 6–2 Striking a coin.

commanded considerable respect, though there were differing opinions in antiquity, and there is some disagreement today. It is possible, of course, that coinage developed as a process, arising slowly and in stages over a length of time, and even that several cultures might deserve credit for the different "steps." It is also possible that such an idea (portable, symbolic bits of metal) ignited tentative innovations in a variety of directions when it appeared, and that some of them turned out to be "dead ends." An early stage could have been the use of metal lumps having similar size and weight. Another would have been when the traders or craftsmen who dealt in such lumps placed their own stamp on individual pieces as a guarantee of quality. In the end, the very mechanism of trade itself would have standardized shapes and weights, and given us (sooner or later) the sort of object we call a "coin."

A famous Greek city in Asia Minor provides an example of this. Coins found deposited in the earth beneath the temple of Artemis at Ephesus show all the styles or stages we have just mentioned. Unstamped metal lumps in standard sizes are likely the earliest of the pieces found. Next would come lumps that have been punched on one side, followed by those showing a punch as well as a scratch-mark of some sort on the reverse. Last are true coins—stamped with some device on both sides. While it is hard to say how many decades this tale might span, we can at least guess that "money was not invented in a day, nor in any one place" (Burn, 1936 and 1966:183).

We shall come back to this question of origins later, when we reach the question of a coin's value as evidence for understanding specific events in ancient history. We must first think a little about something more general: what basic sort of thing can a coin tell a historian?

Professor Tom Bard Jones is one of those who have shown most clearly how a coin can function both as artifact and as document. Its first capacity is as an object: we can use coins in the same way we would employ other material remains.

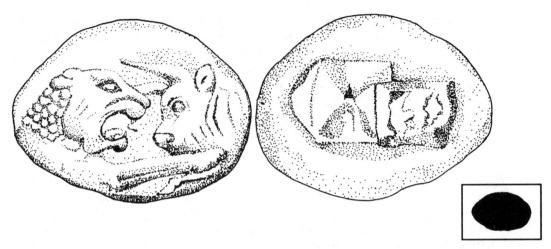

FIGURE 6–3 The early coins remaining from the reign of Croesus in Lydia prove that a great deal of symbolic energy can be concentrated in small and workmanlike spaces. Lydian coins were little icons of pride, ambition, and wealth—of all those things, in short, which Croesus intended his kingdom to be. (Note insert of the silhouette showing the gold coin's actual size.)

- Coins help us mark out a date for the strata in which we find them.
- They can (especially if they are unique) suggest to us the names of otherwise anonymous sites.
- If we can follow or chart the distribution of coins issued by a particular state or city we may begin to glimpse its commercial or political relationships. One state will not adopt another state's coinage, after all, unless some commercial or political reason drives it to.
- If we examine how the distribution of coins changes over the years, we may be able to guess at other changes as well. When the coins of some neighboring state become suddenly abundant or disappear at a site, we may suspect that some considerable change in the relationship between the two places has taken place.
- The quantity and quality of coins at a particular place gives us a gauge of its general economic condition in the past, and if we can date its coins very precisely we can even begin to sketch its economic history. When baser metals become far more prevalent in the mintings, for example, or when metals become increasingly diluted into alloys, we have a strong reason to suspect the economy has hit a slump, and probably the originating culture was struggling. That may, in turn, suggest new ways of understanding other kinds of evidence.

But it is as documents that coins provide really specific data. The stamps that give them individual character are designs or *devices*, known technically as *types*. A coin's obverse side (what we call its front, or *head*) bore the primary pattern—usually, in the earliest periods, a stylized portrait of the head of some person or animal. On the obverse of their earliest coins, Greeks would see the portrait of a patron deity, and they knew from it which city-state had struck the metal. Lydian coins minted during Croesus' reign were a little different, bearing the faces and front quarters of a lion and bull gazing at one another. On their reverse (or "back") the Greeks' own coins would often show a symbol belonging to the deity pictured on the front: an owl for Athena, an eagle for Zeus—the heraldry, in a sense, of the gods who guarded the Greek cities.

These little icons obviously tell us important things about the religion and politics of each city-state. They also carry (especially for historians of art) an aesthetic message—we can guess what color imagination and myth gave to ordinary trade (just as the antique, engraved solidity of all those old presidents and buildings on American money suggests a certain atmosphere to us as we use it). When an object of art famous in ancient times has become lost, the old coins may offer another windfall to an art historian. The sculpture reproduced on the obverse of a city's coins may very well be an image of its most famous statue of the patron deity; a poor shadow of some original masterpiece perhaps, but sometimes all that we still have of it.

At some point in a culture's history the portraits on the front of its coins may change from divinities to contemporary human beings, and when that happens historians inherit yet another wealth of information. These portraits may be stylized, but they are often meant at least to approximate the actual appearance on some ancient individual. We can finally begin to see the people whose lives we are reconstructing. (This will become extremely important in Chapter Eight, since coins bearing the image of Philip II of Macedon have been some of the main ammunition in the argument over who is really buried in the Vergina tombs.)

Coins that carry inscriptions (somewhat confusingly called legends) give us even more kinds of data. We learn (or at least have a hint of) the language of the people who issued the coins. If we can date them properly, the inscriptions are useful for deducing changes in the forms of letters, and in the construction of grammar. When we put together both legend and type, light falls on the kind of propaganda once spread by the authorities who minted them. Suppose, for instance, that the most striking thing about a gold coin thought to commemorate a battle fought in 280 B.C. is the pensive, regretful pose of the Heracles on its front. We may be meant to feel the hero's (and the culture's) sadness over the many loved ones who died in that battle. So, a special coin may also be struck to mark a particularly moving event. (Even today there are special issues of coins that are prompted as much by human feeling and the landmarks of history as they are by the needs of trade.) The curious thing is how the centuries have turned this relationship on its head, at least for historians. Great events once created the coins; now the coins tell us the events were there, and suggest the weight they once had in the flow of their culture's history. Without them, we would sometimes never have known of the event at all.

So it is that, according to Michael Crawford, "coins are naturally a potential source of great importance for the history of the ancient world. Neither their use nor the evaluation of this use is particularly difficult" (1983:187). The important thing, he adds, is that one begin by asking the right questions: "of what does a particular coinage consist, what is its date, where was it produced, what can it tell us, how does one interpret this information?" (1983:187). Herman Bengtson (who has become a classic analyst of the sources of the distant past) calls numismatics one of the three fundamental disciplines in the study of ancient history. As he sees it, coinage can tell us five kinds of things:

1. It tells us who had the right to mint coins. Exercising the "power to mint" was in ancient times equivalent to political independence.
2. Coins represent historical events in their types and legends.

3. Numismatics illustrates the patterns of religious history, especially when cults were sanctioned by the state.
4. It preserves the flavor and substance of ancient propaganda.
5. It gives us the skeleton of a good ancient chronology, based on rulers, eras, and even artistic styles. (1970:145)

Nonetheless, we should remember to use the evidence of coins very carefully lest, as with other seemingly "easy" forms of data, we allow speed and enthusiasm to lead us astray. In the first place, the community of scholars still does not have access to the full range of evidence because so much of it has never been published. Even when coins do appear in publication they are often defective as artifacts, and it is not always clear how defective they are unless the publication includes a good picture of the coin. After long circulation a coin (like any piece of worked metal) will have become worn and therefore open to misinterpretation. In antiquity, currency might easily be left in circulation for several centuries, and be severely worn before it found some hiding place that might preserve it for the modern archaeologist or collector. One student of ancient economies makes the point that there existed in those days a "tendency to consider a coin a permanent possession once it had been acquired by a private person" (Starr, 1977:114). Thus a coin's owner felt perfectly free to overstrike it with his own device. An authority would not mint new coins if it had the (far simpler) opportunity to re-use old ones by running them under the hammer again, and of course the weight and content of such overstruck coins would conform to some older standard, not to the current one. Finally, and perhaps worst, we must remember that forgery was an ancient as well as a modern art.

A second (and equally disturbing) trait that coins share with other artifacts is their random preservation. Can a single coin be considered really typical of anything? Should the very fact that an improbable string of chances has kept it intact until discovered in modern times make us suspicious? The normal fate of coin, after all, is to be used until it is worn out, or to be melted down and used for something else. Even its context might lie: most ancient coins were undated and carry no indication of where they were struck—can we assume that the location of a single survivor tells us anything we can be sure of? A light-fingered soldier in some long-forgotten invasion may have carried it off in a looted hoard, and then dropped it by accident anywhere on his way home.

If we are lucky enough to find a hoard, though, we actually have fewer of these problems. A *hoard* is "a group of coins the circumstances of whose discovery—for example, in a purse or other container—make it clear that the hoard was deliberately buried in a group" (Crawford, 1983:191). But hoards, for obvious reasons, are not common remains for any time before 500 B.C., and even as their frequency increases they bring their own unique riddles. If a single coin can be found out of context, so can a single hoard. It might very well have been laid in hiding because its contents were special (and so a very poor guide to its time or culture), and it may have been placed in an extremely misleading place because hoards are not meant to be found. Hoards that have been found often contain coins whose dates extend over several decades—or even centuries—which makes any guess about when they were hidden a perilous one. It is not even true (though it sounds like a very practical rule of thumb) that the least worn coins are the newest.

And if the physical evidence itself leaves us fretting with questions, how should we approach the complex and trap-strewn business of interpreting it? A hoard is not likely to give up many secrets about the person who collected it or hid it (they may not be the same), or about the motives involved. What was the long-dead owner's name? What did he do? To what social class did he or she or they belong? Xenophon gave the sensible answer: "When men possess a great deal of [wealth], they bury the part which they do not want" (*Ways and Means*:4.7), but we do not know quite how valid his view has ever been.

Such a long list of cautions and alarms might suggest that real ancient history were best done with very little reliance on the numismatic evidence. That would be a serious mistake. The clouds are not quite so dark as they seem. Recent scientific developments have first of all proven helpful, since they allow us to analyze the metal content of ancient coins, and so determine where the metal has come from. In a spectrographic test, an electric charge "zaps" and volatilizes a tiny sample along with some graphite. The light thrown off by this violent little reaction refracts onto a viewing screen, and experts can tell from the spectrum of colors shown there the makeup of elements in the metal. Peculiar metallic ion mixes can often be traced to a particular ore-bearing region, and thus to the mining-area of a particular culture.

Perhaps even more interesting is the possibility of recreating the shape of an older coin "type" beneath an "overstrike" layer, which seems to be telling us, on first sight, that we are looking at a newer one. Thus a single coin can be used as evidence for a relative sequence of dates—a very neat archaeological trick.

Finally, when we are lucky enough to have a number of coins from the same source, it becomes a little easier to recognize changes in the style of a device or in the strokes of the lettering over time. This is duller detective work than the preceding two techniques, but it allows us to assign approximate dates to the issue of coins, and so to tie them closer to the history of the people who made them.

Most important of all, though, is that we know the context—the real historical backdrop—of the coins we are trying to interpret. The more we know of such things already, the more weight we can give to the evidence of the coins; the less we know, the more deceptive they become. Crawford puts this with particular firmness: "Ancient coinage is a distinct class of ancient material, to which distinctive methods of study are appropriate. But it can *never* be satisfactorily studied in isolation from other material" (Crawford, 1983:228. The italics are our own). He goes on to describe several disasters of interpretation that resulted simply from lack of attention, or from ignorance of a coin's historical context. The point is this: our goal should be to understand antiquity as fully as we can, making as much as possible out of the proper interplay of our different categories of evidence. We should never find ourselves pushing an "easy" category of evidence too far because the others seem difficult, or dry, or likely to create trouble. Perhaps a concrete instance of such interwoven evidence might help, especially if we can tie it into our examination of the origins of coinage. Let us take a closer look at the Lydians.

Modern scholars may not agree about who invented coinage, but they might be willing to compromise on this lesser claim: perhaps "ascription to the Lydians is true in the sense that development of coinage was continuous in the Aegean thereafter" (Starr, 1977:108). We have good reason to think that several of the stages in the development of true coins (as we described them earlier) did indeed take place there. While Croesus was king, Lydia did begin to issue various coins of pure gold and silver, and each of these replaced (or coexisted with older) coins of electrum alloy. We know that the standards of weight and metal equivalence used in Lydia were very precise.

It was also about this time that Lydia reached the high point of its territorial spread and political importance. The gifts that the Greeks remembered flowing from the wealth of Croesus reflect a real wealth; Lydia was a powerful place. It is not surprising that we also know Croesus sent such gifts as part of a plan for even greater expansion. He needed the divine advice of the Oracle at Delphi because he meant to engage Lydia in battle against the rising power of a Persian empire that seemed every morning to loom a little nearer and a little larger on his eastern frontier.

He got an answer. Croesus might attack the Persians if he wished, the Oracle said, but if he did so a great empire would be destroyed. Croesus took heart at the prophecy, and full of grand imaginings he "prepared an expedition against Cappadocia, sure of success in bringing down the power of Cyrus and the Persians" (Herodotus:I.71). The dark fate of his expedition remained famous throughout ancient (and most of modern) history: the empire that Croesus destroyed in battle was his own. Lydia, lost on a gamble, sank to the status of a Persian province in 546 B.C.

In defeat, Lydia lost both its political independence and, so far as we can tell, the right to mint its own coins. The evidence that has survived suggests that not long after the army of Croesus vanished into the badlands of Cappadocia, the coinage of his royal line ceased. There were, for a while, coins struck in the "Croesus style" by some Persian moneyer, but he used a lighter standard of metal, and the locals must have felt the sting of their disgrace every time they made a purchase. As the sixth century passed, the Persians began minting their own gold *darics* and silver *sigloi* on weight standards of their own, stamping them with the insignia of their irresistible power.

Persia went on growing in the years that followed, casting its net across new lands, gathering in fresh supplies of wealth, until its strength seemed as unshakable as a force of nature. What finally shook it was the sudden arrival of an odd young man, unexpected as a thunderclap, from the north of Greece. Alexander, as he tore through the heart of the empire in a few short years, came again and again upon immense hoards of treasure and coin. At Arbela he discovered 3,000 talents of silver; at Susa, 9,000 talents in minted darics, and some 40,000 talents of gold and silver bullion. At Persepolis, a Persian capital that Greek architects had once helped to build, great vaults were packed full of silver and gold—the total value being something like 120,000 silver talents (since the gold was estimated in "silver" terms; figures supplied by the first century B.C. historian Diodorus: 17.64, 17.66, and 17.71).

If we drew only the most cautious of conclusions, it might be that those metallic symbols of "Lydian invention" had, transplanted in the exotic soil of Persia, found a fertile place to grow.

This is not to say that there were no fertile "soils" in Greece. Coinage spread like brushfire among the bustling, trade-minded Greek city-states during the sixth century B.C. One's own coin was a badge of civic independence, and its quick adoption illustrates the rapid development of the individual poleis and that intense, local Greek loyalty to them which other cultures found so hard to understand. We do not possess coins from every one of these multiplying city-states (some were astonishingly small), but we know that a

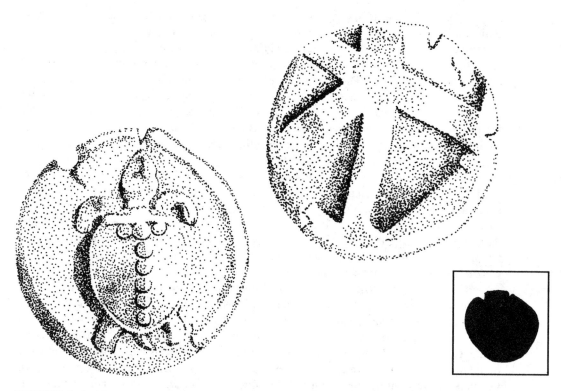

FIGURE 6–4 Many early Greek coins provide icons of their minting *poleis* rather less restless than the lion and the bull of Croesus. This "turtle" is from sea-bound Aegina, where Pheidon is supposed to have struck his first coins. From its origin, money "announced" its point of origin. (Note insert of the silhouette showing the silver coin's actual size.)

great many established their own systems. The rather untidy consequence of this is that we cannot talk about "Greek coinage" in the same holistic, culture-wide manner we use about Lydia or Persia.

The picture becomes even more complicated because many of the poleis caught on to the practice of minting coin almost simultaneously. The historian who wants a clear consensus of evidence on the origins of coinage in Greece will find a tangled mare's-nest. The evidence suggests only a few, tentative, conclusions.

In antiquity itself, the honor of minting the first Greek coins was often granted to the city of Argos, during the rule of the political innovator Pheidon. Strabo, who wrote in the first century B.C., cited the far older expert Ephorus (fourth century) as authority for the claim that "silver was first minted in Aegina by Pheidon" (8.6.16). A work of the far later Byzantine period (called the *Etymologicum Magnum*) based its fuller account on sources from the first century A.D.: "Pheidon of Argos was the first man of all to mint coin (and he did so) in Aegina. Distributing the coin and taking back the spits, he dedicated them to Argive Hera" (III.613.13).

Rejecting all this testimony, the modern numismatist Percy Gardner collected enough contrary arguments in 1918 to decide that neither Pheidon of Argos, nor the city of Athens (another claimant) deserved the glory; both, to him, being "now out of court" (67). Donald Kagan reexamined the issue historically in 1960 and (at least partially) disagreed: "The case for Pheidon is not finally proved, but it is supported by a credible and plausible tradition. The burden of proof must properly be shouldered by those who would attack it" (136).

We should be very foolish to try choosing between (or even reconciling) these opposite conclusions unless we find evidence for doing so in the coins themselves, and maintain along with it a clear picture of the historical context. We might embark on a sketch of the context, for simplicity's sake, in Argos.

Pheidon seems to have succeeded to his position in the city-state by old-fashioned inheritance, but his career in the years after seems, by the older accounts, to have become extraordinarily dynamic. He rapidly expanded the Argive territory—no mean feat in an Archaic Greece where every tiny community clung to its independence with a tenacity like that of the medieval Swiss cantons. He pushed hard to recover first what he called "the heritage of Temenos" (an ancestral, or even a half-forgotten Mycenaean claim?), and after that the even larger "inheritance of Herakles" (Strabo: 8.358). According to tradition the two towering events of his career were his capture of Olympia (he celebrated an Olympic games with himself as "president"), and his victory over the Spartan army in open battle at Hysiai (a little southwest of Argos). The two events may date to 668 and 669 B.C. respectively, which might thus make one the consequence of the other.

Pheidon was also credited, as we said earlier, with inventing systems both of measure and coinage. These, put together with the political legends, add up to a remarkable burst of Argive power in the early classical era, and they cannot be very easily dismissed, nor can Pheidon's part in them. Greeks did not easily grant glory to someone other than their own folk in an uncertain matter. Aristotle, who interpreted the best political data he could gather with a cold and plausible eye, made the career of Pheidon a significant episode in Greek history, developing the theory that though he began his reign in Argos as a king, he ended it as a tyrant.

Tyrannos is an interesting word. It is not Greek, but seems to have been imported from Lydia. Its earliest recorded use in a Greek source (that we have discovered so far) was in a lyric of the warrior-poet Archilochus, who sang proudly that:

> *For Gyges gold I do not care,*
> *I do not envy him or dare*
> *High heaven, nor lust for tyrannis*
> *Far from my eyes are things like this.*
> —(trans. Colin Edmonson)

Gyges was first in the line of Lydian kings that ended with Croesus.

The plot thickens, for the Argives may have borrowed more than a word from Asia Minor. At some debatable point, most likely in the first half of the seventh century B.C., Greeks began to replace the old individual combats between representatives of armies with a new and broader-based kind of warfare. In the new armies (which for many city-states were very small), heavily armed footsoldiers, pressed into side-by-side formations, were marshalled by a commander with some expertise in drill. Each soldier carried—as far as he could afford it—a standard kit of equipment: greaves, a corselet, a helmet, and both a long stabbing-spear and a short stabbing-sword. Battle doctrine required that the formation stay tight and try to push back—to overpower and perhaps to rupture—the opposing front line. The soldiers who bore this equipment and fought in these new formations were called *hoplites*—from the name for their shield. As near as we can tell, Argos was the first city-state among the mainland Greeks to combine the new tactics with the new equipment. The advantage the Argives thus won, though brief, gains excellent testimony from the traditional victories of Pheidon.

This new form of warfare seems to have been built upon the borrowing of several critical things. The helmet may have been Near Eastern rather than Greek. Three more distinctive innovations seem to have come, according to the traveled "researches" of Herodotus, from the Carians of Asia Minor: the fitting of crests on the helmets for identification in battle, the painting of heraldic devices on the shields for glory and group morale, and the making of shields with a braced (off-center) arm-handle. Caria was an old kingdom that lay along the southern border of Lydia.

Lydia itself, as we saw at the chapter's outset, commanded great respect in western Asia Minor, its armies noted far and wide for their tenacity. A Greek poet living in the region during the seventh century thought the highest boast he could make of his father's fighting skill was that he once "broke the close ranks of the Lydian horsemen." This reputation came to the Greek mainland very quickly (the new Greek revival was heavily dependent on a stable Asia Minor to anchor its trade routes), and so Lydia may well have provided the model for the new close-order battle techniques. That is only speculation; what we know for certain is that many of the Lydian military campaigns were directed squarely against the Greek poleis of Asia Minor.

And even so we have not quite exhausted the "Lydian connection," for elements of both the Asian-style tyrannis and the military innovations may be linked to the rising use of coinage. There is a growing consensus among ancient historians that the earliest coins were not intended only, or even primarily, to ease the flow of commerce. The largest denominations did not circulate very far from the area in which they were minted, and attempts to trace both the circulation of goods and of coins do not reveal that the patterns of one overlapped those of the other in quite the expected way. Coins of small denomination, which might have been really useful in local trade, did not very often exist in the earliest years. Although it is hard to deny that true coinage quickened and sophisticated the trade of the Aegean world, that effect could have been a byproduct rather than an original goal.

Might the first-intended use of coins have been to simplify the accounting techniques of Asia Minor's archaic kings? Coins are easily stored, kept track of, and (when necessary) negotiated for value. They do a variety of things for the authority that mints them, and that authority was always, in these early years, a state. The kings of Lydia seem to have placed particular store in them as a means of paying their newly organized troops.

The reader may by now have begun to notice how often this study seems to resolve into a sort of triad—money, tyranny, military innovation. It surely cannot be an accident that all three are firmly attested in the historical traditions of both Lydia and Argos. The conclusion that forms almost irresistibly on the horizon, though, remains tenuous until the coins themselves provide evidence for it. Did Lydian coins exist early enough for Pheidon to have known about them?

A first answer to this lies in the relative dates of the coins that have been unearthed from the foundation levels of the temple of Artemis at Ephesus (near the coast of Asia Minor). Historians usually agree that these are the earliest true coins we have found, but they do not agree so easily about the exact dating that the coins imply. E. S. G. Robinson's expert opinion is that the foundation deposit dates from around 600 B.C. Mixed within it are both true coins and metal pieces representing many of the pre-coinage types. Robinson finds this convincing. The sampling discovered, he says, "compels the conclusion that we are very near in time to [coinage's] invention...this great event can hardly have taken place much more than a generation earlier" (1951:163).

This presents a problem. Many scholars now believe that Pheidon of Argos was a historical figure, and that his career unfolded during the second quarter of the seventh century. If so, he could hardly have been alive (he would at best have been in extreme old age) when the "great event"—the culture-changing development of coins—began.

But there is more than one reconstruction of Pheidon's career. That already mentioned places the taking of Olympia and the great victory at Hysiai toward the end of his life. Donald Kagan has made a good case that such events make more sense near the start of Pheidon's reign, and has reminded us that Pheidon probably did not die till around 620 B.C. His years of activity would then fall significantly later, and overlap with the last important steps in the emergence of "the true coin." This would be correct even if the Artemisian deposit really does date to 600 B.C., but therein lies another of the question's tantalizing wrinkles. The dating, as Kagan points out, is only approximate.

> If the assumption be made that the Basis deposit was closed not precisely in 600 but even about 610 and the development period was not thirty-five but fifty or sixty years, then the invention of coinage would be dated ca. 670–660. Such a guess is certainly no less likely than the one made by Robinson. Neither is sufficiently well founded to affirm or deny the Pheidonian claim. (1960:125)

To support this line of reasoning we must also find some plausible connection between Argos and Lydia that dates to about the middle of the seventh century—some "wire" along which these new techniques might travel like sparks from one terminal of the resurgent Aegean civilization to the other. We might find it in the alliances between these states during the earliest decades after 700 B.C.. Argos, interestingly, seems to have been the really energetic partner of the two. Here is one reconstruction:

> ...with the accession of Pheidon, Argos became a power to be reckoned with. Pheidon first extended his influence by supporting the revolt of Megara from Corinth; then, when a struggle broke out between Aegina on the one side and Athens and Epidaurus on the other, Pheidon came to the aid of Aegina. Samos sided with Athens and Epidaurus against her rival and sent a naval expedition to raid Aegina. Corinth, angered by the revolt of Megara and frightened by the rise of Argive power, joined in and sent Ameinocles [a noted shipbuilder of triremes] to help the Samians. Nevertheless, the Athenians were defeated and Pheidon gained control of Epidaurus and Aegina. He fostered Aeginetan trade and struck there the first coinage in Greece. Through his enmity with Samos, he became friendly with Miletus. (Bradeen, 1947:239)

The scenario we have been trying to build rests of course most strongly upon that last sentence, but the preceding narrative puts our hypothetical tie between Argos and

Miletus into context. Perhaps it was through the river-port city of Miletus that Pheidon learned about those little, strangely useful lumps of standardized metal that were the ancestors of the "true coins." And Miletus did have the strongest possible ties (for an independent and harassed city-state) with the kingdom of Lydia. It was Croesus' grandfather who began campaigning against Miletus, and the attempts at conquest continued under his father. Each year the Lydian army marched into the Milesian farmlands just as the crops were getting ripe; when it had destroyed what it could not eat, it retreated back northward (Herodotus:I.17). Some of Miletus' neighbors fared no better. This crippling and rhythmic pressure on many of the Ionian Greek city-states seems to have begun as early as the middle of the seventh century. Seldom, as history has suggested again and again, does one learn any quicker or more indelibly than from the innovations of one's enemies. The "wire" running from Lydia to Miletus to Argos was a live one indeed.

Let us sum up. We have excellent historical reasons to credit the Lydians with the invention of coinage. We are also certain that the Greek polis of Miletus was in direct (and painful) contact with Lydia during the seventh century, and that—spurred by the constant harassment of the Lydians themselves—it would have had both motive and opportunity to learn about the usefulness of those odd lumps of hoarded metal with the fixed weights.

Then there is also the strong tradition that Pheidon of Argos struck the first coins in the mainland of Greece. As he pressed his coins into circulation, he will have begun to replace an earlier medium of exchange, the old "spits" of iron by which the metal craftsmen conducted their trade. We also know that he dedicated a number of these iron spits to the temple of Hera at Argos (and so took them out of circulation). The picture we have been trying to build in this chapter might suggest several of his reasons: he could make quite clear on a public occasion his official support for the new medium, he could demonstrate (also in public) the ratio of exchange between his new coins and the old spits, and he could offer a time-honored gift to the patron goddess of his polis. We may close by noting that a bundle of such iron spits has been discovered beneath the Argive temple.

But there is always another side to things (it is perhaps the gods' way of keeping historians humble and close to their evidence). No coins were found anywhere near the bundle of spits at Argos, and so any verdict based tightly on the numismatic evidence alone must remain "case not proved." An entirely numismatic solution to the mystery would only be possible if some truly datable coins bearing some clear device identifiable with Argos were suddenly to come to light near the Argive temple of Hera, or perhaps at Aegina. If we were to show a real numismatic connection to Lydia, we would have to find strong parallels of form, weight, standard, or punch-marks between the Argive and Lydian coins (or proto-coins). Given the scarcity of these earliest materials, and the great difficulties of naming a real date or location for such mintings, we would be unrealistic to hope for very much.

It is just a little likelier (though it would cast only the faintest glint of light in the darkness surrounding our present question) that we might demonstrate a connection between Lydia and Persia. The last melancholy mintings of the "Croesseid" coins and the ominous issue of the first "darics" both occurred in a slightly later generation than Pheidon's, one in which a real dating by the methods of modern scholarship becomes a little more possible. If we could achieve such a feat we should have a few of the answers to critical questions about how, and why, and how fast the "Lydian invention" of coinage spread once its culture was flooded by the mainstream of Mediterranean civilization. We would then know far more about the equation of political independence and about the right and power to mint coins. With even more evidence, we might be able to tell the tale of those coins as they moved across the expanses of Lydian and Persian history, to chart their uses and the patterns of their circulation. We might even hope—since, for all their bustling and strident local-mindedness, the world of the Greeks intersected constantly with the worlds of Lydia and Persia—that these answers might begin to loop back into the little realms of the Aegean, and to tell us more about lost pioneers like Pheidon.

FURTHER READING

The chapters by Tom B. Jones and Michael Crawford are excellent introductions to the subject of numismatics. The accounts occur, respectively, in *Paths to the Ancient Past: Applications of the Historical Method to Ancient History* (New York: The Free Press, 1967), and *Sources for Ancient History* (Cambridge: Cambridge University Press, 1983).

Chapter Seven

Word Portraits of Socrates

The legends on coins, as we noted in the last chapter, are sometimes propaganda. This is only to say that they tell us more or less what someone once meant them to tell us, and so there may be more "good" news on a coin than "bad." Such coins thus become a tool as historically reliable as any propaganda, holding out a new wealth of information and laying a trap at the same time: for while they are records, they are also arguments in disguise.

But if simple declarative evidence like inscriptions on coinage can present such hidden trouble, what must we expect when we move on to longer written accounts? Must not we expect that any written narrative once had a purpose in its composing, and so—since the teller's purposes affect how things are told and even how they are remembered—might be coloring the truth? Can we take no written account at face value?

Perhaps we could if only we knew precisely what sort of "face" some particular ancient document really meant to present to us. We need to know in what "spirit" its author wrote. As early cultures became more and more reliant on the new skills of writing, they explored its possibilities in a widening array of new directions and forms: genres were being born. The first famous written products of Greece were the *Iliad* and the *Odyssey*, both epic poems, and both alive with the moving breath of the speaking voice. By the middle of the fifth century B.C., though, there were dozens of written forms—each with its own new business to be about, and each building its own practical and artistic rules. There were short business records and the briefs of cases in court; tragedies and comedies meant for civic audiences; treatises in philosophy, science, and practical economy; medical accounts, histories, and personal reflections.

The Classical Age (500 - 400)

Date B.C.	Greek Events	Around the Mediterranean	Artifacts & Art
500 --	(492) Persians under Darius invade Greece (aiming at Athens) to teach it a "lesson"; a storm foils them. (490) Athenians defeat Persians at the Battle of Marathon in NE Attica. (480) The Spartans slow the Persians at the Battle of Thermopylae. Xerxes passes Thermopylae, and sacks Athens. The Athenian and allied fleets	(499) Ionian cities revolt against Persia (helped by some Greeks like Athens) until 494. (486) Darius I of Persia dead. His son Xerxes inherits the throne. (480) Persians under Xerxes invade Greece again, this time indirectly from the north; some Greek cities joining	(c. 484) Herodotus the historian born. (c. 477) Myron (sculptor of the "Discus Thrower") fl. (472) Aeschylus presents his drama "The Persians."
475 --	defeat the Persian navy at the Battle of Salamis. -- The Delian League is founded. This is supposed to be a defensive naval league against Persia under Athenian leadership. It will slowly become an "Athenian Empire." (c. 469) Socrates born. (461) Pericles comes to power at Athens. (454) Treasury of the Delian League transferred to Athens.	them. -- Carthage invades Sicily; repulsed by the Greek cities there. (c. 470) Carthaginian leader Hanno sails down African coast as far as Cameroon. (c. 460) Persians complete the great palace complex at Persepolis.	(c.) Pheidias begins sculpting. (467) Sophocles' whole play cycle on Oedipus performed at Athens. (458) Aeschylus: Agamemnon trilogy presented at Athens (the "Oresteia"). (456) Death of
450 --	Athens embarks on great civic building projects. The short roads to its port city of Piraeus are fortified by the Long Walls. Socrates is teaching his followers (by dialogues) at the grove of Academe. Athens begins using force to maintain its Delian League. Sparta leads the opposition.	(c. 453) Herodotus perhaps visits Egypt. (Trad. 451) Publication of the 12 Tables of Laws at Rome.	Aeschylus, writer of plays (political and moral tragedies). Athens begins the Parthenon (447) and many other temples on its hilltop acropolis. (445) Herodotus (historian) reads some of his works publicly at Athens.
425 --	(433) Corcyra & Corinth quarrel: Athens intervenes, Sparta opposes. (431) The Peloponnesian War begins. (430) Plague at Athens; Pericles dead the next year. (415 - 413) Disastrous Athenian expedition against Spartan ally Syracuse. (404) Athens surrenders to Sparta; the city is occupied, its walls destroyed. (399) Trial and execution of Socrates by an Athenian court.	(c. 423) Artaxerxes I of Persia dead. Darius II becomes the Great King. (c. 406) Carthage begins to gain a landhold in Sicily (at Agrigentum). (c. 401 - 399) Expedition of Xenophon's "10,000" Greek mercenaries deep into Persia; their retreat after treachery through hostile country back to the Black Sea coastlands. (c. 400) Egypt frees itself from Persian rule.	(423) Aristophanes' comedy "The Clouds" performed at Athens. (421) "Dramatic" setting of Xenophon's *Symposium*. (416) "Dramatic" setting of Plato's *Symposium*. (406) Tragedians Sophocles and Euripides both dead.

One fascinating Athenian was famous (or notorious) enough to provoke enduring descriptions by his near contemporaries in at least three of these genres. Perhaps he provoked more, but this trio (by three different authors) has survived fairly intact, and so we have an unusually well-faceted chance to look at a single life in the old world and to test the prejudices or insights hidden in the various kinds of writing. The subject is Socrates, a man thought so remarkable even in his own day that men who knew him were moved to apply their new literate skills to depict him—to catch what was different, or inspiring, or exasperating about the way he lived, the way he talked, the things he valued.

The trouble is that these accounts seem to differ significantly. The result is almost unfair: we finally have ancient writing sufficiently developed and an ancient personality sufficiently notable, so that one can give us a really rounded view of the other, but instead we inherit a quarrel in our sources. What was Socrates like? Are we dealing with propaganda? Can we trust any of it?

A firm answer to any of those questions would be a godsend since the issue is not only Socrates' strange personal charisma, but also his earthshaking importance in the stream of Greek thought. For centuries now scholars have swarmed like carpenter ants around the proud old edifice of the Greek achievement and still Socrates remains standing at the pivotal center of Greek philosophy. Running through all that ancient "edifice" and giving it its highest life was the "stream" of Greek thought, and Socrates was the "engineer" who changed the banks of that stream. The classicist Francis Cornford once titled an excellent introduction to Greek philosophy *Before and After Socrates.*

Until Socrates' era, the more precise efforts of Greek thought had focused on attempts to explain the nature of the universe: what was it made of? how did it originate? why did it act as it did? Socrates himself seems to have begun with a curiosity about such things, but during his lifetime—and largely due to his own persistent, public, and witty inquiries—many Greeks turned instead to study a smaller, nearer piece of the cosmos. They directed their scrutiny onto humans. Where do people fit in the universe? What makes them behave the way they do? Why do they ask so many questions, and speak with such an uncertain voice about the answers? How do they relate to one another? After Socrates, philosophers pursuing the trails he had blazed looked hard at the very springs of human knowledge itself. The worry that lined the eyes of both Plato and Aristotle (though each arrived at a different conclusion) was whether humans ever truly come to understand anything.

We may allow Socrates, then, a crucial role in the history of Greek philosophy, but we shall run into more controversy over his historical role in his own culture and his own times. Socrates lived perhaps between 469 and 399 B.C., during both the height of the Greek Golden Age and its end, and ends are always a dangerous time for men who ask questions. The Golden Age comes by its name rather more honestly than most historical periods: the Greeks themselves treasured it while it lasted and realized its loss very quickly once it had gone—they called it the *arché.* Earlier in the fifth century (in 480 B.C. and again in 479), various little armies of the mainland Greek city-states had gone out into battle against the vast and organized war machine of the advancing Persian army, and (unlike Croesus) they managed miraculously to beat it to a standstill. The Persians never took the land of Greece, and every hoplite who came back to his city from those heady campaigns must have felt like an American colonist just after his part in the victory over the mighty British Empire.

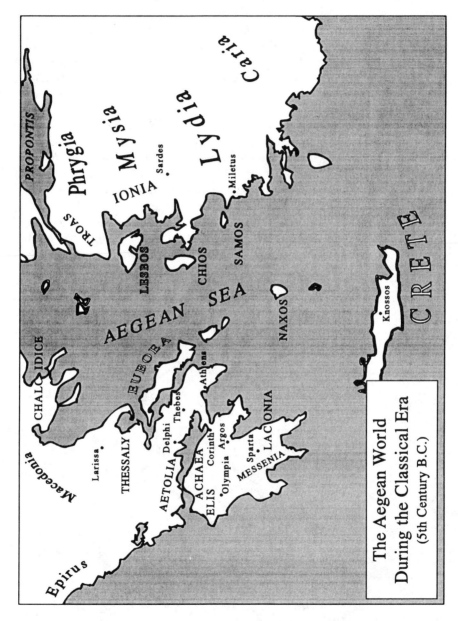

FIGURE 7–1 The Aegean World During the Classical Era

In the wake of those victories, the Greek city-states produced for a generation or two one of the most vibrant cultural explosions in human history. Confidence meant experiment and optimism and creativity, and what gave that creativity its peculiar flavor was the view developed in each individual state that every citizen achieved his greatest worth by plunging himself into his community, bettering it, and increasing its glory. Out of this belief and the sudden success of the Persian wars tumbled an almost pell-mell string of innovations: participatory democracy, wealth invested in the brilliance of one's city instead of one's family, and the building of a magnificent urban culture that was directed at, and could be shared by, the entire citizen populace.

It was Athens, where Socrates was born and lived out his life, that led the way in these headlong achievements. In the dialogues of one of his students, Socrates says, hectoring the point almost like an evangelist, that the state means far more even than a mother or a father. Not surprising, then, that historians and philosophers frown to find him saying elsewhere that he, Socrates, will serve his state best by taking a different course than it demands of him. He does not intend to focus on that public life by which all the other citizens kept their state in being. He intends instead to be the gadfly—the burr under the saddle of every other participant—watchdogging (whether they ask him or no) their mental and moral honesty and wisdom.

FIGURE 7–2 What Socrates left behind him in Athens was not so much one great shadow of memory as many shadows. Accounts written about him were profuse; many more were written than have survived. So also the popular portrait busts produced after his death were profuse, and Socrates looks a little different in each, just as the words of Socrates mingled differently with the thought of each individual he taught.

Such a calling might surely be commendable (though it is easy to imagine some Athenians instantly taking offense to it), but will it square with the belief that each citizen belongs to the state first and to himself only second? If this sort of Socrates was the real one, did he not deserve some blame for the painful breakdown of all those values that had made a Golden Age possible? They did break down. Their protracted crash during the later years of Socrates' life reads like slow torture to all but the most cold-hearted historian. Is it partly Socrates' fault that the city-state culture of Greece dissolved quickly in the fourth century B.C. and was replaced by a world of private individualisms, or was it coincidence? It is odd sometimes how every reexamination of Socrates becomes another trial.

SOCRATES

All the descriptions of Socrates that survive agree upon one thing: he was a landmark personality, the sort of man who left his friends feeling that they had not merely been taught but changed, the sort of person about whom no one could be neutral. This is indisputable in those most familiar recollections of him that we inherit from his student, Plato. Socrates plays the fundamental role in most of Plato's early and middle dialogues and continues as a deeply felt presence even in the late ones. It is only in the *Laws* that he is not mentioned (and the "Athenian Stranger" in that book has obviously learned from him, though sad experience has caused him to think twice about the lessons). Perhaps the *Apology* is the most famous of Plato's Socratic pictures. The teacher, now old and harassed by the suspicions of several changes in government, stands trial on charges of impiety and corrupting the city's youth. A defendant pled his own case in classical Athens, and the city demands that Socrates explain himself. He rises and speaks:

> I have never lived an ordinary quiet life. I did not care for the things that most people care about: making money, having a comfortable home, high military or civil rank, and all the other activities—political appointments, secret societies, party organization—which go on in our city; I thought that I was really too strict in my principles to survive if I went in for this sort of thing. So instead of taking a course which would have done no good either to you or to me, I set myself to do you individually in private what I hold to be the greatest possible service: I tried to persuade each one of you not to think more of practical advantages than of his mental and moral well-being, or in general to think more of advantage than of well-being in the case of the state or of anything else. (36B–C, Tredennick trans.)

For all this service he was immodest (and perhaps tired or ironic) enough to suggest "free maintenance by the State" as "an appropriate penalty...strictly in accordance with justice" (37A). As he seems to have expected, this did not "go over" very well. He was found guilty and sentenced to die, but even after he had burnt his bridges, Socrates used the minutes remaining to him on the court's water clock for one last attempt at teaching. He said that his death would not sweep the critics of everything Athenian from Athens' streets, nor the habit of criticism from her reputation. He talked about what death was (death is a human thing), and suggested that his life had a goal and meaning that the rejection by the city could not end. He finished in the language of enigma:

> Now it is time that we were going, I to die and you to live; but which of us has the happier prospect is unknown to anyone but God. (42A)

This is a moving exit, worthy of grand tragedy. Even if nothing else had survived about his moral and ethical beliefs, this almost visual portrait would have been enough to place Socrates' memory among those treasured over the centuries, eras, and cultures that have followed. It gives a steel-edged pungency to our memories of classical Athens: one of the martyrs she had at the end of her prime was her own greatest teacher. But this is not the only sort of portrait left to us. Socrates had a number of followers and several who wrote. Xenophon's *Memoirs of Socrates* have also survived, sketching a remembered thinker and friend not wholly unlike Plato's. There is the same insistence on that self-knowledge that men so easily assume they have, and so seldom really attain:

> And isn't this obvious, that people derive most of their benefits from knowing themselves, and most of their misfortunes from being self-deceived? Those who know themselves know what is appropriate for them and can distinguish what they can and cannot do; and by doing what they understand they both supply their needs and enjoy success, while by refraining from doing things that they don't understand they avoid making mistakes and escape misfortune. (iv.2.26, Tredennick trans.)

This emphasis is an authentic one in both men's recollections of the master, but it seems in each to bear rather a different shading. Xenophon had known a teacher who "used to help people with honorable ambitions by making them apply themselves to the objects of those ambitions" (II.1.1). Self-knowledge meant fewer illusions, wiser goals, and better means to achieve them. His Socrates had, significantly, pressed one of Plato's cousins away from a private life and back toward involvement in the city on just these grounds—that it was where his talents lay if only he had the self-knowledge to realize it (*Memorabilia*:III.vii.9). Perhaps it comes as no surprise that the ambitions of the Socratic students Xenophon knew were normal, practical ones, bound up in the everyday life of ordinary people. His Socrates praised the virtues of self-control just as Plato's had in the *Gorgias*, but his made a special point of it. Everywhere in Xenophon's recollections, Socrates is urging quarrellers to reconcile, frustrated youths to respect their elders, political enemies to find common ground. He advises, where he can, on financial matters, and where he cannot he finds someone to advise him. He urges the fitness and training of the body, and makes a joke of his own tendency toward flabbiness.

These very sensible bits of coffee-house advice may have been charming or even audacious enough in their own setting but they do not often attract the best translators today. And they do seem continually to provoke heartfelt little outbursts of irritation from modern "Socratics." Around the beginning of the nineteenth century, the grand German authority Niebuhr pronounced Xenophon worthless in all his works, and the afterclaps of his thunder are still rattling among his literary descendants:

> Those who know Socrates only from Plato's dialogues may find Xenophon's *Memorabilia* a little disappointing. Some of the magic has disappeared. Socrates is still a highly impressive character, but it is not so easy to see why he had such a compelling influence upon the minds and hearts of many (including some of the unlikeliest) of his fellow-citizens. (Tredennick, 1970:7)

But Plato and Xenophon do not exhaust the surviving accounts of Socrates. The bandy-legged little philosopher also made a "starring" appearance in Aristophanes' *Clouds*, as a kind of idiot technocrat running a conspiratorial school for intellectual lunatics in a dark corner of Athens. The *Clouds* is one of Aristophanes' strangest plays: really a dark, bitterly humorous tragedy, the sort of thing—had it been made in the twentieth century—that would probably have fallen into the category of *film noir*. Socrates made his first appearance in it lolling in a suspended basket, while singing "I tread on air and contemplate the sun."

The action turns upon Socrates' agreeing to instruct an extravagant young wastrel who cannot stay away from the racetrack. He promises the boy's fuming father that his son will return as a brilliant Sophist, an expert in the new "sophia" or technical wisdom that was all the rage among Athenian men of affairs. Teachers in these arts were a recent and wildly successful phenomenon in the Greek world, and as Athens became the center of an empire, they gravitated toward her like moths, each clamoring to advertise himself as a unique source of expertise in everything. Almost none of them really belonged to a Greek state, they traveled from city to city taking fees for teaching on a variety of topics, but staking their reputation upon their success as political consultants. Their students supposedly gained the ultimate key to Greek public life: no one could beat them at argument, and verbal argument was the engine on which every political level of the state still operated. Athens and every smaller city around her remained largely creatures of an oral culture. The claim which made the Sophist both a famous and a heated creature was that he could teach anyone to win at this game, to manipulate the herd at the popular assembly to his heart's content.

Aristophanes presents us with Socrates as just such a Sophist, grinning and rubbing his hands together as he promises that old Strepsiades' son will "surely learn both Logics—the Better, whatever that is, and the Worse, to overturn the Better by crooked speech. If he can't learn both, he must by all means learn the Wrong" (Moses Hadas trans.). The play ends almost in a spiral of comic horror: Strepsiades is ruined and takes his revenge by burning down Socrates' school around his ears, laughing at the old fool's cries of "Dear, dear! I'm choking to death, most miserably." Not a speck of the Platonic magic gleams from this tawdry picture. Which of these portraits—if any—is correct? What sort of criteria would allow us to trust any of them?

We can turn for help to the "mosaic" level of fragmentary historical fact. A rag-tag variety of sources that verify one another (including many of the sorts of evidence discussed in previous chapters) can be culled together, with snippets of detail that give us the outlines of a picture. We can say pretty safely that Socrates was born in 470 or 469 B.C. in Athens. His parents were a sculptor named Sophroniscus and a sometime midwife named Phaenarete. As the son of a citizen, Socrates would have been registered in his *deme* (Alopece) where, once he grew to manhood, he would enlist for service in the hoplite army. His *deme* was grouped with others into one of the ten "tribes" on which the political organization of the polis was based; he voted in the tribe Antiochis. It is generally also accepted that he did actually serve with the Athenian army on several occasions (always as ordinary infantry)—his age during the Peloponnesian War put him in the prime category of older recruits.

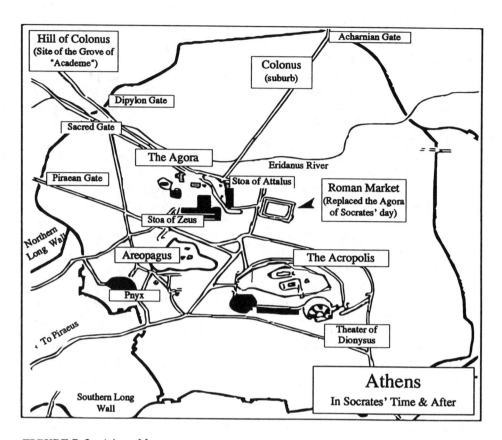

FIGURE 7–3 Athens Map

There is also evidence (which most modern scholars find plausible) that Socrates served a term on the Council of 500 during the fateful year 406–405 B.C., and that he happened to be the one-day chairman over its deliberations on an ominous occasion. Eight Athenian generals who had won a naval victory (at Arginusae, off the coast of Asia Minor) had, on their return to Athens, been unexpectedly charged by their political enemies with murder and sacrilege: faced with a chance to pursue and solidify their success, they had failed to rescue some sailors shipwrecked in the water around them. The war had not been going entirely well, and the political opposition hoped, by a coup in court, to swing popular opinion toward themselves: the actual charge of the two against the "Arginusae Admirals" was sacrilege—undermining the "luck" of the state by angering the gods.

According to the story as we have it, Socrates was the only member of the Council to vote against the prosecution's cleverest maneuver. A majority of them wanted to find the officers guilty as a "block," to require that all the generals be tried together *en masse*; the guilt of one would suffice to kill them all. Socrates objected to this on the grounds that it was both illegal and unjust, thus requiring the rest of the Council to override him—and so to embarrass themselves—in public (Xenophon, *Hellenica*:I.7.15). The admirals were then rapidly convicted and the six who were then in Athens were executed.

Very soon, as Xenophon tells it, "the Athenians repented and voted that preliminary complaints be lodged against those who had deceived the people" (I.7.35). Even so resentment against Socrates hung in the air.

We gain something from this troubling episode beyond what it tells us about Socrates the man and the "gadfly." We also catch a glimpse of that bitter, guilt-ridden confusion that plagued the last years of the Peloponnesian War. The arché in Greece was no more durable than such grand eras have been in other cultures. She tore herself morally and physically to pieces in the years between 431 and 404 B.C. It is against such a backdrop that one better understands the later career of Socrates.

He himself finally faced trial in 399 B.C. on charges of not worshipping the same gods that Athens did, of introducing innovations into the old religion, and of corrupting the Athenian youth. That we know a fair amount of Athens' legal system helps us to reconstruct an authentic picture of Socrates' trial. We know how many jurors there were. We understand that the charge of impiety meant a public legal action; Socrates had offended against the state. He would have defended himself—there were no attorneys to represent defendant and plaintiff, though at least one of his accusers (Lykon) happened to be a court professional. His jury would have been selected by lot from 6,000 citizens who had agreed to serve as jurors over the course of that particular year. After they had heard speeches from the accusers and the accused, and once the witnesses had testified, they would decide first on guilt or innocence and then on penalty. Socrates was found guilty: a majority of 60 votes, we are told, out of a normal 501-man jury, declared against him. He spent a month in jail and then (since Athens worried about the blood-guilt of its executions), he was required to drink hemlock, to die by his own hand. He was survived by his wife, three sons, and a number of devoted pupils.

Since Socrates was thus famous or infamous, his image became a regular product in the Athenian (and later widespread) industry that produced molded knick-knack statuettes for domestic use. So we have yet another category of reasonably certain evidence: most of the portraits (as well as later, more serious statuary) agree with the few passing descriptions in the written sources. Classical Athens, which prided itself on physical beauty, could not have considered Socrates one of its "glories." His nose was flat, the nostrils splayed a little; his eyes were almost comically big and round; he was accused by one of his wilder acquaintances of strutting like a waterfowl and hunching like a satyr. Xenophon (who himself sadly agreed with the "satyr" jibe) recalled that Socrates wanted dancing lessons for the exercise—his stomach was always getting too large. His usual cloak was of poor quality (though, as at Agathon's "dinner party" in Plato, he could dress up when he really wanted to). He very seldom wore shoes.

This is the sort of thing one can draw from surviving portraits of Socrates; enough for a political cartoonist, perhaps, but not even the beginning of what we would really want. The details are such little ones; so eccentric and merely amusing, so empty of grandeur, as though Socrates were someone's crank uncle! This was a man of extraordinary mind and wit, a teacher who lived for seventy years in the leading state of one of Western history's most brilliant cultures. His questions and his integrity (and his death) shook the lives of his students. How can our picture of such a man be so vague, or even so quaint? Victor Ehrenberg called him "Socrates, the greatest, and the least known, among the great men of that unique period" (1968 and 1973:371).

If there is any detail that we have missed among our literary sources, we surely need it. Let us take a second look, and try this time to glean a little more from our knowledge of the kind of work we are reading in each case. Y. Garlan made a point on the ancient literature about slavery and slaves that bears applying to other topics: "We should be in danger of fundamentally misunderstanding them [the texts] if we sought to interpret them outside the context of the literary genres to which they belong and, even more important, without reference to the place that they occupy within one or another system of representation" (1988:15). Throughout most of Western (and perhaps most of human) literary history, authors have taken the different categories or kinds of writing almost as solid worlds in their own right, having their own rules and styles whether any individual human entirely recognizes them or not. A writer approached a category "by accommodating himself to it,..." learning to love its own particular tools, crafting the thing he had to say to fit it, not wrestling the genre to fit what he wished to say.

We may start simply. Certain key characteristics mark specific literary "kinds," making it possible for us to distinguish between a romantic novel, a scientific treatise, and, say, a biography. The three major portrayals of Socrates we have inherited fall into three distinct categories or genres, though two are not so different from each other as they are from the third.

Aristophanes' meant his raucous and barbed comic plays to be performed; even when he himself intended a play to be dark or frightening (as in the *Clouds*), he still had always to please a "comedy audience." His dramas consequently always attempt to weave together a fugue of at least two melodies: a prominent surface series of high-speed, improbable (often bawdy) adventures that stay close to folktale wisdom and never shy away from a cheap laugh; and a deeper, harder-edged and often bitter commentary on social and political issues.

Xenophon's accounts of Socrates are reconstructed memoirs of conversations that strike one, on first sight, as the hastily arranged contents of an old notebook. On almost every occasion they seem both more literate (meaning less poetic) and more ordinary than any similar passage in Plato. The impression, though, is a carefully patterned illusion: the *Memorabilia* is structured, as the German scholar Erbse once demonstrated, like a classic defense speech ("Die Architectonik," *Hermes* 89, p. 261*ff.*). Xenophon used ordinary conversation to vindicate the memory of his old master. He wrote that "since Socrates was as I have described him, in my opinion he deserved to be honoured by the state rather than executed" (I.2.62). As the book progresses, Xenophon gives short, everyday vignettes of Socrates in his early career, dining or lunching in small places with a few of his friends, trying to answer large questions and small with the help of the company present. We earlier called Xenophon's a "coffee-house" Socrates; he is also a homely one (in the best old sense of that word), and he does not appeal to everyone. Those who prefer their history full of sublime triumphs and dark, earthshaking catastrophes—those who, as Leo Strauss noticed, prefer Dostoyevsky rather than Jane Austen—are not likely to get much from the picture. J. B. Bury described it, not over-kindly, as "a portrait such as a journalist with a commonplace mind might contribute to a gallery of 'good men'" (Bury, 1927 and 1935:386). As rebuttal we may use the comment of M. Hemardinquer, which, though it also goes a little too far, might be doing so along the correct trail:

> It seems that Xenophon composed his writings on the model of the conversations of Socrates, free, rapid, touching on all subjects, with an interior unity but without visible connection, always unforeseen, lovely as much as just, removed from all that which could resemble a methodical composition, book or discourse. (*La Cyropédie*, 1872:40)

Plato's dialogues present unique problems since in them Plato has invented, and mastered, a new genre of his own. Somewhere in the borderland common to drama, memoir, philosophical speculation, myth, and forensic speech Plato found for himself a style that allowed him to explore his memories of Socrates' more extended inquiries and to embed them in some reconstructed moments of superb and satisfying artistry. Each piece explores some basic issue—justice, education, beauty, affection—in the form of dialogue (though, strictly speaking, there are nearly always more than two speakers). It spins that issue from the varied speculations of Socrates' companions through increasing fine examinations into some final grasped truth that Socrates has had his eye upon from the beginning. The beauty of Plato's effortless art at painting lively, witty, cultured conversation is that the speakers become characters for us, and keep their personality even when Plato has decided to reexamine the issue of an earlier dialogue—where he has changed his mind or feels he has come to understand differently some old teaching of his master. The forcible and gentle rationality of Socrates' logic and his sure hand with character traits and humor (both of them far harder to do lightly than many people realize) make us almost feel that we have participated in the enlightenment of his climaxes. It does no harm, of course, that Plato's writing style is a joy to read. Not only Socrates, but all except the most boorish speakers in his works have a captivating ease and eloquence.

Perhaps the only real exceptions to this pervasive conversational brilliance in Plato's dialogues are the rather abrasive *Apology*, where we know a man is about to be condemned whatever he says, and the *Laws* (where time, wisdom, and experience of the world have all left their acid marks). Even in these we seem to see through (or hear through) Plato's style and grasp the palpable, original speakers of Athens. His essence has been captured by the modern French scholar J. de Romilly: "It combines the most perfect transparency and intellectual rigor with the warmth of poetry" (1985:154).

But we are weaving together too many strands at once. Taking the order of chronology, let us begin with the portrait of Socrates in the Old Comedy. Aristophanes' *Clouds* was first performed in 423 B.C., about four years after he first pressed himself into the world of drama. The history of the play, as of much of Aristophanes' early career, seems to have been a rocky one; it was not jovial enough for the rather broad tastes of the judges—in the contest at the Dionysia festival for 423 it placed third of the three comedies performed. Aristophanes reacted bitterly to this but although Aristophanes revised it rather drastically it seems never to have been performed at home in Athens again. The revised version is the one that has survived to us.

Aristophanes is virtually our only source for the kind of drama we call *Old Comedy,* and even this is a bit ironic since a remark or two in Aristotle suggest that he had already begun to change the genre himself. We know the names of other comic playwrights who competed at the Athenian Dionysia, but their plays have perished. We have only fragments of their dialogues and a few plot synopses by later collectors by which to judge them, and by which to weigh the eleven plays of Aristophanes that remain. Indeed, we even know that Aristophanes produced thirty-three other plays, and so we really have only fragments of him, though they are chosen and largely complete fragments.

Later writers provide us with a little additional information about what the Old Comedy was. Aristotle's *On the Art of Poetry* is especially important since he compares the genre specifically with epic and tragedy. Valuable too, in a simpler way, is his distinction in the *Nichomachean Ethics* (iv. 8.1128a20) between Old Comedy which preferred plain old indecent language, and New Comedy, which preferred innuendo.

Early in his *Art of Poetry*, Aristotle derives the word "comedy" from "comazein," meaning "to revel." He connects it with the "Comus"—a writhing, wandering dance in which the phallic worshippers of Dionysus defused the "spiritual tensions" of Archaic Greek folk by mocking them and their gods in bawdy song. So, while comedy may have developed a serious social purpose by the fifth century, its origins lay in rollicking and uncontrolled revelry. Aristophanes can, in fact, be at his most eloquent when he is boasting of his own role as an innovator. It is he who has made it artistic and, as his renaissance admirers used to say, "full of high sentence." In his later play *Peace*, one of the actors breaks character for a moment to praise him:

> *It was he that indignantly swept from the stage the*
>   *paltry ignoble device*
> *Of a Heracles needy and seedy and greedy, a vagabond*
>   *sturdy and stout,*
> *Now baking his bread, now swindling instead, now beaten*
>   *and battered about.*
> *And freedom he gave to the lachrymose slave who was*
>   *wont with a howl to rush in,*
> *And all for the sake of a joke which they make on the*
>   *wounds that disfigure the skin;*
> *"Why, how now, my poor knave?" so they bawl to the*
>   *slave, "has the whipcord invaded your back,*
> *Spreading havoc around, hacking trees to the ground*
>   *with a savage resistless attack?"*
> *Such vulgar contemptible lumber at once he bade from*
>   *the drama depart,*
> *And then like an edifice stately and grand, he raised*
>   *and ennobled the Art.*
> *High thoughts and high language he brought on the*
>   *stage, a humour exalted and rare,*
> *Nor stopped with a scurrilous jest to assail some small*
>   *man and woman affair.*
> *No, he at the mightiest quarry of all with the soul of*
>   *a Heracles flew,*
> *And he braved the vile scent of the tar-pit, and went*
>   *through foul-mouthed revelings for you.*
>   (B. B. Rogers trans.)

It can be said that Aristophanes considerably refined the presented technique of the Old Comedy, if he did not refine much of its manner. The genre had, like tragedy, seen individual actors slowly emerge to play distinct parts out of the old homogeneous mass of the chorus. One might tell a story while the chorus provided descant, and broke in to lean heavily on a specially important moment; two or three actors created the possibility of interaction with the twenty-four man chorus.

The plots of the early plays were not especially elaborate, and it may have been at first that an author planned the broad sweep of the play (writing a few important speeches as well) but also allowed his actors to improvise the details as the performance developed. The skeleton that applies to some of Aristophanes' work was this: at the start, a scene with two or three actors "creates" the setting and the "story so far," but they are hustled off the stage by the chorus singing its entrance song. In the play proper, two or more rival actors compete with each other by arguing opposing schemes for getting over some comic difficulty, and one of them of course wins (though how he does it should be a surprise, and funny as well). The "great song" of the chorus follows. The play then goes into its late innings, in which various actors reappear in short scenes full of rapid-fire repartee, the chorus popping in repeatedly to give them a breath. A final ode from the chorus ends the presentation.

Old Attic comedy has been aptly compared to light opera at its best, though we have not perhaps since the age of Pope and Dryden given such a savage bite to it. The features that mark Aristophanes' comic era include an almost harlequin wildness of costume; a blunt appeal to the simplest, readiest passions; a love for whimsical, frenetic, and even surreal situations; a minimal plot whose basic turnings no one can mistake; and as much extra buffoonery as the stage and judges will bear. The last ingredient is important. However elevated Aristophanes might make out his plays to be, he never tried to survive without the old elements of dance, music, and ribald slapstick. Aristotle, struggling to seriously define such a thing in his *Poetics* (1449a), called it "an artistic imitation of men of an inferior moral bent; faulty, however, not in any or every way, but only in so far as their shortcomings are ludicrous" (trans. Lane Cooper). That is the genre at its best—"artistic" as well as "ludicrous."

This definition is not to deny that in the hands of a poet as quick-witted and skilled as Aristophanes the languages of the comedies could sometimes be very graceful. There are moments when his own lyric passages could be almost breathtakingly lovely. Consider this reverent summons to the gods in the great choral song from the *Clouds*:

> *Zeus king of gods who rules on high,*
> *Thee first to our dance do I summon;*
> *Then thee, mighty wielder of the trident,*
> *Untamed upheaver of the briny deep;*
> *And thee, our father of great name,*
> *Revered Ether, nurturer of all;*
> *And thee, driver of horses, who floods*
> *Earth's plain with shining rays, divinity great*
> *Among gods and mortals alike.*
>
> (Moses Hadas trans.)

The music too must have been carefully crafted, though no hint of it has survived.

Aristophanes' comedy is famous for its political bent: both its intent and underlying purpose are to press Aristophanes' views about everything wrong with current Athenian government and society. If it were an issue facing Athenians in the last quarter of the fifth century—even if it were a potential issue or a passing fad—our comic's opinions on it are probably to be found advertised and debated (with a motley of pratfalls for his opponents) in one of the plays. War and peace are, in a sense, two of his most constant actors. Every political and judicial mechanism in the state is referred to in barbed little asides, if not in full-fledged scenes. Aristophanes, as we might expect, had no qualms about attacking individuals directly. His only invariable rule (unless he broke it near the end of the *Clouds*) was to keep things funny.

Given these textures of the genre and this personality in the playwright, can we learn anything more from Aristophanes' portrait of Socrates? We might first of all use the "portrait" more carefully. Thomas Nast did not sketch "portraits" of Boss Tweed; Olifant's chisel-nosed Richard Nixon and MacNelly's tooth-happy Jimmy Carter were meant as essays in a slightly different genre. There must be some correspondence, with the real person, though, or a cartoon—whether drama or pencil sketch—will fail utterly. Thus, in Aristophanes, Socrates lives a life of poverty as he does in every other account of him. He is also an irrepressible talker, and a person with a wide (and perhaps therefore scandalous) range of interests. There is even some evidence that the rather Anaxagoran interests in astronomy and physics attributed to him early in the first act were in fact authentic ones at the beginning of his career.

But when push comes to shove in the play, he is only a character type. The Socrates of the *Clouds* is a philosopher-stooge of just exactly the kind that witty belle-lettrists have always imagined. He is also in Aristophanes' precise economy of effort, a Sophist. He exists so that the playwright can kill as many birds as he can with a single stone. The larger topic of the *Clouds*—the issue Aristophanes really means to sharpen his knife for—is the sort of nothing, the superficial technique, Sophists teach, and how they take your money for it (not like in the old days), and what they do to your children. The topic is also, one regrets to say, how a Sophist squeals when he dies.

The crux of the playwright's issue is Right and Wrong (or, depending on the translator, Just Cause and Unjust Cause or Right and Wrong Logic). Everyone knows in his heart of hearts what Right is (it was simpler in the old days), and so Wrong needs a lawyer, or at least a mouthpiece, and into that breach steps the Sophist, smiling and selling his amoral skills. Aristophanes probably did really regard such instructors as threats to the health of the state—the scene in which Socrates' "Thinkery" gets burned down was one of his deliberate revisions. It is also true that Socrates was famous enough to be made a symbol for the whole class of Sophists, if only he could be mistaken for one.

And, though Socratics in every age have been ready to rush forward in their teacher's defense at this assertion, there is fact in it. If you wish to catch and hold an audience's sympathy, your character or issue must be something worth the viewers' attention. The Socrates in the *Clouds*, unless we are to regard its author as an incompetent, must probably have been reasonably close to the Socrates of Athenian public opinion. If he had not been, the 17,000-odd citizens in the theater would have turned to something more interesting. J. B. Bury found this "phantom Socrates" quite culturally plausible:

> The Athenians, with the exception of his personal friends, were quite unconscious of his greatness...the contemporary man in the market-place of Athens probably remembered him merely as an eccentric Sophist. One can imagine what he would have said: "Socrates—yes, an incessant talker, who fancied himself as a good-mixer. He was really an expert bore, preaching for ever about virtue and other wearisome things. He got at last what he probably had richly deserved." (1927 and 1935:397)

Even so, the comic "portrait" cannot be accurate. Just as comic actors used masks that were larger and wilder than life, so characters and their traits grew huge and broad and exotic to succeed on the stage. Socrates taught, but he never had one of the sophistic little schoolhouses that Aristophanes set fire to in his last act. Socrates had a regular circle of friends (and admission to it was an easy, gracious thing); there were no secret, hermetic initiations like the hugger-muggery sketched in the *Clouds*. And Socrates was poor, partly because he did not accept the fees that his counterpart demanded in the play. But what is consistency worth in comedy anyway?

Some scholars are troubled that Xenophon seems to have written his *Memoirs of Socrates* over a period of years; perhaps ten or fifteen years separated the completion of his recollections of the teacher from Xenophon's last contact with Socrates. Thus, for some, there is a real "question of how genuine the reminiscences are" (Tredennick: 17*f.*). At the very least, as we noted earlier, there is that nagging sense that we are dealing with notes, and not even always—as the author himself admits in his *Apology* (26.32)— Xenophon's own notes. Was he, as Werner Jaeger thought, just an outsider trying to muscle his way into the charmed circle?

J. B. Bury's answer will again do for the negative extreme: "for appreciating the personality of Socrates his [Xenophon's] book is almost negligible, while for most of the bare external incidents of his life that are interesting and which a biographer ought to supply, we go to him in vain" (386). It is useless to object that (as our present study might suggest) Xenophon was not writing biography, or that, even so, he provides more details about the private life of Socrates than any other contemporary source.

Tredennick (one of Xenophon's classicist translators) offers a more agnostic conclusion, poised between fairness and disappointment: "Since Socrates was obviously impressive and Xenophon equally impressionable, he may really have remembered the substance of a number of conversations with reasonable accuracy" (18). It is of course cold comfort, since Tredennick need not mean that Xenophon ever actually remembered anything authentic (despite the plain and painful honesty by which he includes only those episodes about himself that show him foolish or mistaken); it implies only that he could have.

Here, to finish the balance, is one of Xenophon's defenders. W. E. Higgins has traced in a recent book how Socrates' concern to discover exactly what things really are finds its echo in Xenophon's unusually precise and economic descriptions of scenes; and how Socrates' habitual and quiet irony is reflected in Xenophon's graceful habit of silently laying a real person or scheme alongside the claims they have made. He concludes that the bond, and the authenticity of the recollections, have a firm foundation:

> The effect of the relationship on Xenophon was profound. In everything he wrote, it has been justly observed, the mark of Socrates can be seen; the dominant influence of his intellectual life was the power exerted by this unique individual. (1976:21)

The key to sorting through these conflicting testimonies must lie in how well we understand the genres (there were many of them) in which Xenophon wrote.

Of the three earliest Greek historians whose works have survived, Xenophon ranks third in time and third in reputation. This rank might (if he were allowed a "close third") be no mean praise. Few historians can (or ever could) object if placed in value close behind

Herodotus and Thucydides. But what critics in the last two centuries have often meant by that "third" has been far less kind. Insisting that he have the same goals as Thucydides, they find his historical explanations superficial. Certain that he intended to provide a Herodotean omnibus of data, they object that their favorite facts have fallen out of the narrative. The issue is from the beginning exactly one of genres, for there are many kinds of history. When we begin to guess the kind that Xenophon intended to write, his skill, as Higgins found, becomes far clearer.

Xenophon also differs from his two predecessors by the range of genres in which he worked. He took up his historical accounting, as we have mentioned, at the end of the Peloponnesian War, making a particular examination of many of the grand schemes for "saving Greece" that circulated in the postwar years, watching how each seemed to transform as the pressures of reality and human nature revealed its true colors. Thus his history was a form of political criticism, and he followed this genre further—in the Socratic manner of "claim versus reality"—with ironic and questioning essays on the life of his Spartan friend Agesilaos and on the constitutions of various states. In addition, he wrote a war memoir (still one of the best-selling classics of its kind), practical essays on horsemanship, cavalry, and the economic maintenance of a farm. He tried his hand at the broader economic problem of developing Attica, utilizing its resources so that Athenians in the postwar era could begin actually to live on their patrimony instead of levying tribute from the patrimonies of others. He took a turn, finally, at imaginative historical fiction (and "utopian literature"), trying to sum up in his *Education of Cyrus the Persian* all the qualities he thought were overlooked in Greek life.

The common thread running all through this kaleidoscope of writing is Xenophon's concern with what men actually are, why they behave as they do, how they have been governed, and how they have responded. Beside each of these questions he sets the claims men make on the subject. Thus his *Hellenica* explores how men claimed they would govern, and how they actually governed, in the dying years of the Classical Age. His *Constitution of the Lacedaemonians* details (with considerable irony) how the government of Sparta claims to work, and how things actually happen in that strange, inbred community. In both the *Oeconomicus* and the *Ways and Means*, he plunges beneath the common dinner-table and assembly-meeting platitudes about practical economy and tries to unravel the real complications of, respectively, managing a household and increasing the wealth derived from the natural resources of Athens.

His *Anabasis*, or *March Up Country*, is a sad recollection of how this business of seeming versus reality once taught him lessons in the harsh world of military life. It is on its surface, a ripping yarn of adventure, the tale of how he joined a band of Greek mercenaries on an expedition into Persia, and how they had to extricate themselves from the heart of hostile territory when the mission went sour. It is also, under its surface, an almost heartbreaking examination of how external pressure might mold a body of men into a community, and how the coming of easier times could spark its disintegration. The *Anabasis* is both adventure and political tragedy. Lastly, the *Cyrus* tries, in a sort of legendary romance, to make a mythic picture of the leadership qualities a ruler would encompass if he really lived up to the claims that all leaders make.

With this varied but unified background in mind, let us return to Xenophon's Socrates—that disappointing man with his simple and practical virtues. Xenophon intended the *Memorabilia* from the beginning as a defense of his teacher, but it is also a defense of a way of life. Socrates, that is, governs himself in a myriad of different settings in a way that comes very close to his modest claims. The same holds true for his involvement in the polis of Athens: claim for once need not shrink from reality. Xenophon is anxious to show that Socrates propagated this integrity; he describes by what "sort of conversation and conduct Socrates made those who came into contact with him better men" (IV.4.25). "Believing that self-discipline was a good thing for anyone to have who intended to achieve a creditable result, in the first place he let his companions see clearly that he himself kept the strictest training that anyone could; and in the second, in his conversation he was always urging his companions on to self-discipline" (IV.5.1). Rather than taking a smug satisfaction in his own virtue, or advertising to share its secrets for a sum, Socrates tried to spread that form of excellence "which makes both states and households well administered" (I.2.64).

This is clearly a man concerned with virtue and training in the skills by which free men benefit their city. Unlike Aristophanes' eccentric dwarf, he keeps no schoolhouse, sharing out useless clevernesses for a fee. Xenophon's Socrates is not a scientist, though his conversation with Chaerophon in the *Memorabilia* shows that he might once have been, and that he is still curious about (and delighted by) the world.

It is also possible that Xenophon's Socrates is a quieter, homelier figure than his roustabout shade was in the Old Comedy. Those who want their wise men to be spectacular would probably provoke from Xenophon only a warning about claim and reality, boast and fact. The ironic man, after all, is the man who claims less than he has, and Socrates was an ironic man.

But we may miss a little of the thunder. Even faced with an abrasive questioner, Xenophon's Socrates can be maddeningly gentle. Once, when talking the hot-headed Euthydemus out of his rather cynical views about the world, he asked, "Tell me, Euthydemus, has it ever occurred to you to reflect how carefully the gods have supplied all human needs?" When Euthydemus replies, "No, as a matter of fact it hasn't," Socrates continues, "Well, you know that in the first place we need light, with which the gods supply us." Socrates then goes on to ask about the usefulness of light and darkness, the value of food and water, and other commonplace curiosities which are often the only persistent evidences in the ordinary person's world that the universe is not empty or hostile or absurd. All this is well and good, but even if the translation were not so lame it seems at length to grow wearisome. Is this all there was of the true Socrates? How could this Socrates attract a dashing and mindless man like Alcibiades into the outskirts of his circle?

It is easier to understand how a rake like Alcibiades, or a social lion like Callias or a playwright like Agathon might be attracted to Socrates if he were more like his portrait in Plato's writings. One of the best modern scholars of the era concluded that "no doubt Plato created the most beautiful portrait of Socrates; through him and as the man he described, Socrates became immortal" (Ehrenberg 1967 and 1973:373). But Ehrenberg, to his credit, did not allow himself to be swept wholly away by the eloquence of Plato's speech:

It has often been said that Plato's genius went deeper than others, as it certainly did, and that therefore he provided a truth more profound than reality. That is dangerous ground for the historian. He is bound to remain skeptical; he must try, as best as he can, to separate history from the infiltration by another, even the greatest, mind. (373)

Ehrenberg, secure in the certainty of his doubts, refused to make a final decision about the "real" Socrates. We may applaud his prudence for this and yet ask whether he did not give up too soon. Are there any further clues that might help us assess, with clear heads and a moderated admiration in our eye, just how reliable the Platonic picture may be?

We must first of all steer clear of the extravagant claims made by really romantic Platonists. To argue that Plato's Socrates is "the only Socrates worth talking about" is, as Gregory Vlastos admitted, wishful thinking (1971:2). It is indeed an especially dangerous position since instead of merely dwelling upon its favorite "wished reality" it tries to win its case by pretending that no competitors exist. Vlastos himself does believe that Plato's portrait is the "right" one, but he has a far more respectable reason to think so. He argues that men like Critias and Alcibiades (and presumably also some of the followers who really learned something from Socrates) would never have been attracted to Socrates unless he were more exciting than Xenophon lets on. Critias (who went on to die as a political tyrant) and Alcibiades (who was well on his way to becoming the greatest scandal and the most famous manic traitor in Athenian history) are crucial to this argument, since they are the sort of men who could have been plausibly indicted for things like blasphemy and subversion of morals, and it seems likely that Socrates was accused of such things because he was associated with them.

The *Apology* may add further weight to Plato's depiction. It was certainly written when many of those who had witnessed the trial were still alive (once again within ten or fifteen years after the death of Socrates), and it thus stood exposed to expert criticism. Its style (like that of the *Crito*) is moreover much sharper, less easy and polished than Plato's usual manner (even in most of his fairly early dialogues), thus distancing itself from Ehrenberg's worry about a Platonic Socrates who speaks too well to be true. It also does not claim (as Xenophon's *Apology* does) to be taken down from notes.

We must weigh in the equation the fundamental effects of Socrates in causing Plato's own philosophy, a creation that would have unquestionable importance throughout the following ages of Western history. Alfred North Whitehead put it that "the safest general characterization of the European philosophical tradition is that it consists of a series of footnotes to Plato" (*Process and Reality*). At the very center of Plato's philosophy lies the doctrine that truth must be sought, and that if a person finally understands the true and the good, he will be unable to act against that knowledge. This goes far to explain many seemingly dictatorial assertions in Plato: they are in fact only an attempt to build real human life on Socrates' old inquiry into what things really are. Thus, when he is defining what makes the Guardians worthy leaders in his *Republic*, Plato has Socrates reason:

> Well, there can be no question whether a guardian who is to keep watch over anything needs to be keen-sighted or blind. And is not blindness precisely the condition of men who are entirely cut off from knowledge of any reality, and have in their soul no clear pattern of perfect truth...?

> One trait of the philosophic nature we must take as already granted: a constant passion for any knowledge that will reveal to them something of that reality which endures for ever.... And, we may add, their desire is to know the whole of that reality.... Is there not another trait which the nature we are seeking cannot fail to possess—truthfulness, a love of truth and a hatred of falsehood that will not tolerate untruth in any form? (VI.484, Cornford trans.)

The key is that it is still Socrates who says these things, though the *Republic* was written well into the middle of Plato's maturity as a philosopher, when he had a school and a reputation in his own right, and when Socrates had been dead for a decade or two. By placing Socrates at the center of those discussions in which he was evolving his own conception of the world and the forces which moved it, Plato spoke eloquently about the debt owed to one man. As his own philosophy developed rapidly beyond those ideas most scholars would credit to Socrates, he still insisted that the germs of those ideas were Socratic. Socrates concentrated upon rigorous general definitions of things in his quest to learn what they really were. He even (if we can allow the most authenticity to Plato's earliest dialogues) gave a hint that such definitions were a shadow of some greater truth about the nature of each object and act in the world. But it was Plato whom we credit with the true Theory of Forms—that absolutes such as beauty, truth, and justice exist as concepts on earth only because they are the shadows of true and solid things in heaven. Obviously here Plato has traveled very far beyond the old seed of Socratic definition, but he has not gone off in a direction of his own, either. How do we separate the intermingled characters of the man who sowed and the man who reaped?

There is another side to this question, which springs from that enormous raw energy of individual pride that fueled the fires of Greek culture from underneath. We speak very easily of Greeks "submerging" themselves in their states, but they did so out of an intense and strident personal loyalty to something that was theirs. No Greek of the classical period naturally yielded first place to someone else. He insisted on glory for his own triumphs, profit from his own transactions, and credit for his own ideas. In the earliest epic accounts it may have been strength, or craftiness, or some invulnerable magic that gave Achilles or Odysseus the success of heroes, but it was an unquenchable hunger for personal fame that made them truly admirable Greek heroes. Thus when a Greek allotted credit to his predecessor, he believed his predecessor to be truly of a heroic mold. Homer was one such figure; the Spartan Lycurgus another; Socrates was a third. The curious thing about the last man in the trio was how quickly he reached heroic status. Socrates did not compose poetry like Homer and he did not steer the course of states with a Lycurgan deftness. He was even, in a culture that prized beauty, an amusingly ugly person. His status derived from the richness and color and honesty of his mind.

Plato, Xenophon, and Aristophanes were not the only ones who recognized the quality of genius in Socrates' mind. The various sources that describe Socrates' circle of followers tell us that Athenians of many sorts and many ages clustered around him, at least briefly, intrigued by his questions. Among the most notorious were Critias and Charmides (both relatives of Plato), and Alcibiades—all three of them major figures in the tragicomedy of Athens' late fifth-century downfall, and all guilty of harming their state as much as they helped it. Bright Athenian youths like Plato and Xenophon were glad to be called his pupils. They were glad to do so, remember, when the savage portrayal in Aristophanes' *Clouds* had already endangered and darkened his public reputation.

If we can rely on the recollected dinner-party group of friends in Plato's *Symposium*, we can fill out one of the more up-scale Socratic "circles" with a few more acquaintances. Agathon, the writer of tragedies, credited Socrates with some germinal idea in his prize-winning play. Aristophanes, the comic poet, was there—an astonishing tribute to the speed with which simple graciousness can undo a host of prejudices (Socrates always seems to have had an utterly un-Athenian slowness to take offense). There was also Eryximachus, the long-winded society doctor; Phaedrus, a crusty bohemian and spartiate all at once (he grumbles a little like Graham Greene in the dialogue); Chaerophon, the gawky little "philosophic nerd," who found one of his only friends in Socrates and never deserted him. And, of course, crashing late and drunkenly upon the party, missing every point but leering, laughing, poking his elbow into everyone's ribs, was Alcibiades.

These were not all. By the late fifth century the "walls" of the state were beginning to crack, and word of the strange, thoughtful little company within Athens seems to have spread. Non-Athenians came to talk and to listen: Antisthenes, the founder of the Cynic school, was a frequent visitor. Aristippus of Cyrene, Eucleides of Megara (where the Socratics would flee after Socrates' death), and Phaedo of Eretria were others. So great a reputation among so diverse a scattering of contemporaries strengthens our suspicion that Socrates could show a streak of genius and engender some part of it within his circle. Such a phenomenon is sometimes, but not often, a shared thing.

The feel of it—of Socrates in a swirl of dialogue catching the words of each of his companions and spinning them into a gradual and surprising truth—must have carried magic of its own. At the gracious dinners of his most cultured friends, when the genre appropriate to the evening was higher and more poetic than his practical talk and definition, Socrates could call on an alchemy of oral speculation that enchanted his listeners and made them feel that they were seeing some new truth just in the same moment as he saw it. Meno, in the dialogue that bears his name, describes himself as stunned by the lyric force of such speech when he complains to Socrates that:

> At this moment I feel you are exercising magic and witchcraft upon me and positively laying me under your spell until I am just a mass of helplessness. If I may be flippant, I think that not only in outward appearance but in other respects as well you are exactly like the flat sting ray that one meets in the sea. Whenever anyone comes into contact with it, it numbs him, and that is the sort of thing that you seem to be doing to me now. My mind and my lips are literally numb, and I have nothing to reply to you. (80A, Guthrie trans.)

We may not go far wrong if we travel backward a chapter or two to our discussion of oral poetry and call the magic of Socrates his "winged words." We have noted that he produced no written accounts; he lived instead largely within the still-vibrant residue of oral culture that made up most of Athens in the second half of the fifth century B.C. This dual-tongued culture, poised between oral communication and literate records, could demonstrate an almost mythic flexibility of language at every turn. Within it grew the history of Herodotus (where legend walks hand-in-hand with shrewd-eyed skepticism); the tragedy of Aeschylus and Sophocles (in which the characters of myth question and sometimes overturn the inherited lessons of myth); the comedy of Aristophanes with its lyric country hymns constantly intruding upon a lunatic world; and the odd, multi-faceted search of the little, goggle-eyed Socrates for the truth embedded in the cosmos and in humans.

Every one of these pursuits have been preserved for us in writing. In Socrates' case, the preservation was lucky enough to pass in part through the hand and ear of an ingenious literary artist. We should never let our anxiety over the exactness of our sources cloud the richness of that fact: we are not the poorer because Plato's language has a poetry and majesty of his own crafting. The scholar who currently holds the chair of poetry at Oxford, hunting for an ideal example of Greek epigram, has singled out Plato's lines on the soul (they are almost a sonnet):

> Even in life, what makes each one of us to be what we are is only the soul; and when we are dead, the bodies of the dead are rightly said to be our shades or images; for the true and immortal being of each one of us, which is called the soul, goes on her way to other gods, that before them she may give an account. (Levi:384)

These haunting lines come from the *Laws*, one of Plato's sternest and least whimsical dialogues, written long after his youth and after the first fires of his Socratic enthusiasm had been dulled a little by time. The beauty and forcible expression, though, are the same as those with which Socrates and the best of his companions speak in the early dialogues; they are a melding of the genius in the composer *and* of the grandeur in the singer from whom he once learned. Every dialogue that comes from Plato's hand is both a drama and an essay hunting to uncover some philosophic truth, and while the alchemic magic in Plato's own mind was very strong, it is exceedingly unlikely that he would have simply fabricated the figure around which his own mental career took focus. Even the nastiest antagonists in his dialogues are seldom straw men.

Socrates teaches through the spoken word (however wildly) in the *Clouds*, and he does so in both Xenophon and Plato as well. There are a homely energy and a power in the conversations of the *Memorabilia*, just as there are a grandeur and a sweep in the speculations of Plato.

A definitive answer may always remain hidden behind this collage of glory and homespun and humor—hidden, in part, because our sources (and perhaps even Socrates himself) worked or spoke in varying genres. But a variety of light is not a curse; it can be refracted back upon itself and uncover secrets that some single illumination might never touch. It allows the possibility of "a truth that must be sought out with some care [that] gives all the more delight when it is discovered" (*Petrarch Opere Latine* ed. A. Bufano et al., Vol. 2, Turin, 1975, p. 1270).

FURTHER READING

The three ancient sources are Aristophanes' *Clouds*, most of the dialogues of Plato, and Xenophon's *Memoirs of Socrates* and *Symposium*. All of these are available in Penguin editions. A. R. Lacey has dealt with these same sources from the perspective of Socrates' thought in "Our Knowledge of Socrates," pp. 22–49 in *The Philosophy of Socrates*, ed. Gregory Vlastos (Garden City, NY: Anchor, 1971). Vlastos' own essay in the same volume, pp. 1–21, examines "The Paradox of Socrates." *Socrates: Ironist and Moral Philosopher* (Ithaca, NY: Cornell University Press, 1991) is the riveting product of long reflection on the subject of this chapter by Professor Vlastos. For a convincing argument about the reality of the Socrates in Aristophanes' play, see Martha Nussbaum "Aristophanes and Socrates on learning practical wisdom," *Yale Classical Studies* 26 (1980), 43–97, especially 71–79.

Chapter Eight

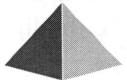

Philip of Macedon: Reconstructing the Pieces

Our attempts to rebuild authentic pictures of the ancient past began in the early chapters of this book with nothing but a few physical remains to use as clues and raw material. With only an enigmatic painting, shreds of an abandoned campsite, a ruined house, we worked as detectives must when there are no eyewitness accounts and no convenient confessions to smooth the reconstruction of a lost scene. Access to oral and written evidence made a revolution in those methods: the figures in our paintings began to speak for themselves.

In the more recent chapters these written and remembered accounts have made our repainted pictures of the past both richer and more reliable, but they have probably made them more confusing as well. Just as in the detection of crimes, the evidence of an eyewitness account or a confession can be very misleading: the case of Socrates in Chapter Seven seemed almost to suggest that three intelligent men who knew the same remarkable figure could look us squarely in the eye and give three utterly incompatible accounts of him. To some frustrated readers, writing as evidence might even seem worse than the meager piles of physical remains with which we tried to understand the late Stone Age. Bones and flint knives may mislead us, but they probably do not lie.

Fortunately, modern historians can often study the world of antiquity without being forced to choose between surviving written works and the material remains. Time, when we are lucky, has left us at least a little of both. Names, places, plotlines, reflections on events speak in authentic old voices from the written accounts; bones, tools, treasures, refuse, and the foundations of ancient buildings give us a physical shape and weight—the "footprints" and "fingerprints," if you like—of the events and actors. The shape of a potsherd will even indicate the dimensions of its pot: in the study of antiquity as in a murder mystery a little clue can tell a large story.

The World of Philip (400 - 336)

Date B.C.	Greek & Macedonian Events	Around the Mediterranean	Artifacts & Art
400 --	(c. 400) The Peloponnesian War is over. A nervous, shifting era of dictators and "brushfire wars" spreads across the Greek world. (379) Thebes (a rather ingrown city in central Greece), after suffering under especially harsh pro-Spartan rule, revolts against its captors. It develops a deceptive new style of phalanx-fighting.	(396) Carthage besieges Syracuse; the tyrant Dionysius I defends it. (c. 395) The Ionian cities (supported by Sparta) attempt another revolt vs. Persia. (390) Rome besieged & sacked by marauding Gauls. (389) Plato visits Sicily hoping to make a "philosopher king" of Dionysius.	Athens is becoming the intellectual instead of the political center of Greece. (c. 386) Plato is teaching at the Academe. He will write the *Republic* about his ideal imaginary government. (385) Aristophanes dies.
375 --	(371) The Battle of Leuctra: Thebes defeats a surprised Spartan army. Soon the Thebans are so overbearing, their allies negotiate with Sparta. (362) The Battle of Mantineia: Thebes defeats "everyone" but loses the only commander (Epaminondas) who really understands its new fighting style. Athens starts re-arming.	(c. 388) Persia tries to regain some of its influence in Greece by dictating peace terms between the various warring cities. (c. 380 - 343) XXXth Dynasty in Egypt (its last native rulers). (359) Artaxerxes III becomes King of Persia.	Plato's student Aristotle will eventually tutor Alexander and then return to teach in Athens at the Lyceum. He will write many books of practical observations, including the *Politics*. (c. 368) Height of Xenophon's writing career begins.
350 --	(359) Philip II becomes King of Macedon. Philip uses the prevailing confusion to gain influence in Greece, posing as the "protector of Delphi." He proves quite adept at "arbitrating" local Greek disputes. His soldiers never seem to lose, and never quite go home either. (343) When Philip takes the rest of the Greek (and Athenian) north, a conference of *poleis* declares war on him once and for all.	(350) Jewish revolt against Persia fails. (343 - 342) Persia reconquers Egypt. (c.) Rome becomes involved in wars with the Samnites & other hill-peoples of central Italy. (c. 345 --) Timoleon of Corinth briefly dominates Syracuse and defeats the Carthaginians in Sicily.	(c. 350) The "Mausoleum" (tomb of Mausolus and "wonder of the world") completed at Halicarnassus. (347) Plato dies. In 342 Aristotle leaves Athens for Macedon, to tutor Philip's young son Alexander. (c. 345) The sculptor Praxiteles fl. (343) The playwright Menander born at Athens; a trendsetter of the more private "New Comedy." Athenian theaters begin running "revivals" of the old playwrights.
340 --	(338) Philip of Macedon defeats Athens, Thebes, and other Greek cities at the Battle of Chaeronea. Three strategic garrisons full of his crack troops watch the locals for signs of rebellion -- their strongholds are called the "Fetters of Greece." (336) Philip suddenly assassinated in Macedonia.	(338) Darius III becomes ruler of Persia.	(335) Aristotle returns to Athens from Macedon. (c. 335) Monument to the dramatic chorus-leader Lysicrates set up at Athens (still standing).

That last point is true not only of artifact remains but even of human bones, and of the earth itself. If we understand the normal erosion of a piece of land, or the usual silting of a particular riverbed (both rate and pattern), we can quite often work back to a very convincing picture of some earlier time and shape in the history of that landscape. If we find the clues locked into human bones about height, age, disease, and wounds, we can sketch the body to which they once belonged, and guess at certain episodes in its "career." All these forms of reconstruction—artifact from fragment, landscape from modern geology, body from telltale bones—have figured in modern attempts to unravel one of the greatest burial and murder mysteries left to us from the ancient world: the case of Philip of Macedon, the father of Alexander the Great.

Modern historians do not want to know about Philip simply because he fathered Alexander. Philip cast his own huge shadow across the breadth of Greek history. He reigned from 359 to 336 B.C., and when he took possession of it, Macedon was an irritating but negligible tribal kingdom on the edge of the Greek north country (its very borders so porous that invading armies used it as a thoroughfare). When he died, Macedon had become the bright and powerful kernel of a tiny, largely Greek, "empire"—its riches already astonishing, its centralized efficiency the envy of brilliant old city-states like Athens and Thebes, its armies feared and irresistible in every corner of Greece. The very poleis that once defined their superiority over all other peoples by the brilliance of their hoplite warriors now invited Macedonian soldiers to resolve their disputes. And what Macedon settled seemed to stay settled, though when Macedon took a hand in a matter, it also usually stayed to keep an eye on the new arrangement. The tragic lesson of the fifth and early fourth centuries in Greece seemed to be that Greeks could not stop killing one another even when their culture was exhausted, or even when they stood to gain more from cooperation. Philip gradually wheeled, dealed, and refereed his way into empire.

What allowed Philip to play this game so efficiently was the tendency of the other players at the table (the Athenians, the Spartans, the Thebans, the host of smaller but equally independent Greek poleis) to distrust each other at least as much as they distrusted him. The Athenian Empire of two or three generations earlier remained fresh and bitter in everyone's minds, as did the Spartan and Theban hegemonies which followed it. Absolute autonomy (or as near the imagined vision of it as one's city could get) was the fire that fueled the inner chambers of the average Greek heart: in this city on this land these people rule themselves. Earlier in this book we called this desire a rule. It might have been better described as a sharp and constant longing; the heat with which Greeks desired it made it a rule. Those who proposed to group the Greek cities into some rational and pragmatic larger form of government inevitably provoked a hornet's nest of resistance.

The Athenians (riding high on their success against the invading Persians) had tried it first. Former allies of the Athenians against the Persians found themselves converted into tribute-paying subjects (one could never tell, the sly and plausible argument ran, whether the "Eastern Menace" might return tomorrow). They smarted under demands from the Athenian political impresario Pericles, and complained, and found their tribute quotas had been raised. As Athens passed unmistakably from their protector, to leader, to overlord, their hostility smoldered hotter and burst into flame. The climax was a surprise, from the Greek point of view, only in its scale. Athens and her empire plunged into a prolonged, bitter, devastating war against her principal rivals—Sparta, Corinth, Thebes—

and every ally they could recruit. The fighting flared on year after endless year, now dying down, now roaring up again, until it almost seemed as though Greece suffered some disease that mimicked the throes of death. It appeared to end in 404 B.C. when Athens—the jewel of the classical era—was surrounded and starved into surrender.

But peace and autonomy had not returned. Sparta had recruited allies with a cry for Greek "freedom." Sparta now tried its hand (a blunter and less disguised fist even than Athens'), at control of Greece. Where Athens had demanded money, Sparta arrived with military garrisons and ill-educated, grasping "commissars" (*harmosts*), settling down like vultures onto their conquests and former allies alike. They even threw a garrison into the northerly city of Thebes, though it had been one of their principal partners in the Peloponnesian War.

Within a decade of that long war's end Sparta had provoked its own backlash of revolt, and out of the ashes of that conflict rose a conquering military elite from Thebes. A quick and skillful thrust of Theban tactical expertise broke the proud, inflexible Spartan army in 371 B.C. Thebes, of course, now intended its own empire. The story reads almost like fits of a recurring madness. The weary land of Greece, in which the margin of survival in hard times had never been a very broad one, found itself reeling—its farmland devastated, its finances drained away, its population decimated. In the end, against the very deepest grain of their own character, some Greeks began to look for rescue outside their own country.

A few of them believed they saw a potential savior on the throne of a small barbarian realm in the cool wooded highlands of northern Greece—north even of Thessaly—in Macedon. An ingenious adventuring prince was putting his own domain in order there, and stringing together a chain of impressive victories against the other barbarians on his borders. Might he not do the same for Greece, thought some, and yet acknowledge himself too simple and too distant to dream of taking Greece for himself?

Philip had ideas of his own. He had been held a political hostage in the city of Thebes during its glory years—from his fifteenth to his eighteenth year. He knew how crystalline, how easily shattered even the most rational diplomatic ties between polis and polis could be. He had seen how quickly city could be split from city along the fissure lines of their innumerable ancient rivalries. Once home and on his throne he played against these "planes of cleavage" at every opportunity and began to break them. The irony was that he often broke them at the invitation of other Greeks.

It was after settling one such Greek dispute in 346 B.C. that Philip (though no one really considered him a Greek) became a voting member in the most prestigious council of Greek states. Every vote he cast had the weight of his armies behind it, and the war-torn city-states of the older Hellenic world could no longer ignore him. Their resistance against Philip came too late, and his army moved south in the campaigning season of 338 B.C., dodging through the passes of Thessaly, confusing and then defeating his most formidable enemies (the Thebans and Athenians) on the field of Chaeronea. Riding on the wings of his success, Philip determined that Greece itself (not merely its petty disputes) be settled down once and for all. It would weld them together in one offensive and defensive alliance with Macedon: the League of Corinth. All states beneath that cloak might still pretend to be autonomous, but the important affairs among them, and with the wider world, would be discussed by delegates in Macedon. Philip determined that Greece would at last be quiet.

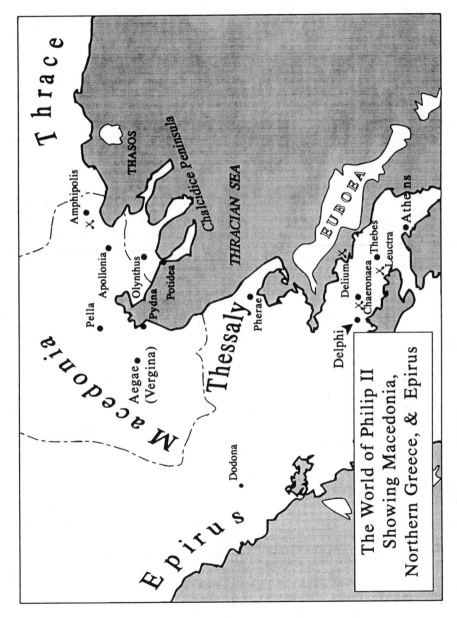

FIGURE 8–1   The World of Phillip II

He had grander plans building now in his mind. The principle item to be discussed by the first meeting of Greek delegates at his capital would be the launching of a massive military campaign against Persia. It was the old Greek enemy; it would focus the attention and hatreds of his new subjects in a new direction, adding to his glory and giving his collaborators in the old Greek city-states something to boast about. He dispatched an advance force across the Hellespont in 336, just shortly before calling his grand council; plans for his grandest gamble were well under way as the delegates arrived in his capital. Then, as the ceremonies opened, someone killed him.

It is probably not fair to say that Alexander the Great would never have conquered so much unless Philip, his father, had planned it first. It is probably fair to say that Alexander could not have carved the shapes of Greece and Macedon so far across the known world if Philip had not fashioned for him many of the tools first, and given him a solid foundation from which to wield them. Alexander had a poised and centralized base of power, half made of eccentric Greek brilliance and half of the simple, feudal loyalties of his ancestral hill-country kingdom. He had a network of fresh alliances at his back, still recovering from the shock of his father's success. He needed only the briefest campaign of his own to keep Greece unbalanced. Alexander was indeed, as he crossed the Hellespont, embarking on his father's campaign; only time would make it his.

History is full of the story of Alexander, but how much do we know of his father Philip, the "barbarian" who mastered Greece, who built a mighty kingdom in the wooded lands of the wild north and sired an invincible son? His great importance was apparent to most contemporaries only late in his life, and thus it sometimes feels as though every clue is tied to the "tail end" of the story. Let us see, working backward, how much we can reconstruct.

PHILIP

When a culture disappears beneath the flood of history it may at first leave a great wrack of material remains upon the waters, but very quickly the random tides of time carry most of these clues away, and confuse the rest. A modern historian's evidence is made up only of that flotsam and jetsam washed ashore in the centuries since. Thus it is that we have the shreds and tatters of cultures that once were whole—driftwood glimpsed as half-buried in the sand, and then recovered.

But these fragments still tell us many of their tales. They suggest relative dates, sometimes an absolute one. They indicate what materials were available in their day for craftsmen to work upon, and what crafted objects their culture desired, and how much skill existed to turn desire into artifact. They tell us which things a culture needed thousands of years ago, and needs can suggest motive forces in the larger story of that people. The tatters of history tell us most, though, when we find them fitting together like the pieces of a puzzle or the clues to a crime, when we can sense that some of them are tiny episodes in a coherent tale. We can even, with great care, use modern methods to fill in the gaps.

Perhaps the greatest modern monument to this technique (though it is only partially a tale of Greek antiquity) has been at Knossos on the island of Crete where Sir Arthur Evans slowly through the first half of the twentieth century rebuilt a grand, rambling Minoan palace. He had the confidence not only to assemble the archaeological fragments of Knossos, but to picture them whole in his own mind and to put them back together.

This is emphatic certainty indeed: scholars since have loved or hated Evans, for he has left them no room to be neutral. After hiking across acres of scattered stone and ruined foundations a visitor at Knossos will come suddenly upon whole buildings towering intact behind their curious "upside-down" Cretan colonnades, the "restored" frescoes gleaming from their walls in brilliant sweeps of color.

Is this an actual sense of the lost Minoan world one is catching, or only a grand tapestry of Evans' imagination? More recent students of Minoan architecture are sometimes appalled by inaccuracies that Evans built permanently into the site. Careful critics of Minoan art can now tell that in some "repainted" frescoes a charming blue monkey or blue boy may have been inferred wholly from some tiny bit of pigment that might once have depicted a tail or a foot. Yet both the architect and the art critic have probably had their deepest sense of what is truly Minoan colored by the sweeping wholeness of Evans' remade palace. Reconstructions speak powerfully to the imagination. Without them we should have far less sense of the texture and wholeness of the ancient civilizations, but they can speak almost as eloquently to us when they lie. We must tread carefully.

Almost every possible technique in the wide field of reconstruction has been used upon some part of the mystery of Philip II, King of Macedon. He was a figure so large that his shadow lies all across the middle of the fourth century B.C. If he had not been the father of Alexander we would probably now call him Philip the Great. That he was Alexander's father has knotted every fact we possess about him with unexpected difficulties, since Alexander changed the world around him utterly. Philip was hardly visible to many writers in later years except as the figure who prepared Alexander's way. A little of what he did might remain in view but his goals and personality grew nearly invisible, as though Alexander had in his victories and death become a lens so large that men could never again look into the past without looking through him. What had Philip meant to do?

It has not helped at all that the only surviving written evidence from Philip's own time has generally come from his enemies. Athenian orators like Demosthenes, immersed in the lost days of their own city's tragic glory, could find nothing good to say about the man who had conquered them, and done it so easily. Bad enough if grand civilized Persia had won its war against the bright, bustling city-states where real humanity lived, but to win against Persia and then fall helpless before these crude, bearded, backwoods horsemen from the north—that was a shame not to be borne. Demosthenes called Philip "a damned barbarian from a place where you can't even buy a decent slave" (*Philippic*:III, 31).

But Demosthenes is a contemporary source—one of very few—and we cannot simply ignore him, especially since Macedon itself remained almost "Homeric" in its oral simplicity until well into the fourth century, and no writing of its own exists to argue the other side. The Macedonian state itself, so ably improvised together by one king after another, had no formal administrative techniques or written codes of law at its foundation, but only a shifting mix of personal charisma, rough-hewn leadership, oral tradition, and custom.

Yet these were the only tools Philip seems to have needed as he "forged a nation out of the Macedonian people...the first territorial state on the continent of Europe with a centralized political, military and administrative structure" (Ellis, 1976:43*f.*). In 359 B.C. Perdiccas had been king of Macedon and led 4,000 of his soldiers to their deaths against an invasion from (even less civilized) Illyria. Perdiccas died leaving an infant son in direct line for the throne, but the army elected Philip—his own younger brother—instead. We do not quite know the year (dates are hard to come by in those years when Macedon still lay on the dark fringe of the literate world), but very soon afterward Philip began to make deeply significant changes in the Macedonian army. He had been hostage as a young man in Thebes during the brief, eccentric years of its military glory. He now began to act upon the lessons he had learned there. Armed with new variations on Greek tactics he threw his revamped national (almost feudal) army into a rapid series of nearly simultaneous advances: eastward into Thrace, north and west toward Illyria and the wild tribes of the Balkan mountains (who had begun to unite after their victory over Perdiccas), and—while everyone thought him still engaged on the other two campaigns—southward into Greece.

Philip had not forgotten the political lessons of his time in Greece either when he learned how divided the Greek states were. Playing one against another, his success was meteoric. The crowning moment of this strategic "jujitsu" came in 346 when he was actually asked to bring an army into the central Greece and settle a dispute between several of the poleis. He stayed and, as we have seen, became a voting member in the most prestigious council of Greek states. The older Hellenic world could no longer ignore him either diplomatically or militarily. The armies of the major Greek states finally combined against him in 338, and after repeatedly tricking them off the battleground of their own choosing, Philip defeated them at Chaeronea. He now announced himself the "arbiter" of Greek affairs. By clever accumulation of one individual treaty after another (and finally by creation of his own alliance in exactly the same style of the one that had been made against him), he tried to fuse the Greeks and Macedonians together in a common cause: he would lead them all against Persia. In 336 B.C. he sent a raiding force to gather intelligence in Asia Minor, and in that same year he was murdered. A recent history of Macedon traces the irony:

> Chaeronea was the swan-song of a military career spanning two decades, that had taken a remote border state to the threshold of world power. The train of events started, within a few months of final victory, that would lead to the enterprise of Persia. But the young cub who had covered himself with glory at Chaeronea was fated, as in some Greek drama, to garner those laurels. The old lion took the fatal steps which were to lead to his grave.... (Crossland and Constance:22)

The story of those last fatal steps unfolds with dark drama in the histories of Diodorus Siculus, a Greek who wrote in the first century B.C. Diodorus puts Philip on the stage in Book 16, as Philip organizes to receive his Greek delegations and to give away his daughter's hand in marriage, planning sacrifices to the gods so magnificent they might become the stuff of legends. At last it was the morning of the spectacle, though the sun had not yet risen,

> While it was still dark, the multitude of spectators hastened into the theatre and at sunrise the parade formed. Along with lavish display of every sort, Philip included in the procession statues of the twelve gods wrought with great artistry and adorned with a dazzling show of wealth to strike awe in the beholder, and along with these was conducted a thirteenth statue, suitable for a god, that of Philip himself, so that the king exhibited himself enthroned among the twelve gods.

> Every seat in the theatre was taken when Philip appeared wearing a white cloak, and by his express orders his bodyguard held away from him and followed only at a distance, since he wanted to show publicly that he was protected by the goodwill of all the Greeks, and had no need of a guard of spearmen. Such was the pinnacle of success that he had attained, but as the praises and congratulations of all rang in his ears, suddenly without warning the plot against the king was revealed as death struck....Pausanias saw that the King was left alone, rushed at him, pierced him through his ribs, and stretched him out dead; then ran for the gates and the horses which he had prepared for his flight....Having a good start, Pausanias would have mounted his horse before they could catch him had he not caught his boot in a vine and fallen. As he was scrambling to his feet, Perdiccas and the rest came up with him and killed him with their javelins.
>
> Such was the end of Philip. (xvi.92*ff.*, Welles trans.)

Because we have so few sources, and because these were deeds done and recorded in a land still very near its old ancestral culture of oral tradition, there is a feel of mystery and legend wrapped around the end of Philip. Some of this mystery may never be dispelled (perhaps we should not entirely wish it to be), but a careful historical reconstruction can tell us much before we have finished with it. We may even find ourselves literally face to face with this "barbarian" genius who remade the very structure of classical Greece.

We might start with a (comparatively) plain matter of reconstructing geography. Where was it that so many people (Greek and Macedonian) flocked to attend the celebrations and to pay honor to Philip on the last day of his life? We know the name was "Aegae," but identification of its location is not as simple as it seems. By the twentieth century Aegae was a lost city. No one had known for a long time where it had once been, and several towns could claim they were the "first royal capital of the Macedonians." We knew that up until the reign of Archelaus (413–399 B.C.) Aegae been at the center of the little kingdom. About the end the fifth century Macedon had moved its power and growing wealth into the town of Pella, fortifying it and making it the new capital. Pella was the seat of power when Philip forged his impressive kingdom and when Alexander created his empire. Thus, once the royal residence had been transferred, Aegae retained only sacred associations and its royal burial ground, but these were of scant help to scholars because Macedon is full of burial grounds. Everyone waited for a telltale inscription to appear.

Not all candidates for the site of Aegae were equal, of course. Some made more sense than others, the best guess perhaps being the modern village of Edessa. A look at the index of W. W. Tarn's classic *Antigonus Gonatas* (1913 and 1969), for instance, would show the entry: "Aigai (Edessa)." Much of the evidence for the identification was a plausible interpretation of one passage in the history of Justin, a writer of the second century A.D.. It seemed to equate Aegae with Edessa: "Caranus...urbem Edessam... Aegeas,...vocavit"; "Caranus called the city Edessa, Aegae" (7.1.7).

The reconstruction of Aegae's true identity began when Nicholas Hammond, an expert on topography and climate, became curious about old Macedon. Hammond was educated as an ancient historian, but he has since spent much of his life (both in peace and wartime) hiking through the Balkan countryside, learning its textures and eccentricities with an intimacy no merely technical knowledge could ever have given him. By the late 1960s he was arguing forcibly that Edessa could not possibly correspond well with the ancient descriptions of Aegae. The passage in Justin, so far as he could tell, was simply an attempt to guess where the name "Aegae" came from; it said nothing about what Edessa might or might not have been in the fourth century B.C.. There was enough solid ancient evidence, Hammond insisted, to show that Edessa and Aegae were both cities in that day, and separate ones. He pointed out a passage on weather in the essay *On Winds* (*de Ventis*), written by Aristotle's pupil and successor Theophrastus:

> There also occurs a backlash of winds so that they blow back against themselves when they flow against high places and cannot rise above them. Therefore the clouds sometimes move in the opposite direction to the winds, as in the neighborhood of Aigai in Macedonia, when north wind blows against north wind. (Chap. 27, *de Ventis*)

Hammond knew his Macedonian countryside well enough to realize—and to prove—that this phenomenon did not occur near Edessa, and to add that it did occur near the modern village of Vergina (1972:156*ff.*). Taking that clue as the first loose thread in the mystery, he "pulled," and other clues tumbled out after it. When Plutarch wrote his adventure-filled biography of Pyrrhus of Epirus he added, as one of the minor tales, that Pyrrhus had set up in Aegae "a garrison of Gauls, some of those in his own army, who being insatiably desirous of wealth, instantly dug up the tombs of the kings that lay buried there, and took away the riches, and insolently scattered about their bones" (Chap. 26). When the king of Macedon finally retook his city and avenged this outrage, he rebuilt the burial ground, hallowed it, and covered it deep within a grand tumulus of earth. The episode rings true, for everything we know about them suggests that the Macedonians took death very seriously. And Edessa had no great tumulus; the little village of Vergina did.

Hammond's proposal that Vergina had once been Aegae provoked no immediate chorus of agreement, but the process of unravelling seemed somehow to quicken. A second discovery and the beginnings of reconstruction now lay very near in the future. We must back up for a moment to catch the trail of another career that would soon intersect with Hammond's idea. Manolis Andronikos was a Greek archaeologist who first excavated as a student at Vergina in 1937. He had in those early days been uncovering a Hellenistic palace on a hillside behind the modern village. World War II put a stop to this, but when Andronikos returned in the 1950s his eye kept wandering to a great earthen tumulus near the town that had been a little torn up by the fighting. Fragments of many curious kinds had begun to appear around it, especially tombstones—many of them previously buried.

In 1962 Andronikos formally undertook to dig his way into the strange hill, though it gave him almost uncanny resistance. To follow the old ground level he soon found he had to delve more than twelve meters below its crest. It ran more than 100 meters in diameter and contained tens of thousands of tons of earth. This has not, at least since Schliemann, been the scale in which Greek archaeology likes to work, and it is hardly surprising that Andronikos and his assistants toiled season after season without a spectacular result. The surprise is rather that they kept on.

Hammond gave them a little encouragement, of course, when he began to suggest they were on the trail of old Aegae. There were telltale signs of desecration and plunder inside the tumulus that might point to Plutarch's disastrous tale of the Gauls. Even this, though it were only evidence of looting and destruction, might unlock the secret that this was Aegae if it could be dated to around 280–270 B.C. Better yet, it would show that beneath this tumulus once lay the royal necropolis of Aegae.

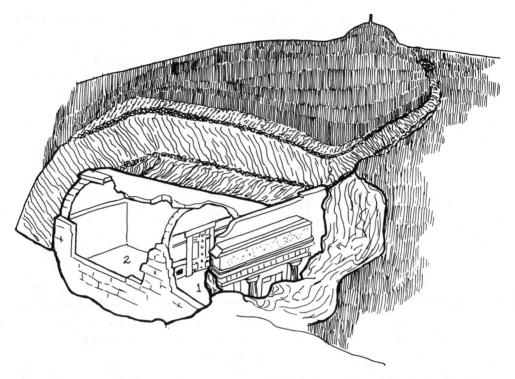

FIGURE 8–2 A schematic diagram of the tomb—possibly Philip II's—which Andronikos found lurking beneath the forgotton tumulus at Vergina. Beneath an impressive and ritual colonnaded doorway, the antechamber (at number 1) contained remains of a cremated woman; the main chamber (at number 2) housed those of a man surrounded by treasures.

At the end of the 1977 season—Andronikos had removed 40,000 tons of earth in that year alone—discovery broke over the weary excavation like a quiet thunderclap. The team had dug at last down through the great exterior tumulus and had gone some four meters into the smaller original tumulus beneath it. They struck the stone roof of an unplundered tomb. A colleague of one of the present authors was working in Athens at the time and suspected that she might be "at least mildly curious about the recent discovery." Colin Edmonson wrote this on December 3, 1977:

> The tomb itself is impressive: a Doric facade with fresh paint preserved on the triglyphs, mutulus, etc., carved marble door (still unopened), and moderately well-preserved fresco on the architrave representing a hunting scene, with several hunters mounted and on foot, dogs, at least one stag, and a lion. ...much has been made of the fact that lion-hunting is a regal pursuit. The painting will be extremely important in any case, and will keep the art historians busy for years, I should expect. The tomb has two chambers, with a burial in each. Entry was made from above into the main chamber, where undisturbed contents were found placed apparently by material (and value?): bronze vessels and weapons in one corner (including several large basins and jugs, several smaller vessels, a shield cover with inlaid decoration in wood, glass, and ivory, spear points, greaves, swords and at least one dagger, silver objects in another corner (mostly vessels of various kinds, but apparently a pair of silver greaves as well), and a variety of things on and around the stone sarcophagus lid, including a cuirass of bronze

with appliqué designs gilded, and gold strips adhering to it vertically, traces of wood, and what has been interpreted as a scepter: a core of bamboo or similar reed sheathed with cloth to which was attached a thin coating of gold, and (at the end?) some decomposed matter which proved on analysis to be feathers, the whole being over a meter and 1/2 long.

The removal of the sarcophagus lid revealed a gold larnax [coffin] 40 × 39 × ? cm, weighing 11 kilos, including the remains of the cremated deceased. Near the skull was a distinctive gold diadem, beautifully wrought, with a knot at the front and careful patterned "hair" all around, adjustable to a range of head sizes, with the back open and joined by a chain (all this is hearsay; I haven't even seen a photo). A similar diadem is represented on portraits of several Macedonian (and later) kings on coins, and on one relief portrait, also regal; this, therefore, is the crown of Macedon. The top of the larnax is decorated with a sort of sun-burst design with a rosette in the center, and Andronikos takes this to be the emblem of the royal house.... The sides of the larnax are divided into three zones, with palmettes in the upper register, rosettes in the middle, and a sort of running leaf pattern below. The feet terminate rather awkwardly in lion paws.

In the prothalamos [antechamber], also entered from above (as I understand it), was another burial, also in a gold larnax, weighing 8 1/2 kilos with contents, again cremated (?—the bones are said to have been wrapped in blue cloth with a design in gold thread, but all this has suffered greatly since discovery). The sex of the occupant has not yet been determined [it has since been shown to have been a woman probably in her twenties] and the only important find from this chamber reported so far is a gold-covered quiver, arrowheads, and some red-figured sherds.

Nearby (in the same tumulus, as I understand it) is another tomb, plundered, but with handsome paintings in the burial chamber representing Hermes Psychopompos leading a chariot in which a wild-haired Pluto is abducting an anguished Persephone, who turns back pleadingly to a stunned female companion behind the chariot. The scene is said to be most striking for the effectiveness of its motion and emotion, and will also doubtless keep the art historians busy, if not happy, for some time.

The main chamber also produced five ivory heads ca. 3 cm high and other fragments of limbs, hands, etc., which Andronikos has identified as Amyntas and Eurydice [the parents of Philip], Philip, Olympias, and Alexander, and he goes on to associate these with the chryselephantine portraits of the same people by Leochares in the Philipeion at Olympia. This group provides him with what he regards as his best evidence for the identification, although the argument is of necessity a cumulative one: the splendour of the tomb (although the main chamber has only a rough, preliminary coating of stucco, and is apparently not finished), the regal sport on the architrave, the wealth of the contents, the diadem, the symbol of the royal house (which also, incidentally, appears on the lid of the otherwise undecorated second gold larnax), the scepter (which is so only if the tomb is in fact royal), the portraits, and (although he makes little of this, since they have been badly battered) the fact that at least one pair of greaves shows a discrepancy of 3 cm in height, and we all know Philip walked with a limp....Oh, yes; Andronikos also emphasizes that all the contents can be dated to 350–320 B.C., and no other King of Macedon was buried in Macedonia in this period.

Other scholars this time agreed quickly and wholeheartedly with Andronikos that Vergina was Aegae, and that this man in the tomb might well be Philip. Hammond, who had done much to keep Andronikos' hounds on the chase, added in 1978 that "the man was certainly a king and the woman a queen" (1978:335). Many were even ready to accept the exact identity of the individuals. Headlines in the Greek press read:

The Bones of Philip (Ta osta tou Philippou)

or, even better:

The Treasure in the Tomb of Philip (o thesauros ston tapho tou philippou)

The article in London's *Sunday Times Magazine* bore the proud banner "The Golden Tomb of Philip II."

But perhaps all this heady success had tumbled forward too quickly. The tomb's location could almost certainly be identified as Aegae now, since Aegae had continued to be the royal necropolis even after Macedon moved its capital to Pella. The dates of the objects could be set with fair confidence in the three decades between 350 and 320 B.C. Philip was in that time the only king buried in Macedon. And, too, there was the type of burial and the types of objects included—all appropriate for a dead king. The construction of the tomb seemed to make the firmest argument of all: while the main chamber had still been under slow deliberate construction, the antechamber had been added to it hastily, perhaps even suddenly. We should have expected exactly such a thing if this were Philip's tomb, since the details tell a story that fits well into the circumstances of his death. Philip was assassinated. Very soon after—perhaps as part of the same chaos—Philip's newest wife (of one year), Cleopatra, was killed by his wife of twenty-one years, Olympias. The female bones in the antechamber could thus easily be Cleopatra's.

But it would take far more reconstruction than this to make such claims with any certainty. Andronikos was candid enough to voice his own doubts to an interviewer in the *New York Times Sunday Magazine* of December 25, 1977:

> He himself expresses the fear that perhaps he should not have attributed the tomb to Philip. "I know I had the right to do so on the basis of the archaeological evidence found so far," he says. "It is what is called in English a "working hypothesis," but if next spring I should find evidence against this hypothesis, I would be the first to say so. Even now I am not absolutely sure." (p. 32)

Debate has, in fact, in the years since swirled around several features of the discovered tomb. Some believe the introduction of the architectural vault was one result of Alexander's campaigns in Asia. Can a vaulted tomb then predate his expedition? The diadem, to some scholarly eyes, has a hint of Asian influence to it. Are we seeing the artistic influence of Alexander's conquest of Persia? Some experts are even willing to argue that not one of the objects found is necessarily a royal possession: the "scepter" might have been a priest's "wand," or a herald's baton; the sun-burst design might well be an emblem of Macedon without being the private property of the Macedonian kings. Might the different length of the two greaves not stem from faulty craftsmanship rather than being individually tailored to a man with uneven legs? Worse yet, some of the artifacts have been confidently dated to years later than 320. Several ceramic salt cellars, as an example, seem to belong to the period 320–290, and some coins found near them have been dated between 315 and 290.

Perhaps inevitably, then, other candidates have been suggested as the real occupants of the tomb. Philip II's son, Philip III (Arrhidaeus) and his wife Eurydice, were both killed in 317 on the orders of Olympias; ancient sources tell us they were buried at Aegae the following year. In 318, after several rounds of civil war, Alexander's son Alexander IV was put to death and also buried at Aegae. While the evidence of Andronikos' discovered tomb does not fit the interment of a 12-year-old boy, it could suit the joint burial of Philip III and Eurydice. They have in recent years become strong contenders as alternative occupants of the "Golden Tomb of Philip," and they have long found a champion in the Macedonian scholar W. Lindsay Adams.

Very recently, in fact, this argument has taken an even stronger line: the authoritative Macedon expert Eugene Borza sees the objects in the tomb as clues that lead away from Philip II.

> The possibility that a sceptre lay among the goods in Tomb II provides a partial basis for suggesting that when Cassander interred Arrhidaeus he buried not only the elder son of Philip II, but also the personal paraphernalia of Alexander, including the scepter of the Argeadae. It was a sign that the Old Order was finished. Within a few years the son and wife of Alexander would be dispatched, and the Argeadae were no more. (1987:116)

This theory has its attractions—it ties several awkward chronological threads into one neat bundle—but its own author admits that it "is not conclusive, and is limited by problematic evidence. Inconsistencies and unanswered questions remain" (119). Any honest scholar must make such an admission in a mystery like this one; the very nature of the evidence probably prevents some of the questions ever being fully answered. But, before we abandon all hope that we shall ever unlock the secrets of Philip or the Vergina tumulus, we might try our hands at one more form of reconstruction. The face of the male buried in Tomb II under the Vergina mound has been re-created from the remains of his skull.

After the unearthing, Andronikos invited three experts to make plaster casts of the male skull found in that tomb. His experts brought three varying fields of skill to their task: J. H. Musgrave is an anatomist and an anthropologist; R. A. H. Neave specializes in forensic anthropology; and A. J. N. W. Prag is a scholar of classical history. They worked deliberately, dividing their procedure into five stages.

- First they prepared plaster casts of those bones that were in good enough condition to draw any firm conclusions from: the frontal bone, the left part of the nasal bone, the left and right halves of the upper jaw, the lower jaw, and the mastoid part of the right temporal bone in the skull.
- They next went on to make wax facsimiles of the cast bones, setting these onto a clay head block where the researchers could move them about as they tried to discover a proper relationship.
- The missing areas between these wax castings were then formed experimentally from clay and fitted in between the other parts. Whenever a result looked promising, they made a finished cast of the entire skull.
- As a fourth step twenty-three pegs were placed on the skull casting that indicated average thicknesses of soft tissue on modern human faces. These pegs were used as guides, the team carefully attempting to add a reasonable average layer of facial tissue to their reconstructed head. This step was of course a very chancy one—critics who intended to dismiss their work would almost certainly accuse them at this stage of "pure invention"—and so they proceeded even more cautiously than before, calling in the advice of two facio-maxillary surgeons and one plastic surgeon.
- Finally, with the soft tissue tentatively in place, the team molded in facial features to accord with the underlying anatomical structure. They patterned the fullness of the lips, for example, upon tooth size and the projection of the jaws. They then made several wax copies of this result (remember that every stage was treated as an extremely experimental process), and on one of these hair and coloring were added by a skilled makeup artist. Though they had been careful not to expect conclusive results, all three members of the team decided in the end that the dead man could be identified as Philip II. Their reconstructed head, though it could easily have been inconclusive (police reconstructions often are), turned out in fact to point strongly toward several conclusions.

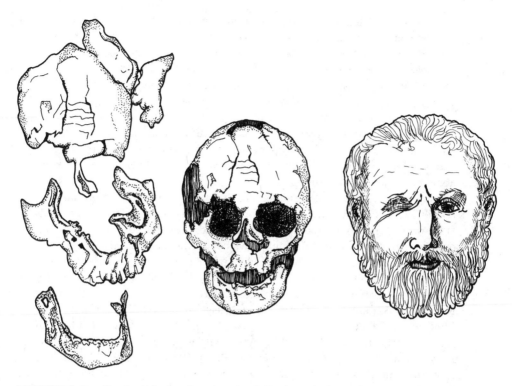

FIGURE 8–3   On the left, the clues; on the right, the culprit—at least according to Musgrave, Neave, and Prag after applying their various skills to the skull fragments found in the main chamber of the Vergina tomb. Note the damage to the right eye.

The reconstructed head corresponded uncannily to ancient descriptions of Philip II, and this in spite the fact that the team had known to guard against such an attractive possibility from the beginning. The most telling clue lay in scarring and in damage to the frontal bone: obviously the right eye which it once protected had been injured seriously some years before its owner's death. Philip, according to reliable literary record, had been struck in the right eye by an arrow during his siege of Methone in 354 B.C. Physicians had cut his right eye out in the process of saving his life. In addition to this, expert forensic examination of the bones placed the dead man's age at between 35 and 55 years; Philip had been murdered when he was 46. Was this in fact the skull of Philip II, the conqueror of Greece? Was that final, fully fleshed reconstruction an almost unnerving shadow of Alexander's monumental father? Could it ever be possible to "close the case"?

Unfortunately, tantalizing as the correspondence was, the official report also admitted that "fresh or healed damage to the bones or changes due to illness could not be established" (Prag, Musgrave, Neave:1984, 61). Nor could the team determine precisely whether there had really been an injury in the region of the right eye (the frontal bone merely looked as though there had). Other little problems clustered around the question. If this were truly Philip, must one expect certain additional indications? Since a prominent traditional facial feature of the Argead lineage had been a noticeable bridge to the nose, had the team played their work false when they added such a bridge to their reconstruction? Nose bones deteriorate beyond recovery, and they had simply added what seemed reasonable. Philip was said to have had dark hair, beard, and eyes; the wax replica had without direct evidence been given dark hair, beard, and eyes. And yet Philip's line had successfully posed as Greek-blooded for generations among the mainland Greeks, who also tended to this coloring. Would not any reasonable reconstruction have followed such lines?

We must constantly remember as we follow this inquiry that there is at least one other candidate for the male occupant of Tomb II at Vergina. Philip III was also an Argead, and thus he might at least in some ways have resembled his father. We know much less about his looks, for the principle feature described by ancient authors was not his face but his mental illness, and some scholars have found a tenuous echo of that condition in the rebuilt skull. Experts had noticed an abnormality—an underdevelopment on the left side—in the upper jaw, and noted that it could have caused a corresponding overdevelopment in the lower jaw. This could have been either congenital or the result of an injury. One of the team wondered, though, why no hint of this appeared in surviving portraits or written descriptions of Philip II. The deformity, he decided, "is not so severe that it need have been apparent or distressing, particularly when covered by the thick beard that Macedonians traditionally wore" (Prag, Musgrave, Neave, 1984:75). It might even add a faint echo of that characteristically rakish character with which Philip II was often remembered, but a nagging doubt remains. Might it also have been a facial deformity that forced men to notice the other defects of Philip III? In a classical Greek culture that put such stock in physical appearance, we might equally expect mention of it in that case (such peculiarities were exactly the sort of thing being noticed in portraits of every sort during that era). Portraiture of the later fourth century had become an art that revealed precise, specific characteristics. Perhaps Philip II would have been powerful enough to suppress this tendency among his artists, but the doubt will not go away.

Let us try to sum up. We cannot wisely conclude that the reconstruction of the "Vergina skull" has allowed us to truly look upon the face of Philip II. We equally have no real reason to lose all hope—to think ourselves no further toward understanding the age of Philip than we were before the discoveries. Aegae is a Macedonian site of critical importance, and we have very surely located it, and can place it in the real landscape of old Macedon. Few scholars now refuse to identify the royal necropolis with this site. As we have discovered the tombs, moreover, we have been able to begin reappraising our picture of life in Macedon. Each item recovered from the lost vaults, whether a treasure or a homely tool, speaks to us not of some crude barbarism, but of a rich and sophisticated culture. As we date and analyze these things we find nothing that forbids us to reasonably conclude we have unearthed the final resting place of Philip II, or Philip III, or Alexander IV—indeed of more than one of these. All of them strode with varying greatness through the thick of the epic history of Macedon.

If we cannot yet allocate an exact occupant to each tomb without provoking debate, that is a bargain price to pay for the dramatic advances of the last twenty years. Not so very long ago, only a little attention was paid to any part or period of ancient Macedon. It was the merest chance discovery that found Pella in 1957. But the recent renaissance in Macedonian topography and archaeology, together with the exploratory reconstruction we have recounted in this chapter, allow us the confidence that we stand at last upon a new threshold. Professor Borza (Barr-Sharrar and Borza, 1982:27) said it well: "One may predict that an age of fulfillment in Macedonian studies is about to begin."

FURTHER READING

Manolis Andronikos, the excavator of the Vergina tombs, has published an account, *The Royal Graves at Vergina* (Athens, 1978). The discussion of the bones can be found in N. I. Xirotiris and F. Langenscheidt, "The Cremations from the Royal Macedonian Tombs of Vergina," *Archailogika Ephemeris* 1981, 142–60. The attempt at reconstruction is presented by A. J. N. W. Prag, J. H. Musgrave and R. A. H. Neave, "The Skull from Tomb II at Vergina: King Philip II of Macedon," *Journal of Hellenic Studies* 104 (1984), 60–78. A new, less disfigured version of the reconstructed head is pictured and described by A. J. N. W. Prag, "Reconstructing King Philip II: The 'Nice' Version," *AJA* 94 (1990), 237–47.

One of the newest theories is that of E. N. Borza, "The Royal Macedonian Tombs and the Paraphernalia of Alexander the Great," *Phoenix* 41 (1987), 105–21.

Chapter Nine

Psychohistory: In Search of Alexander

Just what this distressing young man thought he was doing, and why, I really can't say. I doubt if he could have clarified the subject to any appreciable extent. He had a habit of knitting his brows. And no wonder.

　　　　　　　—Will Cuppy

It may be exciting enough to sense how close we may have come to seeing the image of Philip's face, or of his tomb, or some true and important site of his ancient kingdom: but what if we could for even a moment glimpse inside him as well? Such vivid re-creations as we discussed in the last chapter can give us only the scantiest, most uncertain image of his inner soul. The greatest danger is perhaps that, having come so far, we might try to cross the final distance by leaping to conclusions. We can feel that the face on the remade skull is concretely joyous, or serious, or brooding—after knowing so little about so many intriguing ancient figures we find responses to this one tumbling from ourselves even though we are aware we are still dealing only with a model.

　　　Any written account contemporary with an ancient life (or, if we are lucky enough, written by the very person in question) should of course place us in more intimate and reliable contact with that person. We get, as we said some chapters earlier, a chance to hear them think. And yet, as the case of Socrates proved, it is hard to know just how much we can rely on any particular piece of ancient writing, and harder when there are several such pieces on a single topic that do not agree. Autobiography should usually reveal more than a biography, but the ancient world has left us very few autobiographies.

　　　One fresh approach to the past holds out to us a hope that we might at least capture the "true personality" of prominent characters who died millennia ago, and that we might do so, in some sense, scientifically. It is called psychohistory. It hopes, by taking what we

The Age of Alexander (336 - 323)

Date B.C.	Alexander & Successors	Other Events	Artifacts & Art
336 -- **330 --**	(336). Alexander becomes king of Macedon. He loses little time invading Persia, stopping only to secure his back (in Greece). (334) Alexander pulls off a nearly disastrous victory at the Granicus against the Persian force blocking his route into Asia Minor. He begins a high-speed "zigzag" campaign across the region, dodging to keep the Persians in the interior while he keeps his other eye on the coasts. (He has no supporting fleet). (333) Alexander at the northeast corner of the Mediterranean coast, finds the Persian army has slipped in behind him. He defeats it again (The Battle of Issus). (332) Alexander besieges Tyre. He takes Egypt and becomes Pharaoh; he founds the city of Alexandria. 331 Alexander catches Darius at Gaugamela, breaking the Persian army in battle. Darius flees. Alexander takes Babylon and ends the Persian Empire. 330 Alexander "dismisses" his Greek allies. He pursues Darius. 329 Darius is dead, but Alexander continues relentlessly northeast until his army finds itself high in the Afghan mountains (near Samarkand). 327 Alexander reaches his limit in India (the mountains of the Hindu Kush). The following year (326), he defeats an Indian army at the Hydaspes River, but afterward his "NCO's" refuse to follow him any further. 325 Alexander's return march to Persia across the Gedrosian Desert. 323 Alexander dies, leaving his generals and family to quarrel over his winnings.	(c. 338) End of the Latin League as a power in Italy; Rome dominates the central peninsula. (333) End of Phoenicia as an "independent" economic power. (331) Persian-backed revolt of Sparta against Macedon fails. (324 - 323) Alexander returns to Athens the treasures looted by Darius during the Persian War. (321) Roman army surprised and defeated by Samnite mountaineers at the Caudine Forks. (c. 320) The Hellenistic Era begins: Egypt going to the family of Ptolemy, Syria to that of Seleucus, Asia to Antiochus, and Macedon to Antigonus. (320) Ptolemy captures Jerusalem; Libya becomes a province of Egypt.	(341) Epicurus (founder of Epicureanism) born on island of Samos. (c. 340) Praxiteles sculpts his "Cnidian Aphrodite." (c. 333) Birth of the philosopher Zeno (founder of Stoicism) on Cyprus. (c.) Beginning of true Greek portrait sculpture. (c. 326) The Temple of Apollo completed at Delphi. (c. 325) Date of the "Olympian Hermes" (sculpted by Praxiteles). (c. 323) Euclid (the mathematician) born. (c.) Date of the "Alexander Sarcophagus" carved with reliefs of Macedonian huntsmen which still carry some original coloring (Sidon). (321) Menander's 1st play produced. (c. 307) Epicurean and Stoic "schools" open in Athens.

know of an ancient person's emotional life and by finding analogies for these emotional patterns in modern psychology, to let us "read" his or her mind—at least as reliably as we can "read" those of human beings today. Some of this is dependent upon how much information we have. As many of the most energetic figures of the ancient world have left us a record more of what they did than of how they felt about it, the material is scarce. But some exists and the possibilities are intriguing. If we had only the ability or evidence to "read" one or two minds from the world of Greece and Rome, whose would we choose?

Alexander III of Macedon must surely be an obvious choice. Almost from his childhood he seems to have driven himself toward the title "Alexander the Great." Indeed any mind that could have launched itself so far, so fast, and so furiously across the known world—to have driven a band of canny and combat-weary Greek soldiers almost beyond its borders—must have brimmed with thoughts and dreams on an epic scale. So it seems. Or was he simply a compulsive and lucky madman?

Philip II dreamed in his last years of leading his Macedonians and Greeks on a grand, unifying campaign against Persia, but before any of it really began he was mysteriously cut down by an assassin. He left his plans behind him, and he left a son who has seemed in the millennia since almost to have been a brilliant and violent dream himself. Alexander gathered his father's dreams into himself and launched a campaign of conquest that drove and darted from Greece into the Near Eastern world like a whirlwind.

Alexander was only eighteen when his father was assassinated; his very claim to the throne of Macedon hung by a slender thread. Other relatives claimed the crown, and the barbarians on his northern flank pressed instantly through the canyons and valleys of that mountainous frontier. The Greeks, crushed only two years earlier by the un-guessed mobility of his father's redesigned Macedonian army, thought they saw a chance to move fast themselves and regain their freedom. Alexander secured his own position quickly in Macedon, declaring a culprit in his father's murder and cementing his own people into key places at court. He made a sudden and unstoppable show of force against the unruly northern barbarians in his "back yard," and then turned quickly and sliced southward into a Greece still bitter and reeling from Philip's successes. A rumor had come to Thebes that the northerners had caught and killed Alexander, and Thebes (wanting desperately to believe it) had revolted. Alexander was not dead; he appeared suddenly outside the walls and his Macedonians destroyed the city so thoroughly it shocked the Greek world into silence. The dream of its own brief supremacy in the days of Philip's childhood had lured Thebes to its death.

It was the very deftness and speed with which Alexander ran these threats to earth and ended them, that gave him a sure seat on his throne. He was a worthy successor to his father. It became instantly obvious that once he determined to deal with something, he could strike silently and suddenly, and that what he struck either accepted his terms or (like the city of Thebes) it vanished. From the time of his first successes, history in the Mediterranean world began to run at a speed like wildfire. Alexander swept his army together and threw it across the Hellespont into Persian Asia Minor in 334 B.C., dodging and striking his unbalanced enemies through Anatolia, down the coast of the Levant, and collapsing the province of Egypt (where some declared him to be a god). He carved through Mesopotamia into the heart of the Persian empire, and took it so rapidly he might almost be said to have possessed it alive: the body had no time to die. Persia remained

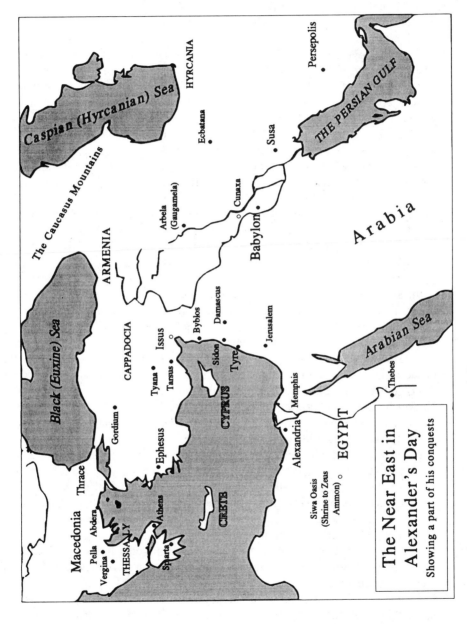

FIGURE 9–1   The Near East in Alexander's Day

"living"—it acted and spoke, its troops, cities, and dress seemed unchanged—but the mind that moved it was Alexander's.

Alexander continued breathlessly, striking northeast across central Asia into the foothill peaks of the Himalayas, and then turning toward India in 326. It was there in western India, in the weariness after another of his pell-mell victories, that his troops stood on the banks of the Indus and refused to go any further. They had come 6,000 miles; for a Greek or Macedonian home must have seemed a whole universe away. Alexander swallowed hard upon his dreams and by 324 he was back in Babylon. Within a year he was dead. Old unhealed wounds ignored in the adrenalin of conquest, or poison, or some exotic germ, had conquered him. He had lived only 33 years, and his plans for keeping and settling the vast lands he had taken were barely formed. But he had conquered the Persian empire and his whirlwind conquests strike the opening hour of the last phase of ancient Greek civilization. We call it the "Hellenistic"—or "Greek-like"—Age.

Grief at the death of Alexander was sharp and real, but a half dozen or so of his most capable generals jostled quickly to fill the void. As they pushed out of the enormous shadow of Alexander, they seemed for a generation or two almost larger than life themselves: for about fifty years they wrestled and carved at the new empire until a handful of "Greek" kingdoms covered the old Persian world. The question at first had been: who will be successor to Alexander? But it became, as the candidates died at one another's hands, who can survive with even a part of what he took?

By 275 B.C., the world of the eastern Mediterranean lay exhausted in the aftermath of the Succession Wars. It looked, to a casual observer, not so very unlike the world before Alexander. Three principal kingdoms—Asian in their bones, Macedonian at heart, Greek in their minds—dominated what became called the "Hellenistic Age": Egypt, Asia (meaning Mesopotamia and the Levant), and Greece/Macedon itself.

The new rulers of the Successor Kingdoms had goals like enough to the old poleis of Greece. They intended to keep their independence. They each intended to become entirely self-sufficient (an attitude like that of the old polis that had striven to be a world to itself within its own narrow walls but stretched across vast boundaries). Each kingdom was also haunted by the addictive memory of Alexander, and dreamed of pressing its territory outward. In a word, the warfare that had run like a smoldering epidemic through classical Greece continued, but its world had now the resources to try it on a massive scale. Elephants trumpeted beside the old Macedonian horse; the exotic specialists of armies from the corners of the known world dealt new forms of death along the fringes of the old Greek phalanx.

Even this brief summary of the force of Alexander's whirlwind career should reveal why we would choose to know his inner thoughts. Few commanders in history have been so fortunate. His military genius, at least on the broad scale of grand strategy and in the fine details of battle tactics, worked too many miracles for us to plausibly doubt its genuineness. A streak of blind recklessness may often have driven him, but Alexander died before the recklessness could cost him a battle.

Alongside his brilliant use of tactics and speed in the field there was his personal leadership. He launched himself even more recklessly into danger than his troops. Perhaps, if we could read his mind, we should know why. Plunging first in a headlong skirmish over the wall of a besieged city in India, Alexander found himself suddenly alone, the spears of his enemies hedging all around him, and his companions still on the wall fighting like madmen to reach him. Alexander very nearly died, but his men roared and rallied behind him, poured across the wall and took the town.

They also feared him, and they had good reason for it. Plutarch tells how Craterus and Hephaestion, two of Alexander's closest friends (both of them valuable officers) began to quarrel. The young king "reconciled them, taking an oath...that he loved them most of all men; but that if he heard of their quarrelling again, he would kill both, or at least the one who began the quarrel" (Alexander:47). As always, the events that swirled around the career of Alexander threaten with each moment to become larger than life and, also, at every moment, to burn out of control. Would a glimpse at the conqueror's mind tell us why?

Some ancient writers believed that Alexander's vision changed (both the horizon for which he hungered and the way he saw himself) as his victories accumulated around him. Did he pass at some point from a feverish, heroic mortality to the belief that he was actually a god? During his time in Egypt he struck out westward with some of his troops across the desert to the oasis-oracle at Siwah, where it is said that the god told him his true father was not Philip II after all; it was the great deity Amon-Re. Worse yet, there was an ominous episode near the end of his life, when he returned to Babylon from his easternmost campaigns and issued an edict to the skeptical, freedom-loving cities of the Greek world that they should regard him in the future as a god.

Trying to undo the tangle of all these cords at the center of Alexander's psyche is a troublesome one, and perhaps impossible. It is as though someone had retied the Gordian Knot from cords of enchanted and nonburnable rope and placed it in the center of a furnace. If we merely find some cold, mechanical solution to the man, we shall have missed the authentic fire at the core of his personality. But if we stare too long at the fire it will dazzle us, and the knot will remain a mystery. To really surmount the text, we must both endure the heat and solve the puzzle. A method that truly lets us read thoughts in the mind of Alexander must give us at least a little success at both endeavors, or it will have failed.

In this chapter we turn to "psychohistory" and give it a try at penetrating both the puzzle and the fire—both the inner character and the motivation of Alexander the Great.

ALEXANDER

If we can trust our ancient witnesses, men (including his father Philip II) could not help seeing the "greatness" of Alexander even in his own lifetime. Plutarch sets the tone early in his biography by telling a tale in archaic, almost heroic style. The young prince, much taken by the sight of a great unbridled, vicious, and headstrong stallion named Bucephalus, boasted that he could tame him. Among the young upland nobility of rustic Macedon this was unmistakably a challenge especially since others had tried and failed; some were hurt in the attempt. The unconquered animal was haltered, the grooms leading him away to be destroyed, when Alexander made his wager: he would make one try to subdue the beast, and pay the whole price of the horse if he failed. With an uncanny magnificence he slid up onto Bucephalus' back. Horse and man seemed in an impossibly brief moment to become one, and Alexander rode smartly up before his father and dismounted. Philip was silent. Tears stood in his eyes, and he "kissed him as he came down from his horse, and in his transport said, 'O my son, look thee out a kingdom equal to and worthy of thyself, for Macedonia is too little for thee'" (VI. 8).

We have sketched Alexander's career at the beginning of this chapter. He lived only the greater part of thirty-three years, and in that time conquered an empire that dwarfed the old mountainside fiefs of Macedon. When he was acclaimed king in 336 B.C. it took him less than two years to consolidate his own position at home, and though that sounds easy when described as quickly as it was a few pages back, one ought to remember how long Philip spent at the same task. By 334 he was master of the southern Balkans, and Macedon was once more the acknowledged overlord of Greece. This is fast foundation-building for so far-flung a series of conquests, but Alexander scarcely looked back, and the structure at home did not fail until after his death.

We have likewise made his departure and the sharp, widening wake of his conquests seem perhaps too easy. He took about 35,000 troops of all kinds with him across the Dardanelles, and with them he defeated the great Persian land armies on three major occasions, in spite of the fact that chance, his reckless speed, and the "interior lines" of his enemy often put him on the less favorable ground. At the Granicus in 334 he had to cross a swift river and attack a stable position on high ground. At Issus in northern Syria (333) he had flung his columns so rapidly around the northeast corner of the Mediterranean that the Persians poured out onto the coastal plain behind him, cutting his line to Greece. He then had to improvise an attack on the spur of the moment. At Gaugamela, east of the Tigris River (in 331), he faced the cream of the Persian imperial reserves—including Darius' elite guard, and a "special weapons" chariot force—without the benefit of surprise. Darius had even had time to have the battleground leveled to suit his chariots. Alexander won, against all reasonable odds. When he plunged on eastward into the further interior of his freshly won empire, he allowed himself and his troops little more than a breathing-halt, while he sat down symbolically on the old throne of Achaemenid Persia and demonstrated the new face of his power.

We said at the opening of this chapter that Alexander took the Persian Empire so quickly that in some senses it had no time to change, but of course from the distant vantage-point of the twentieth century we can see that great blocks of culture were suddenly confronted with change. Enormous alterations were taking place about this time in the shapes of power all through the Greek and Asian worlds, and doing so too quickly for the cultural weight they bore. It was as though the great plates beneath the surface of the earth might begin to move, at some individual's command with men still clinging, living, farming, and fighting, upon their surfaces. At first it was the Persians who saw the change overcoming them. By the end of Alexander's life the worried faces were Macedonian ones. But Alexander pushed on.

He never, in fact, settled onto an easy course. In the eastern hinterland of Persia, Alexander found himself fighting to take towns on the tops of crags and towns in the midst of desert. He turned southward only because he discovered himself emerging finally onto the tall slopes of the Himalayas; he left "Furthest Alexandria" behind him, founded in the high, cold country of the Hindu Kush. Southward he found India, and alien new kings with elephants walking like towers in the dust along their lines of battle.

By 326 B.C. the veterans among the Macedonian infantry decided they would go no further, and insisted wearily that the campaign was over. Alexander stormed and sulked like Achilles in his camp on the Beas River for three days, but he knew at last that he could drive his men no further into India. The epic had yet a little more to run, but its "great episode" had ended. By 324, the Macedonians emerged from a long returning trek through the Gedrosian Desert (Alexander's punishment because they had resigned the role of heroes?) and poured back into the streets of the Persian winter capital at Susa. By the end of another year Alexander had died in Babylon.

He left behind him a breathless new empire that stretched from the Adriatic to the Indus—an unimaginable 3,000 miles—and over it hung his enormous shadow, fading slowly like an apparition, until the smaller winds of the Succession Wars caught and whipped the shadow of that empire into tatters. There were many more factors than the legacy of Alexander in the fourth, third, and second centuries, but even the tatters were often what ruled and defined the eastern Mediterranean and Near Eastern worlds. No European since him has repeated such a catastrophic success. Surely this is a case holding great rewards for the method that might unlock the man's inner goals and motivations. What restless and insatiable force drove Alexander and consumed him beyond the horizons east of Macedon? Did he make his own choices (and how?) or did something impel him from within? What did he see when he looked at the tale of his own success?

These questions fascinated writers almost before Alexander was dead. The few ancient scholars who tried for an answer claimed to have read letters written to, or even, by the conqueror. A "Will of Alexander" was also in circulation, purporting to give his final plans in great detail, and adding a prayer he was supposed to have offered to the Egyptian god Serapis. If only these documents could have been authentic they might tell us much about their author's mind. They are forgeries. Thus we cannot be sure that any evidence in them is genuine, though they can tell us a few reliable things about the very early wish men had to probe the fires that burned behind the turbulent charisma in Alexander's face.

Fortunately, we can pursue that goal along other paths than the forgery of literature. Honest scholars close in time to Alexander were also concerned with the things that fueled his psyche. Plutarch, for instance, perhaps best known for his *Lives* of prominent Greeks and Romans, liked to pair a Greek figure with a Roman and make subtle observations about the counterpoint between their characters. He leaves no doubt of this in the introduction to his *Life of Alexander*: "as portrait painters are more exact in the lines and features of the face, in which the character is seen, than in the other parts of the body, so I must be allowed to give my more particular attention to the marks and indications of the souls of men..." (I. 3, Dryden trans: same trans. used for other references).

Plutarch almost always begins each "Life" with a brief account of his subject's birth, parents, and upbringing. Modern historians often find this a useful approach, since biology and early training do effect some significant moldings of a person's character. Though they do not always admit it, very little but the kind of preferred detail and some technical jargon separate their approach from Plutarch's.

Alexander, even judged by Macedonian standards, certainly had an unusual early life. His own mother, Olympias, was among the wildest of the factors. She had grown up the daughter of the king of Epirus, an initiate into back country forms of the exotic cults of Orpheus and Bacchus—both marked by their rituals of unbridled emotion. Plutarch, himself one of the quietest, most "proper" of all the literary Greeks, could not help but point out the danger in her influence: "Zealously affecting these fanatical and enthusiastic inspirations, to perform them with more barbaric dread, [Olympias] was wont in the dances proper to these ceremonies to have great tame serpents about her, which sometimes creeping out of the ivy in the mystic fans, sometimes winding themselves about the sacred spears, and the women's chaplets, made a spectacle which men could not look upon without terror" (II. 9).

We do not know how early it really is, but by the time Plutarch wrote, a story had been widely accepted that before Olympias consummated her marriage to Philip "she dreamed that a thunderbolt fell upon her body, which kindled a great fire, whose divided flames dispersed themselves all about, and then were extinguished" (II. 3). Olympias, the tale runs, clutched the story of the thunderbolt close to her heart for the rest of her life: the divine fires—not that bluff and hard-drinking, one-eyed Macedonian king—had conceived a child in her, and when he was born she named him Alexander.

Philip, who had no difficulty acknowledging he had fathered Alexander, was himself a remarkable man. The Macedonians had acclaimed him king in the wake of a national disaster: the bulk of the army under the command of his elder brother, the king, had gone into the wild Illyrian hills to stop an invasion, and they had almost been obliterated at the hands of the Illyrian tribesmen. Within two decades of this disgrace Philip had turned Macedon into one of the great powers of the Mediterranean. He had become hegemon or leader of much of the Greek world. He had forged a strong (if uneasy) league between the Greek city-states and Macedon that focused all the internal and divisive energies of the Hellenic world outward against its old enemies in the Persian Empire. Diodorus Siculus, who wrote in the first century B.C., praised Philip (in spite of the feats of his son) as the real miracle worker of his dynasty:

> one who with but the slenderest resources to support his claim to a throne won for himself the greatest empire in the Greek world, while the growth of his position was not due so much to his prowess in arms as to his adroitness and cordiality in diplomacy. Philip himself is said to have been prouder of his grasp of strategy and his diplomatic successes than of his valour in actual battle. (XVI. 95. 2–3; Welles trans.)

So much for the parents; the third great influence in Alexander's life might at first seem more startling. It was Aristotle, whom Plutarch called "the most learned and most celebrated philosopher of his time" (VII. 2). Philip recruited Aristotle from his prominent early position at Plato's Academy in Athens and "rewarded him with a munificence proportionable to and becoming the care he took to instruct his son." It was under Aristotle, Plutarch insisted, that Alexander caught in his being a hot and violent thirst for knowledge which he never satisfied, and which he never escaped in later life.

Even if we limit our reckoning only to these three figures, it is possible to sense the powerful elements that poured into Alexander's genetic inheritance and into his upbringing. He had extraordinary parents. His education was meant to make him elite among the students of the Greek world. We even have a comparison (a "control" as the scientists call it) to bear in mind as we watch Alexander develop. Philip II had another son—Philip Arrhidaeus—who was very nearly the same age as Alexander, and who also became king of Macedon before his death (though he made almost nothing of his chance). Men remembered Arrhidaeus as ineffectual and easily dominated. His own mother, for those who like genetic parallels, was according to Plutarch "an obscure woman of the name of Philinna" (LXXVII. 7). And no one bothered to expose Arrhidaeus to any of Aristotle's teaching.

Could it have been, then, the mere combination of those three elements that made Alexander great? His half-brother had only one of them: the advantage of Philip's fatherhood. That threw Arrhidaeus, whether he had a queen's influence, or education, or nothing at all, into the center of the vicious intrigues that had racked the court of Macedon for generations. And if so, were his disadvantages really due more to some malice working in the shadows? Nurture (in this case a malevolent nurture) rather than nature? A strong rumor outlived Arrhidaeus that "drugs which Olympias gave him had ruined not only his health but his understanding" (Plutarch LXXVII. 8). Obviously more was afoot than genetics and childhood upbringing in the palaces at Pella and Aegae during Alexander's early years. Individuals could wrestle with their own fates and the fates of others.

Let us take another tool and try to probe deeper. The very language of our sources suggested a certain form of analysis to the eminent German political and social historian Victor Ehrenberg. Ehrenberg argued in 1938 that we would get a better look at the psyche of Alexander if we followed a distinctive thread of emotional expression that he has left imprinted indelibly upon his biographies. We know him, in the heat and thunder of his conquests, to have made certain authentic kinds of utterance again and again. A key phrase that recurs is *pothos elambane auton* ("longing seized him"). The word *pothos*, Ehrenberg suggests, is Alexander's own, and it carries the flavor of longing for the unattainable, almost for the undefined. Here was the fire that drove him, Ehrenberg thought, the hunger that flung him toward uncommon—even herculean—horizons. *Pothos* (the "yearning") and *epithymia* (an "unconquerable desire") appear scattered like the counterpoint notes to a melody all through the surviving accounts of Alexander's career. He never defines them. It was as though he craved not only the unknown but adequate words for the unknown as well. Ehrenberg thought it especially telling that the words cried out from passages where the simple literary context would not, by itself, have called for them. They seem to belong to an older tradition of authentic memory and myth that surrounded Alexander, perhaps coming from his own mouth.

Both *pothos* and *epithymia* stand out, for instance, in passages that describe Alexander's hunger to explore the farthest regions of the east, in his anguished attempts to spur his men onward beyond the rivers of western India. They sound like horns through the speeches where, stymied in his desire to go eastward, he throws himself into the dream of exploring the Southern Sea (Indian Ocean). They press his pleas to persist in the conquest of impossible, impregnable sites like the citadel of Aornos. When he visits famous or mythic places like Gordion or the desert oracle of Amon, *pothos* or its cognate words run through the background. They came naturally to him when he founded Alexandria.

And most of these episodes, curiously, are late ones. Alexander spoke early in his campaigns of a "yearning" to visit Gordion, where a mystic knot beckoned him (or suggested a quick chance for fame), but most of the *pothos* narratives belong to occasions after 332 B.C. Ehrenberg believed he had seen the turning point in this tale. He suggested that "Alexander's stay in Egypt, which was epochal for him in so many respects, and above all the expedition to the oasis of Ammon gave him the phrase of *pothos*; and that thereafter time and again he at once veiled and revealed his passionate and boundless schemes in its emotional and iridescent vagueness" (58).

Now *pothos* is not merely some exotic "mystery word" from the dark corners of the Greek vocabulary. It is a perfectly good term in the common tongue meaning a "longing,"

FIGURE 9–2 A bust of Alexander from the Hellenistic capital city of Pergamum, showing the characteristic expression of distant and undefined yearning with which artists crystallized the young conqueror's remembered personality. This, if Ehrenberg is right, may be the "longing," or *pothos,* which Alexander identified as a driving motive deep in his own psyche.

"yearning," or "regret" for someone or something absent or lost. Its secondary meaning is a strenuously felt, but ill-defined, love or desire. Nevertheless, the weight and flavor of *pothos* in the authentic accounts of Alexander is an extraordinary one. Ehrenberg insisted that no casual or cold-eyed explanation would account for it, that "Alexander himself picked out this word to convey a meaning peculiar to him alone, and alien to the mainly rational mind of the Greeks. The reason why he unconsciously chose just this word, seems to have been that it expressed longing for absent things, for things not, or no longer, within reach. This he transformed into longing for things not yet within reach, for the unknown, far distant, unattained" (60). Such longing "grew to become the motive force of the conqueror of the world" (60). Nor were the gentler and homelier subtleties of the word irrelevant. Each such undercurrent in Alexander's speech "reveals the fervent heart of a youth, palpable below all his greatness and all his excesses" (61).

Ehrenberg was himself among that rare breed who are wise as well as learned scholars: he did not insist that his own conclusions were unshakably valid. We cannot be certain whether Alexander used such words or that he was truly driven by vague and irrepressible yearnings. More than one of the cold-hearted conquering tyrants in history have managed to pose as poets or dreamers while they ravaged the lands of their neighbors. We have, in any case, no deliberate writing of Alexander himself to use as ultimate proof. And there are other ways to explain him, born of other methods.

When he made his presidential address to the American Historical Association in December of 1957, William Langer asked "what direction is apt to lead to further progress in historical study," in other words, "the historian's 'next assignment.'" He had an answer, he hoped, in "the urgently needed deepening of our historical understanding through exploitation of the concepts and findings of modern psychology" (Langer:1958). He focused most intently on "psychoanalysis and its later developments and variations as included in the terms 'dynamic' or 'depth psychology.'"

Historians have not quite beaten down Dr. Langer's door in their hurry to pursue this recent approach to the deciphering of history. It has, however, attracted a name of its own—"psychohistory"—and a modest band of ardent disciples. They do undeniably offer us an intriguing tool. If their methods are sound, we may be able to use them as we probe the minds of people lost to us as long ago as Alexander III of Macedon.

By its broadest definition, psychohistory is the application of various psychological theories to the study of historical characters. Just as there are various schools and styles of psychoanalysis, so there are different sorts of "psychohistorians." The common thread in them all is a preoccupation with the nature, faculties, and operations of the human mind. It was Sigmund Freud (1856–1939) who—at least among the moderns—blazed the pioneer's trails across this field, attempting to describe the unconscious and irrational elements in human nature. He asked how these elements have interacted with the conditions nature imposes on humanity, and how they are entwined in the institutions and ideals with which men have developed their cultures. His younger contemporary and student Carl Jung (1875–1961) tried to follow the shared strands of emotional—even of oral and mythic—imagery in the human mind that might suggest some common "mental language," thus giving us a tool for "reading the minds" of vanished eras and cultures.

Within the last fifty years we have seen the discipline of psychology branch quickly out into a great number of areas. One of these is known as "depth psychology," its practitioners concerned to focus beyond those impulses buried within the individual psyche but looking as well toward the larger social context of that individual's cultural era. Freud's successors have thus found themselves examining whole cultures as well as the particular minds within them. Navigating across new ground they have coined new words: *psychobiography* means the psychologist's account of a certain individual within his context; *psychohistory* means a study with a broader scope. Since our own intended goal is to catch some glimpse of the psyche of Alexander, we must begin at the particular or individual level.

Freud himself set out on various occasions to explore the minds both of living subjects and of ones long dead. In 1910 he began the psychological portrait of Leonardo da Vinci, later published as *Leonardo da Vinci: A Study in Psychosexuality*. His objective, as the modern child psychologist Travis Crosby explains it, was both personal and historical:

> The point was to move from the given clinical case to the broader statement, from the specific to the universal—the "laws" Freud mentions. He wanted to move from the apparent, the readily observable, to "deeper layers"—to those unconscious forces he was convinced control just about every aspect of our lives. He wanted to leave the psychiatrists' office and find in the life of a man who was never a patient further evidence that it is correct for analysts to deny that "health and disease, normal and nervous, are sharply distinguished from each other, and that neurotic traits must be considered proofs of a general inferiority." And finally, he wanted to go back far in time, find in the remains, so to speak, of a man of great historical importance—his

words, remarks attributed to him, his sketches and paintings—evidence that explains some of the contradictions and ambiguities of his life. (Cocks and Crosby, 1987:85)

Hidden behind this endeavor is the assumption of one fundamental precept: that human nature has remained in its essence constant at least over the span of historical time. It lies, as the historian Rudolph Binion points out, behind much of the telling of history in general: "Human history is what people did. To understand it is to understand why people did what they did. This is possible because mind is enough of a kind for its workings to be inwardly intelligible at any historic remove" (in Cocks and Crosby:69). The psychohistorian starts, then, by believing that human drives, fears, neuroses, aspirations (both conscious and unconscious) are defined at their essential level by the basic conditions of human life, not by some specific time or place. The human nature of a Macedonian of the fourth century before our era will thus be substantially similar enough to be recognizable to the human nature of an American of the twentieth century. And the modern American has at least the possibility (he may of course be very foolish or misguided in practice) of drawing accurate inferences from the emotional behavior of the Macedonian.

There are dangers in this assumption, since what seems irresistibly to be a deep-seated human drive in one era may seem (may in fact be) nothing of the sort in another. When reading history we seem to feel a strong and distant resonance between some fundamental yearning of our own and that of the culture we are studying; we may not in fact be noticing an "unchanging element" in humanity at all. The long, rolling movement of historical change may by chance have thrown before us some merely apparent similarity between that past and our modern mood. The Scotsman who thought Greek hoplites were sound Presbyterians because they wore kilts had not actually discovered a fundamental cord in our common humanity, but he nevertheless felt much "closer to the past." The premise, as the literary historian C. S. Lewis once put it, is that

> Just as, if we stripped the armour off a medieval knight or the lace off a Caroline courtier we should find beneath them an anatomy identical with our own, so, it is held, if we strip off from Virgil his Roman imperialism, from Sidney his code of honour, from Lucretius his Epicurean philosophy, and from all who have it their religion, we shall find the Unchanging Human Heart, and on this we are to concentrate. (*Preface to Paradise Lost*, 62)

It is as though a gardener were to hand us a pruning-saw and tell us that, until we got all the branches lopped off, and had whittled the trunks down to about our size and shape, we should never get a really good look at his prize trees.

We must, consequently, be very careful as we explore the methods of psychohistory to see which aspects of human behavior or human culture any particular psychologist intends to make his common denominators. Jung's dim mythic symbols of oral memory or Freud's subconscious sexual impulses cannot be made automatically to have been the foundation of past personalities because we find them convincing in the present. They should be required to provide historical evidence of their own. But our present experiment is to see if (taking them as correct for the moment) they can give us fresh and reliable insights into the mind of Alexander the Great.

Accepting this premise of the common human psyche, then, a psychohistorical analyst of the Freudian type will proceed to investigate the interaction between three basic forces: necessities imposed by nature; the polarized instincts toward love and death in an individual; and the institutions and ideas developed in a society. Each of these might be explored very usefully on its own, but it is their mingling that makes them—for a Freudian analyst—the moving dialectic of history. A record of our past becomes the record of the creations, destructions, and ambiguities spun off from the never-resolved interweaving of these forces.

Let us follow this theory a little further, just to see where it leads. The cultural and social structures of a group will, by these rules, condition (both consciously and unconsciously) the personalities of its members, and the way in which those personalities evolve. The historian Paul Friedländer (1978) believes he can identify four ways in which society does this: through its primary institutions, its symbolic systems, its "educative thrust to internalize basic social norms," and its mediation in the constant adaptation of ego to environment.

On the other hand, individuals can also exert their own pressure on their group, especially if they are charismatic enough to make a sharp and noticeable change in their society. This has sometimes seemed so historically important that it has become a definition of what "charismatic" means: "a personality able to internalize and make explicit new norms pertinent to all, or to internalize and revive old norms, whereas the society around him, in its crisis state, was able to perceive neither the new norms nor the old ones" (Friedländer:70). Alexander certainly qualifies as "charismatic" by that definition—the personal fires that drove him made earthshaking changes in the lives of the people he led, and the changes went on rippling out through the lives of Macedonians and non-Macedonians for generations after. How would psychohistory go about trying to uncover those conscious and unconscious forces in Alexander's soul that could explain his charisma?

We must keep very clear from the beginning that in Alexander's case we shall have to make do with very sparse documentation. Although we know the names of twenty individual authors who were Alexander's contemporaries, and who published accounts about him, we have now only six surviving (and rather late) accounts. The very nearest in time to Alexander—Diodorus Siculus—is not what we would have preferred to call "near"; he dates from the first century B.C. Traditions as well as memories could well have changed considerably in 275 years. Perhaps the fullest account is that of Arrian, a Roman senator who wrote in the middle of the second century A.D., nearly half a millennium after his subject had died. But we must use what we have.

Even while Freud was still engaged in building his theory of the human psyche, one of his contemporaries had turned his sights on Alexander. L. Pierce Clark thought that he could see at the heart of our enigmatic figure an authentic human drive, even one much discussed in the ancient world: "we have in the brief life and career of Alexander an excellent example of a colossal narcism dramatized to its tragic conclusion in the conquests of the known world, but he failed to conquer self" (1923:69). That narcissism, he thought, ran with such an enormous current in Alexander that it prevented him even making the emotional adjustments most of us try to make to achieve a balanced life.

All humans are narcissistic to a degree, Clark argued, since they perceive themselves during infancy and youth through their mother's eyes. The mother's love and devotion for her child conditions the child's own emerging view of his or her self. Children "may be said to doubly love themselves: first, because the mother makes them the primary object of tender love, and, second, because self-love is personally pleasurable" (Clark: 66). As a child develops normally, he went on, this emotional aura of personal worth grows weaker. Under abnormal conditions, alternatively, that sense of self might grow out of control, gathering seductive emotional powers into itself, pushing the personality of the individual into regions we call "pathological." Narcissists, having passed beyond the normal definition of self-love, hunger for others to acknowledge their special value. They drive themselves almost in the way that the beloved drives a lover. "Many narcissists seem to build all their love energy into the life ambition to stamp their will upon the world" (Clark, 61).

Those sources that survive tell us of a strong and persisting bond between Alexander and his mother. We can detect an unusual energy in it since the normal love of a mother for her child does not extend to the furthering of her own ambition through that child by dark and violent means such as those practiced by Olympias. We also have very clear evidence that relations between Alexander and Philip were strained on many occasions. During the year before Philip died Alexander was living in self-imposed exile. Philip had in 337 B.C. decided to marry yet another wife (he had several, most of them political conveniences), and everyone sensed somehow that the new wife (Cleopatra) posed a particular threat to the position of the non-Macedonian Olympias and her son. Plutarch tells the tale:

> On the wedding night someone proposed a toast to the hope of a legitimate heir from Cleopatra's womb. Alexander took offense instantly and shouted "But what of me, base wretch? Dost thou take me for a bastard?" Philip intervened with drawn sword but tripped and fell. "Look now, men!" cried Alexander, "Here is one who was preparing to cross from Europe into Asia; and he is upset in trying to cross from couch to couch." (IX. 6–11)

Given such turbulence at home, it would not have been hard for Olympias to add fuel to Alexander's suspicions. What did Philip intend, anyway? Clark proposed that Philip himself may have made it worse by daring, in time-honored and bluff Macedonian fashion, "to speak plainly to the boy of his real faults" (67). Such blunt-nosed needling will only have made Alexander's already excessive self-love even sharper by wounding it, by strengthening that seductive internal voice suggesting that he might as well withdraw and brood upon his ills in a safe place. And that, in turn, will have irritated Philip even further.

It is very possible, Clark continued, that the most dangerous tendencies to narcism in Alexander did not really begin to crop up until late in his career. He could, at first, handle the praise of the crowd. "Alexander evidently possessed a keen, discriminative ability to remain unaffected by the major portion of the adulation he received in adolescence" (67). It might only have been as time (and the blinding accumulation of his victories) went on that "his desire for being considered all powerful had a tendency to reappear with greater force…when his genius gave him full time and opportunity to cultivate it to a more adult purpose" (67).

The implication will have been that those warm, dark hungers for his own worth, which his mother kindled in childhood, were fanned into unmanageable flames by his immense (and of course unpredicted) success as an adult in conquest. Alexander was by that point in his life no longer content to be called the son of a god; he intended that men recognize him as deity itself. "Once thoroughly detached from home ties his love revolved about his own fictitious godhead, and he never swerved from ministering to the latter and its promised fulfillment" (69). As a consequence, it was an "unworthy legacy he left behind" (69).

Clark's thesis has gotten some recent modification from another psychohistorian—Ramon Harris. Olympias still holds her central position as motivation force in Alexander's character, but Harris finds other forms lurking in that core of personality as well, especially a powerful and unconscious hatred.

> The character structure of his mother, cruel, aggressive, jealous, combined with her self-love (narcissism), her envy, and continual competition with Philip, made love of her difficult, if not impossible. However, the love of mother, as the primary love object, is always essential. Even when the mother is unlovable, this need persists and is manifested in the primitive psychological mechanism of identification with the aggressor as a defence against the hostility which must be denied. There are many indications that Alexander had identified himself with his mother in this pathological way. To identify excessively with a female (aggressor) is, for the male, to jeopardize his masculinity. His competition and hostility toward his father (and men) was not like a man's healthy masculine competition with other men. Rather, it was more like his mother's unrelenting hatred of his father; and in his relative indifference to women, he was at the same time manifesting his underlying hostile feelings toward his mother....Emulating such a man [as his father Philip] would have been difficult under any circumstances...when these additional obstacles to a healthy identification with his father were superimposed upon the underlying pathological female identification with an aggressive mother, it intensified the psychological dilemma for Alexander. The inner, unconscious need to prove his masculinity, when it became expressed in the external world, undoubtedly contributed to his very real achievements. (1968 and 1974: 121 *f.*)

We get a very different reconstructed picture of the inner Alexander from the military historian John Keegan, who has explored the psyches of men driven toward, and scarred by, combat enough to be wary of their own limitations. "It is a question that can perhaps be answered about no human being. But it is particularly inappropriate in Alexander's case. In his life, the private and public self, thought and action, reflection and execution, so entwine and interpenetrate that the one cannot be disentangled from the other. Like a great actor in a great role, being and performance merged in his person" (1987:91).

Keegan does not intend a direct criticism of psychohistory, but his remarks do show a weak point in the structure of such analysis. If we are ever successful in probing the depths of "the individual psyche," we must first truly have an individual psyche to probe. By Freud's theory, the three components of the human inner being are the ego, the superego, and the id. Of these three only the ego is fully conscious. The ego, moreover, is according to Freud largely a product of (or at least a derivation from) the id, which in its own mysterious way is the elemental, undifferentiated source of human spiritual energy. From it come both the ego and the libido (emotional or psychic energy). The superego is yet something else—partly conscious, partly unconscious: it does much of the structural work in forming character by building the image of the society's and the parents' rules onto the raw material of human nature, and (once again, by theory—whether it is an adequate theory is not at present the issue) creating the thing we call "conscience."

The result which all this theory leaves us with is that only a third of the human psyche can usefully be called conscious. Most of the elements that drive a personality will be imperceptible to the personality being driven. They burn (for those who hold an organic view of mankind) below the surface like the processes that break down our food and turn it into physical energy; no one can tear them open and really look at them. To those who prefer a mechanistic image of human nature, we are each more like the owner of a ship—capable of giving orders on the bridge, but with all the real machinery that drives the vessel hidden from us (and usually beyond the understanding of any but the experts).

The hope of psychology is that by the right methods those unconscious processes can be prodded or cajoled into revealing themselves. It needs for such prodding the physical presence of the person involved, and there, in turn, lies the difficulty for history. We must, in that person's absence, get hold of the fullest records of their behavior, feelings, and reactions that we can find to serve as substitutes, and even then we shall be diving into very dark waters with only a second-hand (perhaps even a hearsay) chart to guide us. In a case like Alexander's, a direct and proper psychoanalysis is simply not possible. Given the nature of our evidence, even the substitute approach means we will be swimming very blindly.

Thus psychohistory and psychobiography both stumble on a common stone in their approach to history: they derive their "solid facts" from psychoanalytic theory, not from historical data. And that psychoanalytic theory, by a further historical accident, can only have been tested reliably on men and women who have belonged to a comparatively modern world. Practicing historians, by contrast, need to deal as near as possible with the past itself. Character analysis has, to be sure, a definable and useful place in the pursuit of history, but it will tell us only very limited things and those only when it is used with the greatest care.

Most important is the fact that when we are dealing with remote historical periods, we must work very hard to understand the mental workings either of the individuals, or of the entire cultures they contain. And we must hang tightly to a healthy agnosticism about the results we get. Even when there is some evidence about the kind and color and form of psyches in a past time, we will find it impossible to really verify whether it is coming to us "pure," and whether we are understanding it correctly.

On those lucky occasions when we do have enough evidence to draw full portraits of some personality or behavior, we are still likely to run up against another limit inherent in the very fabric of psychoanalysis: it needs a subject, separated reasonably from its background, on which to concentrate. But while individuals can and often do change the makeup and movement of their cultures, those cultures are always and at the same time molding and moving them. Whatever an established culture values, whatever institutions lie at its heart, will shape and channel a human life—especially during infancy and youth. Even during adulthood a set of fundamental social ideals and "norms" (to which of course the values and institutions still add their weight) will structure much of what an individual does and how he or she feels about it. Saul Friedländer may speak as the expert: "The culture and the social structure of a group determine in a specific manner the evolution of the personality of the members of the group, on the level of conscious attitudes but above all on the unconscious level" (1978:35).

Are we, then, trying too hard to understand Alexander in isolation from his culture? Are we examining his intentions and motives like the limbs of a rather striking shrub, and so forgotten to notice that we have in the process uprooted it from the earth in which it belongs?

Alan Samuel has recently had his own try at disentangling the deeds and motives of Alexander and his father Philip, and has tried harder to keep them firmly within their cultural context. He sees parallels between Macedon (before it was affected too much by Greek culture) and the medieval Merovingian Gaul, and he draws from some new insights the encouraging conclusion that "we need no longer demand of Alexander or Philip (or their biographers) lives of consistent policy, for they acted less in pursuit of long-term goals than for the fulfillment of the expectations of their followers" (1988:1286).

Though many historians have casually described the ancient culture of Macedon as "feudal," they seem generally to have forgotten the fact Samuel holds before us. Philip and Alexander, however undeniably charismatic they might have been, were never free to act simply on their own or as they wished. Their own society fairly brimmed with expectations of them (in part because they were so charismatic), and they had to find ways to satisfy these expectations or pay the consequences. Thus we may have discovered a new explanation for Alexander's dismissing so brusquely the advice of his general Parmenio on an occasion when the King of Persia offered terms for a truce. Darius held out generous concessions and Parmenio insisted that, were he Alexander, he would accept them. "Then Alexander answered Parmenio," Arrian recounts, "that he would indeed have done this were he Parmenio, but being Alexander he would reply to Darius in the words he actually used" (2. 25. 1).

This is inarguably a good story, and a good glimpse at Alexander improvising in action. As an explanation for it we are usually reminded of Alexander's hunger for new horizons and for the adventure of further campaigns. Samuel, by contrast, presses the suggestion that Alexander was much more like a Viking king than like an armed explorer, or like a poet. He was compelled to reject Darius' offer because his men had a constant and legitimate demand on him for booty from war. No matter that Plutarch says little of such things; since Plutarch was interested only in the heroic leader whose life he was writing; and he would have cared much less about the wishes of the men Alexander led. In any case, he was also a settled and civilized Greek enjoying a comfortable literary and home life under well-entrenched Roman rule. What could he understand about the dynamics of feudal-barbarian conquest?

There are always the portraits; controversial as ever, but haunting nonetheless. The ancients said that the soul of a person dwells in his eyes. But they are only sculptor's eyes, ringed with *pothos*, and nothing but blank stone within. That road to the inside of Alexander stops as well.

A true window for the mind's eye into the thoughts and feeling of Alexander must certainly be placed very high on the list of things historical that we wish we had. It might prove the golden key to a whole era of mystery and flamboyant change that rolled across the Greek and Near Eastern worlds. We do not have it. Even the materials from which brilliant scholars have tried to smelt such a key are after all only second-hand ore. The alchemists thus far have produced many fascinating things, but they have not opened the lock. Samuel was certainly right when he said that "no aspect of the activity of Alexander the Great has attracted more effort than the attempt to understand his motivations and intentions, his impulse for conquest and his turbulent relations with his officers" (1270). But until we discover the real gold of an authentic, contemporary source or two, we shall never have the resources to truly finish the task. There is always the hope, however faint, that one might be discovered tomorrow. And if a hope so forlorn feels a little like *pothos* and reminds us by simple intuition of Alexander, so much the better. Perhaps a "sympathy" at least is worth achieving.

FURTHER READING

There are useful essays in the collection edited by Geoffrey Cocks and Travis L. Crosby, *Psychohistory: Readings in the Method of Psychology, Psychoanalysis, and History* (New Haven and London: Yale University Press, 1987). Much good sense pervades the discussion of Saul Friedländer, *History and Psychoanalysis,* English trans. Susan Suleiman (New York and London: Holmes and Meier, 1978). Investigation of Alexander's narcissism was undertaken by L. Pierce Clark, "The Narcissism of Alexander the Great," *Psychoanalytic Review* 10 (1923), 56–69. For a range of views on Alexander, see the useful collection edited by Eugene Borza: *The Impact of Alexander the Great* (Krieger, reprinted: 1974).

Chapter Ten

Private Roman Letters: "If you are well, I am well."

For at least 5,000 years the art of writing has run as a theme—sometimes stronger, sometimes less—through the human story. In the second chapter of this book, we examined authentic records of the family of Idin Lagamal. Vivid and practical, they prove how long ago cultures began devising those conventional symbols of sounds and their combinations upon which so much of what we call civilization is built. And though pessimistic historians amuse themselves by speaking now and again about the decline of literate society, it is not likely that any electronic revolution will make the tool obsolete: computers depend as much upon text to "freeze" and manipulate speech as did the clay tablets of Sumeria. Wherever (or in however many places) the secret of writing began, the young civilizations of Egypt and the Near East found soon after 3000 B.C. that they could not live without it.

Indeed, as Bronze Age kingdoms of the Fertile Crescent grew larger, with hundreds of humans in the new urban cultures becoming thousands, they found their lives and fortunes wedded to art of the permanently preserved record. They could not supervise the enterprise or exchange of life within their walls nor the tricky business of relations between cities without it. Permanency of record-keeping became essential. That is why we can reach so far into the past and trace with some exactness the properties and transactions, even something of the domestic story, of one family in Dilbat.

Of course, one may do a lot with writing besides keep records. Acquaintance with the tool brings a litter of other written works: literary pieces both sacred and secular; instruction in skills; wisdom and the lessons of the past; reckoning of time and location; documents, legal and political; speeches; letters. The first civilizations, once they found some folk to serve as scribes, put them (and writing) to all these purposes. What we still

¹⁷⁵

Rome's Earliest Era (700 - 300)

Date B.C.	Roman & Italian Events	Around the Mediterranean	Artifacts & Art
700 --	(Trad. 700) Kings reigning at Rome (Trad. c.) the old Roman civic religion taking form.	(c. 700) Union (synoecism) of Attica.	(c. 700) Earliest monumental sculptures at Athens.
650 --	Rise of major Etruscan influence in Latium. (c.) Permanent settlement of the Forum valley in Rome.	(c. 650 - 610) Development of the Spartan social and military system. (625-621) Drafting of Draco's law code at Athens. (594?) Solon archon at Athens; curbs nobility, abolishes serfdom.	(c. 655) Demaratus (legendary?) migrates from Corinth to Etruria bringing Greek potters and painters. (c.) Trade with coins begins to replace barter in Greece by 670.
600 --	(c.) Etruscan domination of the Italian Coast to Campania. (c.) Beginnings of Roman mastery over the Latins. (c.) Establishment of Rome as a real city-state.	(c. 560) Peisistratus becomes tyrant at Athens; collects and edits works of Homer. (c. 530) Pythagoras (natural philosopher and shaman) emigrates to Croton, in (Greek) southern Italy.	(c. 625) Etruscan "bucchero" pottery and metalwork appear in Rome. (c. 600) Early mud and brick temple at Delphi.
500 --	(Trad. 510) Expulsion of King Tarquinius Superbus from Rome; election of two consuls; Rome governed by the Senate. (c. 500) Roman wars vs. Sabine hillmen. (494 - 493) Secession of the Roman *plebs*; power begins to be re-negotiated in Rome, tribunes elected.	(490) Battle of Marathon; 1st Persian invasion of Greece ends. (480) Battles of Thermopylae and Salamis; 2nd Persian invasion ends.	(c. 560) (c.) Black figure vase painting in Attica. (c. 520) Greek temple at Paestum (colony in W. Italy). (c. 500) Date of the "Capitoline wolf" statue. (468) Temple of Zeus begun at Olympia.
450 --	(Trad. 451) *Laws of the Twelve Tables* published in Rome. (c. 405 - 395) Formative Roman seige of its hill-town rival Veii.	(c. 461) Pericles, popular anti-Spartan leader, begins to dominate Athenian politics. (431 - 404) The Peloponnesian War ravages the *polis* civilizations of Greece.	(448, 447) The Parthenon begun at Athens from proceeds of the new "Athenian Empire." Pheidias is the sculptor.
400 --	(390) The Gauls attack and capture Rome; some Romans hold out on the Capitol. (367) The Sexto-Licinian Laws: *plebians* become eligible for the consulship.	(399) Socrates executed at Athens. Period of shifting alliances and dictatorships in the Greek world. (371 - 362) Battle of Leuctra to the Battle of Mantinea: Thebes briefly dominates Greece.	
350 --	Roman wars with the Samnite mountaineers of central Italy.	(338) Battle of Chaeronea: Philip of Macedon defeats and dominates mainland Greece.	(c. 340) "Mastarna" painting in the Etruscan tomb at Vulci (or by 310). (312) The Appian aqueduct built at Rome.
300 --	(c.) Rome settles peace with the Samnites and other Italian peoples; controls the region of Naples.	(336) Philip assassinated. Alexander consolidates power.	Dates of the oldest house-foundations at Pompeii.

The Later Roman Republic (300 - 31)

Date B.C.	Roman & Italian Events	Around the Mediterranean	Culture & Cicero
250 --	(264 - 241) The 1st Punic War (Rome vs. Carthage); Rome takes Sicily. (227) Sardinia and Corsica become Roman provinces. (226) Rome and Carthage agree to a border between their western interests at the Ebro River in Spain. (218 - 201) 2nd Punic War: Hannibal invades Rome from Spain via the Alps, and wins several sharp victories in Italy. (206) Scipio Africanus seizes Hannibal's base in Spain. (202) Scipio attacks Carthage, lures Hannibal to Africa, and defeats him at Zama.	(247) The Parthian Empire replaces the old Hellenistic kingdom of Persia. (217) The Battle of Raphia: Egypt (under Ptolemy IV) seriously weakens the Seleucid kingdom of Asia (under Antiochus III). (197) Rome defeats Philip V of Macedon (an ally of Hannibal) at Cynoscephalae. (189) Rome defeats Antiochus III, the Hellenistic king of Asia, at Magnesia in Asia Minor.	(c. 250) The geographer Eratosthenes becomes head of the Museum at Alexandria; calculates the circumference of the earth. (c. 240) Drama begins to be performed at Rome. (224) Earthquake on Rhodes; destruction of the giant bronze "colossus." (220) Rome builds the Via Flaminia through the Apennines to NE Italy. (c. 200) The "Anthology" of Greek poets collected and published.
200 --			
100 --	(146) Rome destroys Corinth (for a revolt) and Carthage (the 3rd Punic War). (133 - 123) The Gracchi brothers begin a series of populist revolts at Rome. (107 - 100) Gaius Marius almost continuously Consul; improves the Roman army, and re-organizes it on the basis of personal loyalty.	(166) Israel (under the Maccabees) revolts against Seleucid rule. (148) Rome creates its 1st eastern province (Macedonia).	(168) Rome declares Athens a "free city." (c. 166) The comedies of Terence become popular at Rome. (144) The "Aqua Marcia", the 1st arched-bridge-styled aqueduct, built at Rome.
	(67 - 65) The rise of Pompey as an independent Roman commander; Rome controls the eastern Mediterranean. (60) The 1st Triumvirate: Caesar, Pompey, and Crassus dominate Rome, sidestepping the old Republican forms of government. (49 - 45) Civil War: Caesar vs. Pompey. (44) Caesar assassinated in the Forum at Rome; his aide Antony and his heir Octavian soon enter a "cold" civil war over the Empire.	(66 - 65) Pompey conquers and settles the Hellenistic east as a series of Roman dependencies. (63) Syria, the last Seleucid foothold, becomes a province of Rome. (58 - 49) Caesar campaigns in Gaul, bringing it into the empire; he briefly visits Britain.	(106) Marcus Tullius Cicero born at Arpinum. (90) Cicero comes of age; studies in Rome. (81) Cicero speaks in his 1st legal case. (77) Cicero marries Terentia; his daughter Tullia born in 76.
50 --	(31) The Battle of Actium: Octavian controls the whole empire. (28 - 27) Octavian begins to develop a new imperial government under his title Augustus.	(c.) Antony and Cleopatra (Queen of Egypt, last of the Ptolemies) briefly rule the Roman east as Hellenistic monarchs. (30) Egypt becomes a province of Rome.	(68) Date of Cicero's earliest surviving letter. (65) Cicero's son Marcus born. (45) Tullia dies; Cicero sends his son Marcus to study in Athens.

have of their works are windows, every now and then opened yet a little wider, into particular corners and councils of ancient minds.

The first windows through which we see are, by and large, the minds of cultures rather than of individuals. This is true even when we read the letters left by most ancient civilizations. Kings wrote (or commanded their scribes to write) to other kings or to officials who served them. Hammurabi, when he addressed the Master of the Palace of King Zimrilim of Mari, kept his scribe focused strictly on the moment's business:

> To Bakhdilim, say: thus speaks Hammurabi. I have sent a detachment to Zimrilim. As thou knowest, the distance these men have to cover is long. Concerning the well-being of Zimrilim and that of his troops, and that of the troops I have sent to Zimrilim…continue to send me information! And let thy information reach me regularly! (Moscati:62)

We learn, certainly, how much Hammurabi himself wanted to have the information, but his concern with it was a matter of state. The language of earliest letters is predictably structured; it is very, and nearly always, formal. On occasions, a genuine private concern creeps into a letter. One official of Mari, who could not decide what to do with a rampaging lion, wrote anxiously to his king:

> Now I have been awaiting letters from my lord, and the lion has remained five days in the granary. A dog and a pig have been sent in to him that he may eat. I said to myself: "Perhaps this lion will get away!" I was afraid. I have had the lion put in a wooden cage, loaded on a boat, and sent to my master. (Moscati:63)

For the most part, however, such tones—personal emotion, narrative detail, even (though it was of course a serious crisis) that faint note of comic relief—are the exceptions, not the rule. If we want to glimpse a wealth of personal detail left in writing by an ancient people, we are most likely to find it in the rather less typical correspondence of the world of Rome. Along with satire and a universal idea of law, it is often the writing of private letters that are suggested as Rome's peculiar gifts to civilization. (We might suggest yet a fourth gift in the next chapter.) While not the inventors of the art of correspondence, the Romans extended its practice into a wealth of new shapes, and spoke through it in more homely and vulnerable voices. We shall follow this tool of epistolography along the Roman trail.

The Romans became great letter writers, in part because the extent of their empire took them so far, and so often, away from home. While the minuscule polis defined the compass of life for most ancient Greeks, the Romans quickly extended their horizons in both space and in the administration of it. Rome depended upon written documents of all kinds to regulate its affairs. Thus not only as officials but also as private travelers, Romans communicated with one another through epistles.

The full circuit of the Mediterranean coasts eventually came under the rule of Rome, and as the Roman borders spread, their roads and courts and practical institutions spread like arteries and sinews behind them. The Romans had begun as men of the soil; where they went they put down roots. But even while they settled in to distant lands, it was a burden of imperial survival to forge a constant tie with Rome itself. Rome was both the head and heart of their civilization; embodying a way of life, it provided the means to unify the bewilderingly varied patchwork of cultures the Romans encountered around the Mediterranean.

The momentum toward unification of lands and peoples was partly inherited: Alexander and his successors consciously used many habits and styles of Greek life to try and meld some sort of unity between the Greco-Macedonians and the native populations of their conquered lands. The further flung Hellenistic kingdoms might never have survived without some such bond of "common" culture. All across the eastern world, new cities sprang up that looked very like grand or simple imitations of the old polis of Greece. The administration, the armies, and the imagination of the new metropolitan melting-pots spoke Greek. Greek soldiers were enticed by land grants to settle in the hinterland of the new nations, providing a sort of cultural yeast in times of peace, and a stock of loyal reservists in times of war. Every custom and belief that they brought with them flowed out into the stream of the local culture, mingling with its own way of life, blending more intricately with each generation. The whole of this amalgam—we call it "Hellenistic culture"—had a fiber resilient enough to survive Rome's conquest of the eastern Mediterranean, to make a new and very strong blend with *Romanitas*. This elixir, still very recognizably Greek, outlived the fall of the Romans and became the fire in the veins of the Byzantine Empire. The curtain did not fall on Byzantium until the mid-fifteenth century A.D. As elements in the mixture of western civilization go, "Greekness" had a very long run.

Initially, however, those Lati farm-folk, who founded their little community on the banks of the Tiber, had little thought of expansion. Romans traditionally began the account of their own history in 753 B.C., and, through the early generations, the inhabitants of Rome were few and struggling to hold their own against stronger neighbors on every side: powerful Etruscan city-states that clung, closely walled, to the hilltops to the north; hardy, cattle-raiding Sabine and Samnite mountaineers, who dwelt in the high valleys to the east; quarrelsome Greeks who had spread their poleis to the south.

For at least a hundred years the Romans lost their independence to a succession of Etruscan masters, warlords who came to call themselves kings, until the city dwellers (or the "local folk") expelled them about 500 B.C. (The Republic dated its start to the overthrow of Tarquin the Proud in 509 B.C.) Even as the Greeks were fighting to keep the Persians out of Europe, the Romans were struggling for their own identity on the banks of the Tiber. And yet, the Etruscans had done a service to their subjects during their years of kingship. Rome had begun as an outpost of central Italy (Latium) at a fordable and defensible place in the Tiber River; it became by degrees an important town, a crossroads accustomed to the mingling of cultures. Moreover, the Etruscan opposition had helped forge at least a nascent "Roman" personality.

The Romans levered this advantage into preeminence over the neighboring towns of the Latium plain. They spread, homesteading the land, learning and assimilating the deities of others as they went until they pressed upon the tribal peoples, first in the foothills and soon thereafter in the high mountain valleys of the Apennines. A marauding host of Gauls rocked the Roman thrust back on its heels in 390 B.C., sacking the city and penning its defenders on the fortified "Capitoline" hill, but its people emerged from the disaster with stiffer resolve. Their army reorganized, they pressed, through the fourth century, further north and south in the Italian peninsula. By the early third century, Rome had

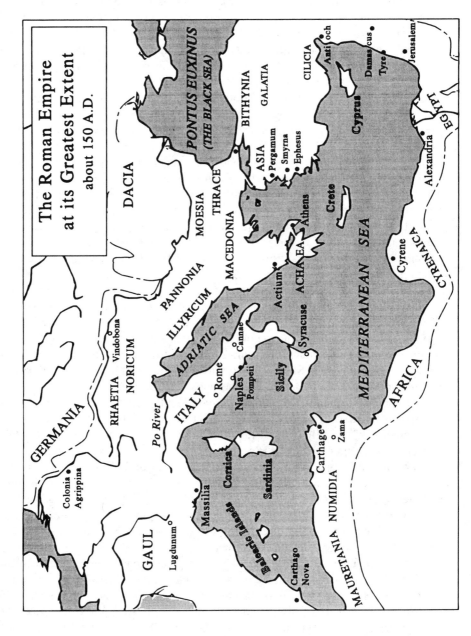

FIGURE 10–1 The Roman Empire at Its Greatest Extent about 150 A.D.

fought off a challenge from one of the descendants of Alexander, Pyrrhus; the disciplined tread of the booted Roman armies was heard in the peninsula's "heel" and "toe," bringing alliances with Greek states long established in southern Italy.

Allying with the Greeks was a mixed blessing. The Greeks had a great many alliances already, with other Greek as well as non-Greek states. A tangled web of treaties carried Roman legions to Sicily where Carthage, anxious to press its influence over the Greek grain-producing towns, engaged them in the First Punic War between 264 and 241 B.C. When the fighting died, Rome had Sicily and Carthage. The Second Punic War—Hannibal's War from 218 to 202—was as much as anything a war of revenge: Hannibal kept a Carthaginian army dodging for a decade through the valleys of Italy itself. A Roman, catching the spirit of Hannibal's own tactics, lured him away and defeated him in Africa.

The outcome was more than a Roman victory. It was as though the continents of power had shifted their balance and weight while few were watching. Each of the old powers in the eastern Mediterranean now had to recognize that Rome was a power in the affairs of the larger Mediterranean world. One reckoned with it, or allied with it, or fell to it. Roman generals were before long squaring the cohorts in their battlelines on fields in Macedon, in Spain, and in Western Asia Minor. In 133 B.C., the old men of the Roman Senate were astonished to find that the last king of Pergamum had simply *willed* his small but brilliant Asian realm to Rome. Better a gift than a conquest.

Before the end of the second century, the Romans found themselves masters of much of the Mediterranean world but to govern they had only administrative tools fit to organize a large city-state or a compact kingdom, a stubborn impromptu legal competence, and a habit of social compromise. They crafted this raw material quickly into more effective tools. To create additional officials, they prolonged the terms of key officials well established within the constitutional structure. Whatever an official might be trusted to do in Rome, he could be called upon a year or two later to do in "the provinces." Throughout the Republic—509 to 31 B.C.—the highest ranked officials were two consuls of equal authority, capable of vetoing one another's actions, and selected for a year's term. As the empire accumulated, those consuls served their traditional year in Rome and then, as proconsuls, were sent out as governors to *provincia* such as Asia, Illyria, Africa, and Spain.

That such a scheme worked at all was due partly to the willingness of these "journeymen" governors to learn from the nations they came to rule. The Roman conquerors became students, especially in the eastern Mediterranean and most particularly of the Greeks. As Rome's own poet Horace put it, captive Greece took her own rough captor captive. Greeks had ruled places further flung than even a Roman general had ever seen, and done so for centuries. It is equally important to remember that the Greek current ran nearly as deep in early Italy as it did in the east. Southern Italy and Sicily had been a prosperous beehive of independent Greek city-states since the great explosion of population in the eighth century B.C. The whole of this amalgam had a fiber resilient enough to persist, in spite of the success of Roman arms. When the Roman arms finally began to fail, some centuries after Christ, the fiber remained, a network battered but still intact enough to gird the eastern provinces for many years.

The Romans recognized that the Greeks had lessons to teach, but to learn by Greek example, Roman officials would need training in Hellenic ways. This process became urgent in the first century B.C. Just when the city of Rome was at last beginning to become

FIGURE 10–2 A bust of Cicero, carved from marble during the first century B.C. (now in the Wellington Museum), showing him as he began to gain weight toward middle age. Based on remaining samples, this was his most productive letter-writing period. As the pace of Roman public life accelerated and grew more precarious in the 50s and 40s B.C., Cicero relied increasingly on the stability and affection of his friends and family.

truly cosmopolitan, its wealthier, better educated aristocracy began to feel that they were "provincial." The Mediterranean around them was ringed with the heritages of old civilizations—Egypt, Asia Minor, Macedon, Greece—and Rome the upstart had not only to rule in their stead, but to win their respect. Romans looked around seriously for the first time seeking places in which they could become cultured without embarrassment, in a style not too "foreign," and in those arts—both of expertise and style—which a player in the grand new game of imperial politics might be able to use. Roman culture would not become simply a later version of Greek culture; the Romans would not be "Greeklings."

The career and home life, the thoughts and ambitions of Marcus Tullius Cicero portray vividly for us all of these struggles to adapt and to be unique, both those struggles caused by the duties of an empire, and by its pressures on an individual soul. In 106 B.C., Cicero was born in a small town far from Rome itself, but he had the advantage of a good education. He had struggled with Greek philosophy, literature, and rhetoric, besides the more traditional Roman subjects like basic mathematics and the great body of traditional law. He made a name for himself in the capital as a skilled speaker in a series of famous and even scandalous legal cases, choosing to reach fame through the courts rather than the army. Though he lacked the blood and political connections of the ancient local families, he aimed for every office a true Roman could hold and won them all in turn, being elected to consulship for the year 63 B.C.

His position was especially significant since he was the first in his family to have gained the honor. His family was now "senatorial," and what he had gained he intended that his son (also Marcus Tullius) should continue. He imagined for his daughter Tullia a role in the family's future just as prominent. The elder Cicero spent considerable thought over both of his children. We know this intimately—his plans, his own private yearnings, his miscalculations and endless worry—because he wrote about them in reams of letters. Sixteen books (each "book" the equivalent of a long chapter in a present-day manuscript) are known as *Ad Familiares*—or "On Family Matters"—and another sixteen are correspondence with Cicero's best friend Atticus, known as *Ad Atticus*—"To Atticus." And there are two shorter collections: three books to his brother Quintus and two to Brutus, one of the assassins of Julius Caesar.

The individual letters give insight into every part of Cicero's life and mind. We will look in two directions: toward his son, Marcus Tullius junior, to suggest the education of a future Roman official; and at his daughter, Tullia, to reveal the "private" domain of women in the Roman Empire. These distinctions are largely artificial, of course. But we must also ask a question about the letters themselves— how far can we trust their contents?

ROMAN LETTERS

To have been born in Rome of the first century B.C. was to occupy center stage of the Mediterranean. Rome had won an empire and was attempting to organize it into a workable community of peoples. Its main resource lay in the ancient families of its governmental classes: birth, wealth, and aristocratic tradition combined to keep decisive political power among heads of the most important families. Though the common *plebs* had increasingly won the right to wield real power in their assembly, the old families of the Senate still did the day to day business of governing the empire. The head of a family was its father, or *pater*; collectively, the powerful fathers were *patres* and their families known as "patrician." New families might join the ranks of the patrician order if the wealth or the career of one of its members warranted. When Marcus Tullius Cicero the younger was born in 65 B.C., his father was but two years away from being elected consul and then gaining fame by defending Rome in that year against one of the great political conspiracies of the city's history. He entered a family on the brink of greatness. His father's success and growing hopes for his son made it imperative that he plan a proper education for the boy. He should, if the gods were just, be one of the great young men in the next generation of Roman leadership.

Some of the traditional education in earlier centuries continued: the father and his peers educated by example, shaping the citizens-to-be in the customary ways, namely *mos maiorum*, "the way of the elders." That way revolved around devotion to the state; it was accomplished by climbing a ladder of duties beginning in early youth with emulation of the Roman elders and heroes, memorizing their exploits and serving at their household shrines. After that came some form of military service beginning from age 19, and then (hopefully) increasingly important offices.

By the first century, however, the education of young Romans had acquired a formal dimension, largely under the influence of Greek habits. At the primary level of ages seven through eleven, teachers (who were often slaves) instructed in the basic skills of reading, writing, and reckoning. A grammarian assumed responsibility during the next four years, instructing in textual studies of various kinds of manuscripts. From sixteen to about nineteen or twenty, Romans were taught the arts of rhetoric, essential for political and judicial oratory as well as military leadership.

All this a foreigner could usually be hired to do, and a foreigner meant a *Greek* foreigner. Nevertheless, wealthy Roman fathers still seem to have felt an element of guilt about no longer seeing to the whole matter themselves. Part of what made Cato the Elder the paragon that he was of grand old curmudgeonly Roman values was the fact that he had educated his child himself, writing his first schoolbooks in big blocky letters with his own hand. In 54 B.C., when young Marcus' cousin Quintus would have been visiting in Rome (the boys would have been eleven and twelve), and Cicero was rather too busy in the courts to father them very much, he nevertheless fussed in his letters about taking up their education himself if he had the slightest chance. He insisted to Quintus' father that:

> I'll do wonders with him if I can get him to myself at leisure, for at Rome there is not time to breathe. (*Ad Familiares*:III, i, 7)

At some point around the turn of the first century B.C., another element entered the mix as a few of the old Athenian schools began surreptitiously to arouse curiosity in Rome. Roman officials and commanders passing through Athens on their way further east developed a habit of stopping at the old Greek schools of the city and dropping in on lectures. Athens made a culturally impressive hotel-stop between Rome and the eastern frontier and there was no real un-Roman embarrassment in picking up a *little* speaking style, a bit of this knowledge or that. The famous orator Licinius Crassus, for example, seems to have been so relentlessly button-holed by an enthusiastic young Marcus Marcellus (either traveling in his retinue or actually "stopping" on his own) that "the elder official" found himself forced to attend any number of classes. The rather conservative orator M. Antonius (Mark Antony's grandfather)—his fleet stuck in Athens by rainy weather—appears standing for hours (in the rain?) to hear the philosopher Charmadas argue with a local politician about the value of rhetoric in statecraft.

The common thread in these glimpses is the old Athenian-sophistic expertise in the powers of oral persuasion and the old Athenian skepticism about its abuse. Both might have seemed like yesterday's news to young Greek locals by this era. But to Romans of the Senatorial class in the late Republic they will have seemed like a sudden burst of scientific light and power into an art upon which one's career, and influence, and life depended—an art which one had practiced up until only yesterday, by means of an old, crude tradition.

It is in this mental and emotional setting that one should see the rise of Roman interest in Athens as the Senatorial "university town." Famous jokes about the clumsiness of the new conquerors as they discovered the intensity of their interest in the Athenian schools look a bit different in its light. Cicero assumed everybody knew that the proconsular governor of 93 B.C., L. Gellius, had "offered" to negotiate a "treaty" between the philosophical academies so they could get on to something more useful with their lives. Both assumed that everyone laughed at this heartily. The schools were offering expertise in the vocal manipulation of mobs like those that were beginning to hold the real political power in Rome. As twilight fell on the oral era of Roman political culture, the Romans discovered the dangerous, seductive power of artful, scientific, verbal persuasion. It was exciting. The possibilities, if the ancient Athenian political expertise and teaching could just be smoothed out and organized on a broad scale, were endless.

Hence, as the Roman market for Greek political expertise grew, there came to be a variety of schools again, something that soon resembled a "university of Athens," with several campuses. Even the schools less useful to the practical expert politician—the Stoic and Epicurean teachings that could insulate a person from the chaos of a civilization where all the old certainties were gone—would be useful, even vital, for Roman sanity all too soon.

Athens could potentially serve a new "socializing" function for its conquerors as well. The elder Cicero had studied in Athens between 79 and 77 B.C.. What verbal tools he could use to keep himself secure in the increasingly wild storms of Roman politics, he believed he had developed when he studied there. And the very quiet of the place appealed to him in memory as the political climate of Rome grew increasingly strident and dangerous. His son Marcus had now reached the proper age, and Cicero rented him a house in Athens and put him under the tutorship of several of the city's leading teachers. Though Athens was far from the centers of trouble for the Romans, Cicero asked friends constantly whether his son were staying away from even such temptations to political or social scandal as Athens might provide. It might not be surprising then if Cicero's letters to Marcus, and Marcus' to him, suggest a growing temptation to love Athens only occasionally as a place to learn, and *primarily* as a retreat—the sort of place Oxford was to be for young English noblemen in the Edwardian years.

But for all that Cicero speaks about any other subject—son, daughter, friends, politics—in the more than 750 of his letters that survive, it cannot be denied that he speaks far the most about himself. To follow these threads we need certainty about the sort of historical evidence that seems to allow us glimpses inside the private souls of late Republican Romans like Cicero. Moreover, if these letters are to be any more reliable than the guesses by analogy that we make in psychohistory, we must suppose that ancient Romans like Cicero exposed their spirits with at least some honesty in their epistles. Many ancient cultures have been curiously reticent to provide us with so deep-cutting a psychological tool.

The letter as a genre is itself a simple thing: a written communication into which a specific author places information intended for a specific reader. The precision of sender and recipient is the key: most kinds of written treatises aim themselves at *anyone* who reads them; a letter is intended for a particular eye, and the information it contains is thus often very particular itself.

Having said so much, it is obvious that the origins of the formal letter as we think of it in the West cannot be called in any sense Roman. Letters in the styles we usually associate with Rome belong really to the broader culture of the ancient Mediterranean—ultimately perhaps to the bureaucracies of the Mesopotamian city-states at which we looked many chapters ago. We have excellent evidence of this (as collected by Tom Jones in his essay "Graecia Capta"). There survive early Mediterranean examples of something that many students of the classics often associate *most* with Roman letters: the formulae that mark the opening and close of "polite" correspondence. "*Vale*"—"be well"—seems in some sense to be the first thing even the simplest Roman letter is *required* to say; it salutes the reader off the page almost like a command, or a spell. It is an injunction that the reader ought be "in good health" (and perhaps that the letter in hand will be no threat to that). *S.V.B.E.* (*si vales bene est*)—"If you are well, it is good"—could appear on a more formal Latin letter, or even *S.V.B.E.E.Q.V.*—"if you are well, so also am I"—in the case of a distant acquaintance. Both formalism and cryptic abbreviation were heartily suited to the thrifty Roman spirit.

But the habit of such openings, and even the formulas, have much older roots. Jones points out that a Hittite king could write to a Kassite ruler and begin by saying,

> I am well, my palace, my wife, my children, my horses, my chariots, everything in my land are well. May all be well with you, your palace,...etc. ("Graecia Capta," p. 65).

Sargon II of Assyria sent home a report on one of his campaigns which he began, "To Ashur...may it be very well." He then applied the same formula to various of his gods, to the city, and the people ("Graecia Capta," p. 66).

The few reliable letters we have from the classical era of Greece do not often follow this formula, though there may be reasons for that. Plato's "Seventh Letter" (whose authenticity few scholars now seem to dispute) opens almost with an argument under way: "You write to me that I must consider your views the same as those of Dion..."(323 e, trans. J. Hayward). If something has not been lost at the beginning of that phrase, we have a glimpse of Plato so intent upon the argument he intends to make that he has no time for niceties: he is formal about his topic, not about his letter. Most Greek letters (more survive from Hellenistic times) begin, "from [the sender] to [the reader], greetings."

All this is of course formality of style: cultures from Sumer through to Rome probably exhibit this continuity of expression for very practical reasons. Formal letters are not simply general purpose communication; they need the attention and probably the action of someone who is distant (perhaps socially as well as geographically) from the sender, and so they need to secure that person's good will. They need for the same reasons to secure some particular form of attention, and so letters in most cultures also show a continuity of formal *types*. Letters intended to plead a diplomatic or legal case, letters commending a project or person to some important reader, letters arranging or accounting for transactions at a distance are all examples of such types. Simple letters between friends or members of a family reporting one's health and perhaps a few interesting events are really the same sort of thing. Each topic tends to *form* the sort of letter written, to create its own formulae and style.

The preserved body of Cicero's letters provide samples of one of these formal types, though as we shall see in a moment these samples are an exception rather than a rule. R. Y. Tyrrell, the classic modern (English-speaking) editor of Cicero's correspondence, notes that the entire thirteenth book of the *Epistolae ad Familiares* ("Letters to Acquaintances, or Friends") is actually made up of "letters of commendation"—a type referred to above, which the Romans called *epistola commendaticia*.

However, the oddity about Cicero's letters in general is that very few of those preserved fit into that mold. A man in Cicero's position must of course have written many formal ones, but (unlike the letters of Hammurabi, or of the Hittite kings, or of Paul in the *New Testament*, or the scraps of Plato's correspondence) formal letters shaped by their topics are not the sort of thing Cicero has largely left to us. Tyrrell pointed out that the first twelve books of the *Ad Familiares* (which he thought formed the original group published after Cicero's death by his freedman Tiro) were a collection "in no way based on any considerations about the nature or subjects of the letters" (pp. 50–56). Four books of additional material were, he thought, added later to the collection we have now:

- the thirteenth, all "letters of commendation" and so forming a sample of Cicero's formal correspondence (letter 68 is in fact a reply to an *epistola commendaticia*).
- the fourteenth, all letters to a particular family (Terentia's) but otherwise collected as randomly as the others.
- the fifteenth, put together exactly in the hodgepodge manner of the first twelve books, with letters touching "politics, art, domestic life,…introduction, etc." all jostling one another for attention. (Tyrroll, p. 55)
- the sixteenth, and the last we now possess, consisting of letters to Tiro, who was probably the editor.

But if this is so, what ties the majority of these collected letters together? It seems to be very little more than Cicero's desire, mixed in constantly with his business, political worries, financial needs, and inquiries about his friends, to talk purely about himself. When the letters of others are included in the collection (those written to Tiro by Cicero's son and others in the sixteenth book, for example) they seem to follow just the same pattern.

What the Romans alone of ancient Mediterranean people have left to us are deliberately published collections of letters in which we are invited to witness a person privately expressing his state of mind. The private Roman letter has something in common with the Roman portraiture explored in the book's final chapter: it seems willing to be remarkably personal and homely.

This is the trail we will follow from here out: Cicero guiding the education of his son, worrying over the life and happiness of his daughter, and generally revealing a less public side of what it meant to be a reflective Roman in the years when the Republic was rolling faster and faster toward its own destruction.

In March of 45 B.C., Cicero, anxious that Marcus settle comfortably and respectably into the life of a student, wrote to Atticus, the best friend he had in Greece, and asked about the handling of money:

> As to my son it seems high time now; but I want to know whether he can get a draft for his allowance changed at Athens or whether he must take it with him; and as regards the whole matter please consider how and when you think he ought to go. (*Epistolae ad Atticus*:XXII, 14)

Cicero thus set up a fairly generous tuition and living allowance for his son Marcus by long-distance transfer (*permutatio*), upon which interest might even be drawn. Athens was becoming a center of banks as well as schools, both functions drawing on the security of a place no longer important in grand political schemes. It all sounds modern enough, as does the fact that Marcus spent his way through it rather too quickly. Cicero added in a later letter,

> About my son I will do as you say. I will leave the time to him. See that he is provided with a bill of exchange for as much as is necessary. (*Epistolae ad Atticus*:XXII, 24)

About the details he was less worried, at least so long as someone looked in on young Marcus occasionally. The fact that he carefully kept them among his *own* correspondence suggests the importance he placed upon the reports of his friends when they passed through the city. One of these is perhaps worth quoting at more length:

Trebonius to Cicero
(Athens, May 25th, 44 B.C.)
If you are well, all is right [*S.V.B.E.*]. I arrived at Athens on May the 22nd and there, as I most particularly hoped to do, I saw your son, who is devoted to the best forms of study, and most highly spoken of for his discreet behaviour; and how much pleasure that gave me you can understand even if I say nothing. For you well know how highly I esteem you, and how much, as befits our very old and sincere affection, I rejoice in any, even the slightest, happiness that befalls you, not to speak of such a blessing as this. Do not think, my dear Cicero, that I am saying this to tickle your ears; your, or rather our young man (for there can be no severance of interests between us) is the most popular fellow in the world among all who are at Athens, and at the same time the most devoted to the arts you yourself love most, to wit, the best. I therefore congratulate you with pleasure also, as I can with sincerity, and myself too no less, on finding that he whom we were bound to love, whatever his character, is the sort of man whom it is also a pleasure to love.

When he threw me a hint in the course of conversation that he would like to visit Asia, I not only invited him to come, but begged him to do so at the best time of all—while I was governing the province; and you must never doubt but that I shall do my duty by him, as you would yourself, with affection and love. Another thing too—I shall be careful to arrange that Cratippus accompanies him, so that you need not think he will have a holiday in Asia from those studies to which he is being urged by your exhortations. For ready as I see he is, and well advanced at full stride, I shall never pause in my own exhortations to him to make further progress day after day in his studies and exercises. (*Ad Familiares*: XXII, 16)

Marcus himself argued his own case in his letters home, and echoed the personal bent of his father, though this is especially evident in those he wrote to Cicero's freedman and secretary Tiro. Such letters suggest occasions when he felt the paternal eye was on him too closely, and that a good report from Tiro was likelier to have a hearing than one of his own. He never says (and one would not expect him to) whether it was the speed with which student life swallowed his allowance that made him write home so indirectly. He and Tiro would have known. It is rather his ease when speaking to an old family servant that gives us one of the best examples of the private style in Roman letters, and also one of our best portraits of Athenian "university life."

(M. Cicero, Junior, Greets His Sweetest Tiro)
(Athens, August or early in September, 44 B.C.)
Since [on some previous occasion] I caused you grief, I shall now guarantee that the joy I give you is double.

I must tell you that my close attachment to Cratippus is not so much that of a pupil as that of a son. For not only do I attend his lectures with enjoyment, but I am greatly fascinated also by the charm of his personality. I spend whole days with him, and often a part of the night.

Indeed I implore him to dine with me as often as possible. Now that we have become so intimate, he often strolls in upon us when we least expect him and are at dinner, and throwing to the winds all austerity as a philosopher, he bandies jokes with us in the most genial manner possible. Lay yourself out, therefore, to win the acquaintance of such a man—so delightful and so distinguished as he is.

As to Bruttius, why should I mention him at all? There is never a moment when I allow him to leave my side. He leads a simple and austere life, but at the same time he is a most delightful man to live with. For there is no ban upon merry talk in our literary discussions and our daily joint researches. I have hired lodgings for him next door, and, as far as I can, alleviate his penury out of my own narrow means.

Besides all this I have begun to practice declaiming in Greek with Cassius; but I like practicing in Latin with Bruttius. I have as daily and intimate companions men whom Cratippus brought with him from Mitylene—men of learning and highly esteemed by him. Epicrates, for instance, the leading man among the Athenians, is much with me, and so is Leonides, and others of that stamp. So much then about myself.

As to what you write about Gorgias, it is true I found him useful in my practice in declamation: but I thought everything else of secondary importance, provided I obeyed my father's instructions, who had written to me in explicit terms to get rid of Gorgias at once. I did not want to temporize, for fear my making too much of the business might strike my father as somewhat suspicious; and besides it occurred to me that it was a serious thing for me to pass judgment on the judgment of my father. (*Ad Familiares*:XVI, 21)

The letters give us insights into more than the lives of individuals. Young Marcus tells us that he was not the only young Roman studying in Athens; in fact aristocratic Roman youth were now arriving in Athens (and elsewhere in the East) for both university time and their "Grand Tours" in large numbers. As a stop on the tour, Athens was essential. One managed it in the guise of business, perhaps attached to the staff of a magistrate, if it proved too difficult as a pleasure. A little study might thus combine nicely with some sightseeing and a bit of financial profit. The poet Catullus on his own admission cut loose from the governor who employed him to "see the famous cities of Asia" (Catullus:xlvi, 6). Whether he included Athens he does not say, but for most other young Roman apprentices in the art of empire it will have been a must. This was especially true of momentary students at the most "gracious" of the philosophical schools. Any young Roman of Epicurean tastes and means, Cicero wrote, tended to "cross the seas and see the sights" (Cicero, *de Repetundis*:I, iii, 6). The "university" was just the sort of thing he wanted. After the Mithridatic Wars, Pompey's settlement of the East into provinces and client kingdoms multiplied the number of Roman dependencies, and so also the number of posts available to the young and politically ambitious. These semidiplomatic tourists must soon have formed quite a body. Athens during the sailing season must have been full of them.

Serious Roman students also poured into the town in larger numbers. Plutarch credits Antony with studying military science in Athens (which would likely have been serious), as well as rhetoric (which might have been half serious and half "culture"). Brutus had just a little earlier been there studying under two speaking teachers, and attending classes at the Academy on the side (Plutarch, *Brutus*:xxiv).

The saddest news for everyone arriving in Athens will have been that several of the most admired old schools in the city were in dire trouble. This was partly because Romans came to Athens with a more old-fashioned set of tastes and a simpler idea of "Greekness" than anyone in the real Greek world had done for generations. Everyone wanted to attend the actual Academy (and often arrived with highly romantic or outdated ideas of who might still be in residence). It came as a melancholy shock to Cicero to find that he and his friends would have to make do with visiting the old site one afternoon—a special hike out toward the little hill of Colonus by themselves. The place was deserted. The very ground was bare. All the lovely, shady, stream-watered trees one could almost *feel* in Plato's later dialogues had been ripped out by Sulla to make artillery for the siege of Athens.

Cicero's "schoolmaster" Antiochus was *scholarch* of the "Academy," and he even meant honestly to restore the old school to a shade of its former self. The ephebic inscriptions of the period no longer mention lectures at either the Academy *or* the Lyceum, originally founded by Aristotle. Scholars suspect that the succession of teachers may actually have lapsed at the Lyceum. Cicero came through in the 70s and heard no one there, though the young Cicero seems to have thought that there might be Peripatetic lectures somewhere in town on the old verbal fireworks of Carneades.

This disappointment must have been severe for many young Romans: the Aristotelian school would have been the one place in Athens where one could hope to get the real, practical, scientific stuff. By comparison the Epicurean schools were full of theoretical "logical positivists" (however good the food was) and wise-eyebrowed, myth-critics, who would tell you for a fee that a proper understanding of your component atoms would cure your anxieties (they called the miracle *ataraxia*). Aristotle had not talked about *ataraxia*, he had talked about *government*, and now there was no one in his place. Cratippus seems to have done some "filling in" in the 40s, but as we have seen he was ready on the slightest suggestion of Cicero to pack up and leave for an Asian tour with Cicero's son if there were a little real money forthcoming.

There were other "university" towns; Athens faced more than a little competition as the Roman Empire had taken on its gigantic dimensions. The Hellenistic capital of the Attalids at Pergamon was Attalid no longer, but it still had a school and library donated by Attalus (protected from looting because it was part of a temple). There was also Rhodes, made especially attractive at the beginning of this period by the fact that Posidonius—reputed by many to have been the greatest polymath of antiquity—was still alive there. Cicero, having had some time in Athens in 79, hurried there to discuss law, history, and anthropology with the old social scientist, and then studied oratory with the famous Apollonius Molon. This kind of curriculum was ideal for a serious, ambitious young Roman with his eye on the government—real stuff for a practical lawmaker and general.

The great competition was of course Alexandria, where true royalty with real wealth still subsidized both the biggest library and the most advanced scientific school in the world. As Tom Jones has pointed out, the advances of the technical Greek sciences by the late Hellenistic and early Imperial periods had gone far beyond the ability of the ordinary talented layman to follow ("Graecia Capta," pp. 67*ff.*). Books he could not follow he did not buy, but the Ptolemies still bought everything. Works of extreme engineering genius and difficulty could only be had there. The best equipment—astrolabes for example—had either to be made there, or their plans copied there. The Library was simply unapproachable by the standards of any other book collector, individual or city. Athens in our era managed to buy a hundred rolls per year for one of its libraries, but the Ptolemies worked on quite another scale.

Romans traveled to all these centers, as officials and as students. And this combination of purposes tells us a great deal about the Romans' management of their empire and their intent in training managers for future generations. While Roman arms had been successful in adding territory to the empire, Romans could learn much from those they had conquered. The legacy from the eastern Mediterranean was particularly valuable in providing administrative tools. Most congenial of all was the Greek legacy. Born into a recently arrived patrician family, trained by his father and tutors in Rome, young Marcus Cicero took his higher education in Athens and, as his father hoped, climbed the ladder to the highest rung of consul in 30 B.C. But the structure against which the ladder rested was crumbling. Only the year before, his co-consul (and real master), Octavian, had finished, in the maneuverings around Actium of the largest armies the Roman world had ever seen, the long process of taking from the office of consulship any of the real glory in which Cicero the elder would have delighted. Only three years later the Republic would effectively end, and Octavian would become Augustus. Cicero himself had died in December of 43.

But if Marcus Cicero did not live up to his father's hopes, it came as little surprise. The elder Cicero struck a usual note when he confided to Atticus after reports of his son's progress in 44 B.C., "Ah well! This is a matter on which I'm even glad to have dust thrown in my eyes, and content to be credulous."

Perhaps young Marcus cannot entirely be blamed. He had his father's tendency to mull too long over a political choice and then choose the wrong side (Marcus accepted a military command under Brutus and Cassius after their flight to Asia). Worse yet, he was surrounded in the dying years of the Republic by hot-hearted, youthful companions (many of them also products of the best Greek political education) for whom the whole dangerous edifice of empire was only an enormous cockpit in which to gamble ruthlessly for personal gain. Oddest of all, very few of these young men seem to have sensed how close to the edge of the volcano they were playing. During the 40s and 30s, a quiet young man, born in the year of Cicero's consulship and thus two years younger than Cicero's son, was carefully watching the final eruption: Octavian, soon to be Augustus, shepherded the changes that ended the Republic and inaugurated the Empire. Cicero knew what was occurring but he, like others, was powerless to effect a different outcome.

But there are brighter moments and better characters close to Cicero in the letters. It was not his son Marcus Tullius but his daughter Tullia who was the apple of her father's eye. She was, as Cicero wrote to his brother (*Ad Quintus*:1, 33), "the effigy of my face, speech, soul." Although no letter by Tullia's hand remains, her actions show a similar and genuine attachment to her father: when he was forced to await Caesar's permission to enter Rome, Tullia came and stood by Cicero publicly at the port of Brundisium. The climate was unhealthy, she had a husband and home to care for, and everyone else awaited Caesar's announcement to make Cicero politically correct again, but Tullia stood where her heart was.

Born in 76 B.C., Cicero's only daughter was named in the usual Roman fashion: she was known by the feminine form of her father's family name—Tullia from Tullius. Since she was the only daughter of the marriage, there was no Tullia minor or major to claim the same name. The power of the family, particularly that of the head of that family, was immense. The oldest living male had absolute legal power over every member of the family: control of property, marriage, divorce, even life and death, were at his discretion. The lives of Tullia, her brother Tullius minor, and even her mother, Terentia, were in the hands of Cicero. The Latin words for Cicero's authority are, in fact, *in manu* or "in the hand."

Cicero was concerned that his daughter's life be a happy one, and he meant "happy" in an old-fashioned Roman sense, which must have seemed almost obsolete in the wild society of wealthy first-century Rome. By "happy" Cicero meant just *that*, but of course he also intended that his daughter should make a successful marriage and produce healthy children. Providing a proper dowry to make such a suitable marriage possible, Cicero transferred care of Tullia to Calpurnius Piso Frugi in 63 B.C. Tullia was then thirteen years of age, the average age for a girl to marry, in part because the life span of women was shorter than that of men. Marriage and childbearing were so important to the Roman state that there came to be penalties for women who were unmarried and childless at the advanced age of twenty. But Tullia was widowed before she could get so far; her husband died in 57 B.C..

Tullia would have returned to her father's legal care somewhat wealthier if she had officially been transferred to the *manus* of her husband (we do not know the details of the marriage), since women married in this manner shared in a husband's estate. Even had she been impoverished, Cicero would have been delighted to have his little Tullia— "Tulliola"—at home. He wrote to his great friend Atticus in April of 56: "…be sure and come yourself, …and bring Pilia with you (which is only fair, besides being Tullia's wish)." Pilia was Atticus' recent bride, probably about the age of Tullia. Cicero hoped to find Tullia a friend, someone with whom she might share pastimes, good conversation, and gossip. They were the sort of things he had always enjoyed with Atticus. Strikingly absent in the letters is crowing on Cicero's part about any money Tullia might have brought home or the expense of having her at home; he seems simply happy to have her near him again.

Remarriage was expected among the important families, so Cicero provided another dowry for the marriage of Tullia to Furius Crassipes. This marriage, too, was short-lived and childless, so Cicero was soon in search of another match for his "adored Tullia." Tiberius Nero, who would someday gain a shadow of fame as father of the Emperor Tiberius, traveled all the way to Cilicia (where Cicero was serving his unhappy governorship) and sued in person for Tullia's hand. Cicero was delighted, but this time things

FIGURE 10–3 An artist's impression of Tullia reading an epistle in the scrolled form. Shorter Roman letters (including much business correspondence) were inscribed on wax-coated tablets bought ready-made in the market.

went wrong. Tullia's mother—"on the site" in Rome and so holding a more practical power—had her own ideas. In August of 50 B.C. he wrote to Atticus:

> While in my province I was paying every mark of respect to Appius, I suddenly found myself the father-in-law of his accuser Dolabella! "Heaven's blessing on the match!" you say; and so say I, and know you are sincere. But, believe me, it came as a complete surprise to me; indeed, I had sent trusted messengers to Terentia and Tullia about Tiberius Nero, who had made a proposal to me, but they arrived at Rome to find Tullia already engaged. However, I hope this will turn out better;.... (*Ad Atticus*:VI, b, 1 Wilkinson trans.)

Absolute power of the father? How had Cicero lost control? Or had he? The apparent discrepancy points up a true discrepancy in Roman social and legal affairs: while officially without power, women's influence could be immense. They could inherit property even though the amounts were limited by law; they were not sequestered and, consequently, gathered frequently for religious ceremonies, and social gatherings and even to demand official action. Cornelia, the wife and later widow of Scipio Aemilianus, presided over and set the intellectual tone of her family's political faction for a generation. And as education became more prized, its value for girls as well as boys became apparent. Since girls married early, their instruction would normally occur in the home through private tutors. But we know of women authors and even literary salons presided over by women. Cicero so praises the intelligence of Tullia that we are justified in believing that he encouraged, perhaps personally oversaw, her education.

Women also influenced Roman affairs through their children. There are too many stories of lasting affection between mothers and their children to discount their significance. And in the first century B.C., funeral orations delivered at the death of Roman matrons became common. Julius Caesar made an early impression on his fellow citizens in the oration he delivered on the occasion of his aunt's funeral in 69 B.C. Perhaps the most famous of all surviving Roman funerary tributes is the *Laudatio Turiae*, a passionate tribute by an ordinary and rather unlucky official of the late Republic to a wife who hid and fed him when he was outlawed, who defended their home against bandits, and who herself hunted the murderers of her parents to justice through the courts. Our own ideas of "matronly virtue" may be, for the Roman world, a bit stodgier than the evidence allows. As fathers were occupied in the administration of empire, mothers were the abiding presence in the home. But then the culture of Rome was built, in traditional theory, not around its forum but around its home.

Tullia had not yet achieved (perhaps she had not sought) this means of influence but Cicero was delighted when in May of 49 B.C. he could write to Atticus:

> My dear Tullia had a baby, on May 19, a seven-months' boy. She had a good delivery, which is something to be thankful for; but as for the infant, it is a puny creature. (*Ad Atticus*:X, 18, 1–2, Wilkinson trans.)

The marriage to Dolabella, though he was not the best of husbands, *was* more successful at first than Cicero had expected. Within a year, however, he confided to Atticus:

> I am frightened to death by Tullia's illness and delicate physique. But I know you are taking great care of her, and am most grateful. (*Ad Atticus*:XI, 6, 2–5, Wilkinson trans.)

Cicero had good reason to fear for his daughter's health following childbirth, so often fatal to Roman mothers. Tullia recovered, only to find that her marriage was no longer secure. To Atticus in July 47, Cicero begged:

> ...Do please give your mind to my poor girl's affairs, both about the matter I mentioned the other day, so that something may be done to keep her from destitution, and also about the will itself....Now it looks as if Dolabella were going to begin proceedings for divorce himself. (*Ad Atticus:* XI, 23, 3, Wilkinson trans.)

The fear was justified: by 46, Tullia and Dolabella were separated. Divorce was not difficult, especially for the husband: if the usual grounds of sterility, adultery, poisoning of children or counterfeiting of keys were not appropriate, other grounds would serve. Only in this case, the divorced wife would gain half of her husband's property. We do not know the details in Tullia's situation. Even if she had gained financially, she was weakened by all the recent troubles and died in 45.

Four years earlier, Cicero had written of "darling Tullia, who is more than life to me." Letters following on Tullia's death attest the genuineness of that statement. When he recovered sufficiently to make any sort of plans, his attention fixed on Tullia's memory. He wrote to Atticus in March of 45:

> In trying to escape from memories which make me eat out my heart, I am taking refuge in telling you something. Whatever you think of it, please forgive me....I am referring to the shrine to Tullia, and I hope you will give it as much thought as you have affection for me....I mean to consecrate her memory to the highest degree possible in this highly enlightened age, with every kind of memorial derived from the whole artistic achievement of Greece and Rome. (*Ad Atticus:* XII, 18, 1, Wilkinson trans.)

For a measure of his affection, we have only to contrast the tone of a letter sent to Cicero by one of the renowned jurists of the day, Servius Sulpicius, who sent his formal condolences in March of 45:

> When I was told of the death of your daughter Tullia, I was of course as grieved and upset as I was bound to be; I felt that it was my tragedy too, and if I had been there, I should have been at your side, and should have expressed my sympathy to you in person.
>
> Do try, if you will, to fix your attention on [the idea that you were born a mortal]. Lately, at one and the same time, many outstanding men perished, the Roman people suffered a crippling loss, and all our overseas possessions were shaken: are you then so distressed for the loss of the little life of one poor woman? If she had not died now, she would have had to die a few years later, since she was born mortal.
>
> Then take you your mind too off these things, and turn to thoughts worthy of your role: that she lived while life had anything to give her; that she lived as long as we were still a free people; that she saw you, her father, hold office as praetor, consul, and augur; that she was married to young men of the foremost rank; that she experienced almost every happiness; and that when the Republic was falling, she departed this life. What possible quarrel could you or she have with fortune on that score? (*Ad Familiares:* IV, 5, Wilkinson trans.)

The contrast between the tone of these last two samples returns us to the question we asked about the value of this category of evidence. What kind of evidence do letters provide? How reliable is it?

Cicero's letters are private letters; even when they deal with international or national matters, they describe one man's reaction to events and issues. Many have nothing official about them, dealing with domestic issues and the writer's own emotions. To Atticus he once commanded, "Write, if only to say that you have nothing to say!" (xii:44, 4). Many scholars have felt that Cicero reveals a heart laid bare, divulging such unworthy sentiments as conceit, timidity, and duplicity alongside the honorable qualities of patriotism, love, and industrious energy on the behalf of others. But do these sensations truly come unbidden from his heart?

An answer rests on the issue of publication: did Cicero write with an eye to many more readers than the recipients of actual individual letters? Most people write private notes to friends quite differently than they compose letters intended for publication. A letter to Atticus (xvi:5, 5) alludes to a project of publication. However, it seems almost universally agreed that publication was not Cicero's project. Certainly the collections did not appear in his own lifetime. We know, by contrast, that Cicero's great rival in the field of surviving Roman letters, Pliny the Younger, managed to get his own letters published during his lifetime.

Even so, can we find unblemished emotion in the words of this great artist of Latin prose? Some letters are chatty and colloquial, others employ artificial literary language. Often when he is writing to political figures, Cicero sprinkles the discussion with Greek words. He makes no effort to hide these affectations when he uses them, and on some occasions the only word for the thing he wants to say was a Greek one. Still, the question remains a legitimate one. Perhaps we have only a variety of literary efforts?

Perhaps, but the very mix of topics and tones in Cicero's correspondence echoes the life of a Roman citizen who was, first of all, a private citizen with his roots firmly set in a powerful family structure. Second, he was a political servant of the Roman commonwealth. Third, he was someone who had to come to terms with a vast array of foreign cultures and peoples. Variety of form and language need not mean artificiality. We might consider Cicero's letter just months before he was slain by Mark Antony:

> Do not infer, I beseech you, from these strange jests that I have ceased to care for my country. Believe me, dear friend, day and night all my thoughts and endeavours are set upon this, how to save the lives and the freedom of my countrymen. I let slip no change of warning, pleading, and planning on their behalf. And my resolve is, that if in thus watching and working I am called to lay down my life, I will count it a glorious ending.(*Ad Familiares*:IX, 24, 4)

And about Tullia's death, Cicero's grief, and the matter of the shrine—we might then hazard not too unkind a guess. Under the weight of deep and poignant emotion, he wondered on previous occasions about the survival of something divine after death in someone he truly revered. The *Somnium Scipionis*, a quiet and poetic dream at the end of his *Republic*, testifies to the depth and honesty of that train in his thought. He seems from the admission of his letters to have brooded for some weeks while staying in the little house at Astura, on the dank edge of the Pomptine marshes, on what Fowler called "the survival of the godlike element in his daughter." His Stoic teachers in Athens so many years earlier would have taught him to ask the questions. He seems to have done so, moreover, with an anguish Roman fathers did not admit to in public, and to have wished to envelop that "godlike element" in a shrine.

I wish to have a shrine built, and that wish cannot be rooted out of my heart. I am anxious to avoid any likelihood to a tomb…in order to attain as nearly as possible to an apotheosis. (*Ad Atticus*:XII, 36)

Such thoughts are made of the same spirit that impelled Cicero to educate his son Tullius so carefully, hoping that he might stay alive and out of political danger long enough to succeed his father in service to Rome. And his love of country nourished family loyalties like that to his beloved Tullia. "If Rome be well, I (and mine) are well."

FURTHER READING

The most important ancient sources for a study of Roman letters are of course books of Roman letters. See any modern edition of Cicero's letters. One such collection is *Letters of Cicero: A Selection in Translation* (trans. and ed. by L. P. Wilkinson) (New York: Norton, 1966). Plutarch's *Life of Cicero* makes excellent, if gossipy, companion reading. The letters of Pliny the Younger, a civil servant who served the empire in a variety of capacities under Trajan, make an excellent contrast. On the rule of women, J. P. V. D. Balsdon, *Roman Women: Their History and Habits* (London: Bodley Head, 1962) and Sarah Pomeroy's *Goddesses, Whores, Wives and Slaves: Women in Classical Antiquity* (New York: Schocken Books, 1975) provide informative reading. Though it is now rather old, W. Warde Fowler's *Social Life at Rome in the Age of Cicero* (New York: Macmillan, 1915) is still a very good and beautifully written overview of the era.

Chapter Eleven

We See by Their Eyes...

When we sought with the tool of psychohistory to unlock a long-dead personality, we chose Alexander the Great. The choice was an obvious one—a flamboyant leader who threw his luck and his armies against the wildest odds that nature and Persia could contrive. In the act of succeeding, he blended the landscapes and peoples of Greece, Macedon, and Persia into the patterns of a new era. What he could not do seemed, in the shadow cast by his death, almost not worth doing; what he had left unconquered hardly worth conquering—until the Romans conquered it.

They began as a handful of people dwelling in a hilltop village beside the Tiber: their hamlet was an outpost of the Latin agricultural tribes of central western Italy, stationed by the border with the more advanced, and more dangerous, Etruscans to the north. They were in fact dominated by those Etruscans, but when they had learned enough sophistication to fight like their overlords they rebelled and became an independent city. The story thereafter is one of headlong expansion—both by conquest and by colonization—first through Italy, then around the Mediterranean. They took the Greek lands on the heel of the Italian "boot," Sicily, the southern shores of Gaul and Spain and (by stages like the rise of a tide) most of the territories of the Hellenistic East. Their empire lasted more than half a thousand years and left a legacy that every later European power of grand ambition—from the Holy Roman Empire of Charlemagne to the Kaisers' Germany of the twentieth century—would feel obliged to echo, or to compare itself against.

The Romans themselves gradually recognized on how vast a canvas they were painting history. Virgil, the poet whose epic adventure the *Aeneid* marked the formal opening of their imperial era, counselled:

The Roman Empire (31 B.C. - A.D. 476)

Date A.D.	Roman Emperors	Around the Mediterranean	Artifacts & Art
31 B.C.	(27 B.C. - A.D. 14) Augustus (the first emperor) rules as *princeps*, or first citizen of Rome, followed by his stepson Tiberius. Their heirs are the Julio-Claudians (to 69). (43) Claudius extends the Empire to Britain.	(20 B.C.) Rome and Parthia agree to a common border; Augustus calls a halt to expansion. (c. 5 B.C.) Jesus Christ born in Judaea. (c. A.D. 29) The crucifixion of Christ at Jerusalem.	(c. 25 B.C. and after) Augustus attempting to restore old Roman religion and values. (19) Virgil dead; author of the Roman epic *Aeneid*.
A.D.50	(69 - 96) Age of the Flavian emperors: Vespasian, Titus, Domitian. (79) Vesuvius erupts, destroying Pompeii and Herculaneum.	(A.D. 64) Under Nero, a fire destroys much of Rome. (70) Titus takes and destroys Jerusalem.	(A.D. 64) Nero begins construction of his palatial "Golden House" below the Palatine. (80) Titus opens the Colosseum (the "Flavian Amphitheater") at Rome.
100 --	(96 - 180) The Age of the "Good Emperors": Nerva, Trajan, Hadrian, Antoninus, Marcus Aurelius. (114 - 117) Trajan attacks Parthia.	(115) Trajan captures the Parthian capital of Ctesiphon. (123) Hadrian pulls back from territory beyond the Euphrates.	(c. 100) Principal writing career of the historian Tacitus: *Agricola*, *Germania*, his *Histories* finished about 108. (c. 113) Pliny the Younger dead; publication of his letters. (c. 120) Completion of Plutarch's book of biographies. (c. 180) Marcus Aurelius: *The Meditations*.
200 --	(168) Marcus Aurelius repulses the 1st serious Germanic invasion of the Empire. (212) Caracalla extends Roman citizenship to all residents of the Empire.	(227) The Sassanid Persians take over the old Parthian Empire. (c. 250) Increasing persecution of Christians in the Empire. (259) The Sassanids capture the emperor Valerian during a failed campaign. (271) Aurelian finds it necessary to fortify Rome.	(c. 229) The Roman *Histories* of Dio Cassius published (in Greek).
300 --	(235 or earlier - 284) Period of the "Barracks Emperors": increasing disintegration, short reigns, numerous external attacks. (284 - 305) Diocletian reorganizes and defends the empire. (312 or later - 337) Constantine uses Christianity to pull the Empire together. (c. 330) Constantine moves the capital to Constantinople in the East. (360 - 363) Julian the Apostate; last pagan emperor.	(301) Diocletian freezes all wages and prices in the Empire; persecution of Christians becomes systematic (303 - 311). (312) Constantine converts to Christianity. (376) The Battle of Adrianople: Goths overwhelm and kill the emperor Valens.	(c. 335) Art treasures being removed from Athens to Constantinople. (355) Julian studying in Athens, is initiated into the Eleusinian Mysteries.
400 --	(410) Visigoths led by Alaric sack Rome. (476) Death of Romulus Augustulus, last emperor of Rome.	(438) Emperor Theodosius collects and codifies the body of Roman law.	(382) Altar of Victory removed from Senate-house in Rome. (400) Augustine writes his *Confessions*.

> But, Romans, never forget that government is your medium!
> Be this your art: to practice men in the habit of peace,
> Generosity to the conquered, and firmness against aggressors. (851–53)

In his *Fourth Eclogue*, Virgil claimed a huge victory:

> Ours is the crowning era foretold in prophecy:
> Born of Time, a great new cycle of centuries begins.
> Justice returns to earth, the Golden Age Returns,
>   and its first-born comes down from heaven above. (4–7)

Just as historians who examine the past would pay dearly to know what drove Alexander, so would they pay equally to know what fueled the drive and character of the Romans' rise to empire.

The acquisition of empire was quick and often unplanned. About the middle of the third century B.C., Rome was master of nearly one-fifth of the Italian peninsula. Little more than a century later, eastern kings were willing their states to Roman control. By the first century B.C., the scale of her successes had become so broad that Sulla fought along the southern coasts of the Black Sea, Pompey defeated the Seleucid kings of Asia, and Julius Caesar slashed northward through what is modern France. Then he tested the resistance of a still-independent Egypt.

The centripetal strain was too much. The date of 133 B.C. marks the start of a new period in Roman history, known both as the Late Republic and the century of revolution. Changed circumstances arose in every respect of life as the result of territorial expansion. No administrative base existed for the control of the rambling empire; consequently, aristocratic leadership was confirmed but actual decision making was increasingly in the hands of powerful military leaders. Sulla fought Caesar's uncle in the streets of Rome as well as kings in foreign lands. The demands of empire had created a new social order, a middle class of businessmen, while the fruits of war yielded slaves in massive numbers. Culturally, too, Rome was adapting to the influences of foreign cultures, particularly Greece. Down to 27 B.C., would-be rulers sought solutions to these developments often by fighting one another, as Marius struggled against Sulla, and Caesar fought Pompey. On the verge of one resolution, Julius Caesar was assassinated. His nearest peers would not tolerate a king in the eastern mold. And so, the civil war continued among the next generation of leaders.

Rome had been a republic but, under Caesar's adopted nephew Octavian (who ruled from 27 B.C. to A.D. 14), it emerged from its civil wars as an empire. Octavian renamed himself Augustus, defined the Empire, organized its defense, and declared "peace" upon it. It grew less rapidly as it sought to recover its balance in the first and second centuries A.D., but boundaries were expanded in the most plausible of the lands along the periphery. The south of Britain, the west fringe of Germany, and deep, shifting slices of the Near East joined the Empire, and as each became a province, were stirred to think of participating in it. "Citizenship," which had once been the most local and particular possession imaginable in the Greek world, was now held by Asians, Spaniards, and Africans who would never see a street of Rome. One and then another emperor considered extending citizenship to the whole of the realm; Caracalla made it law in the third century A.D.

But even with no more than this peripheral and civil expansion, the strain of maintaining the imperial peace—the "*Pax Romana*"—was heavy. Augustus had held power merely as "princeps" or "first citizen." His successors grew in time first to resemble great, traveling warlords, and eventually distant, semi-divine monarchs of Asia. Beyond more efficient administrative means and military force, the Romans welded the empire together by extending their culture of law, their agriculture, and their administrative cities in the west. When they found an older Greek culture already rooted in the east, they left it largely intact. The common bond came to be the cult of Rome itself and, in time, of its emperor's person.

These efforts nearly failed in the third century of our era as the empire was again wracked by civil wars and political catastrophes. Rome had twenty-five recognized rulers in fifty years, and another fifty pretenders besides. One of these managed to die a natural death. Diocletian ended this collapse into fragments only by an insuperable effort of will. He grasped, wrestled, and stabilized every corner of the empire: he, at the end of the third century, and Constantine at the beginning of the fourth, established the last semblance of balance. Each in his own way (Diocletian using Mithraic paganism and Constantine, Christianity) ruled as absolute master, not as "first citizen." Upon the laws that proceeded from their courts, they fixed rigidly the social status, the economy, the occupations, the inheritance, and the civic duties of everyone within their borders. They gripped the "peace" to their empire as though with a vise. The old confidence had ebbed.

The Roman empire went on, albeit in very different form. It had a new capital, in Constantinople—the Christian polis of Constantine—at the very eastern reach of Europe. Here, with only the memory and the name of Rome, an eastern Roman Empire would persist while its western counterpart fought, reeled, and was changed by streams of invading Goths, Huns, and Vandals. In A.D. 476, a German warlord named Odoacer took the place of the last Roman emperor in the west. The name of the last emperor rings like a knell at the end of the "classic" chapter of the Roman story. He was Romulus Augustulus, namesake of the founder and the second founder, although the "ulus" made him a "little Augustus." Tradition endured, however, in the world of Rome when all other things were dead. The span between 753 B.C. to A.D. 476 is a measure of its resilience. What manner of people held to it so tenaciously?

"THE VIEW THROUGH THEIR EYES"

The tool we have to help us in this search is one which the Romans themselves refined. Portraits had been done in many other times and places, but portraiture as an art is peculiarly Roman. It allows us, if we use care, to read in the collective mind of these lawyers and generals, shopkeepers and conquerors.

> ...when Greek art had run its course; when beauty of form had well-nigh been exhausted or begun to pall; certain artists, presumably Greeks, but working for Romans, began to produce portrait work of quite a new and wonderful sort:...beautiful portraits of ugly old men, of snub-nosed little boys...things which ought to be so ugly and yet are so beautiful. And the secret of the beauty of these...busts,...is that the beauty is quite different in kind from the beauty of Greek ideal sculpture, and obtained by quite different means.

This was the verdict in 1884 of Violet Paget, writing under the pseudonym of Vernon Lee. Her assessment focused upon several observations often expressed in discussions of Roman portraiture from the late nineteenth century to the present. She insisted most of all on the differences between Greek and Roman art when it could be considered portraiture. The Romans borrowed much from the Greeks, but what they made of the portrait was their own. She arrests the reader with words like "ugly"—making a quality or even a style of it. Some of the best examples show sly, wrinkled old men or arrogant, half-idiotic little Caesar brats. It is a realism that often insists upon, requires, and even advertises certain kinds of deformity. A distinctive mark of the Roman work, realism clearly distinguishes Roman from Greek portraiture.

A desire to show the Romans as near "actual life" as possible is a goal critical to any historian who wishes to deal in their world, not simply to historians of art. The importance goes beyond outward appearance; the realism of Roman heads reveal inner qualities, emotions. One head of Julius Caesar shows "the true reticence of genius, the touch of suffering and of isolation inseparable perhaps from greatness. The highly intellectual features are eloquent of some hidden pain, whose traces furrow the delicate mouth and chin, and bestow upon this head an austere charm" (Strong:353). Or listen to the word portrait of a head of Lucius Verus, the adoptive brother of Marcus Aurelius: "The brooding eyes and loose mouth belong to an irresponsible egoist stricken with the insanity that has held so many autocrats" (Goldsteiner: 1940, p.7 quoting G. Richter). Have we another means than psychohistory to find inner character, the very souls of these redoubtable empire builders?

The potential of this historical tool has long been recognized. Alan J. B. Wace, better known for his investigations into Bronze Age Greece, succinctly traced the clues it offers ninety years ago. The journal which carried his article ceased to be published in 1914; thus the study is neither readily available nor well known. We hoped to do a double service by reprinting it, both enlarging our historical toolkit and bringing that account within reach once again.

The Evolution of Art in Roman Portraiture
by
A. J. B. Wace

Roman portrait busts have been long neglected. Those that bear no names are passed by with silent contempt; those that have been baptized, usually quite wrongly, with the names of Emperors or other famous men are regarded merely as sentimental curiosities, and not as works of art. The object of the present paper is to attempt to point out the artistic qualities of Roman portrait busts and to trace the evolution of art in them. This would be a comparatively easy task, if we could be more or less certain of the chronological order of any considerable number of portraits. Fortunately this is possible. From the heads of the emperors on their coins especially the gold *aurei* and the large brass, we can identify busts of most of the Emperors of the first and second centuries, and some of those of the third century. We have thus a foundation for determining the style of any particular period. In this we derive great assistance from the conclusions of Bienkowski on the development of the shape of busts. He shows that the bust is small in the republican period and gradually grows larger during the empire. Accordingly we may divide the development of the bust into the following periods.

(1). Republican, Augustan and Julio-Claudian [i.e. through 54 A.D.]: the bust just includes the collar bone and the parts around it. Naturally in the later period the bust grows slightly larger.
(2). Neronian, and Flavian [54–96 A.D.]: the bust includes the edges of the shoulders and of the breast.
(3). Trajanic [98–117 A.D.]: the bust includes the armpits.
(4). Hadrianic [117–138 A.D.]: the bust includes the whole shoulder with a small part of the upper arm.
(5). Antonine and Aurelian [138–192 A.D.]: the bust includes most of the upper arm.
(6). Third century: all shapes are in use, but the most characteristic shapes are the large busts with the right arm, or half-figures.

This classification of the bust-shapes coupled with the study of style founded on Imperial portraits is of the highest importance in enabling us to arrange chronologically nameless private portraits.

Next, as regards female portraits, the coins of the Empresses enable us to see clearly in what order the different fashions of hairdressing succeeded one another. Two additional points should be observed. The eyes up to the Hadrianic period are usually quite plain. Occasionally they are rendered plastically by a simple, incised semicircle, or rarely by a dot within a diamond. From the time of Hadrian—occasionally in his time the eyes are plain—the eye is always represented plastically by two drill holes within a semicircle. Lastly, as regards male busts, we may note how the fashion of wearing a beard changed, though it must always be remembered that members of the lower and middle classes were probably always bearded, and at least never strictly followed the court fashion. From the Republican times to the Trajanic period it was the fashion to be clean shaven; from Hadrian to Diocletian with the sole exception of Valerian, the emperors are bearded; then Constantine again started the fashion of being clean-shaven.

Republican Period till 30 B.C.

It is well known that in the Republican period it was the custom for Romans to keep in their houses portraits in wax of famous ancestors, which were paraded at funerals. The possession of such portraits indicated noble descent, and the *ius imaginum* or right to own them, was jealously guarded. These waxen portraits were doubtless painted to increase their likeness to the deceased. These are of course the predecessors of the marble busts, which we intend to discuss in this paper. It is only natural to assume that, when the Romans first began to make portraits in marble, they should imitate the waxen technique. Consequently we can clearly distinguish a waxen style in the earlier republican portraits. In such heads every line, every detail of the face is rendered in a smooth, even manner, which suggests a cast taken direct from the living model, as no doubt wax busts were usually made. In this waxen style we can trace one distinct development. The artist in working in marble

FIGURE 11–1 Busts. A Roman upholds the honor of his forefathers by carrying their busts in a funeral procession. These, and the accumulated wisdom they represented, were also prominent features of the inner rooms of a Roman home. Respect for a straightforward sort of virtue set the tone for these busts, and created much of the honesty in early Roman portraiture. (First Century B.C., Museo Barbarini, Rome)

in his anxiety to render faithfully every detail of the face makes all the lines hard. The hair, which in the earlier busts is merely a slightly raised and roughened surface to be completed by paint, is in the later scratched in with firm chisel strokes. The resulting style is stern, unyielding and wooden: an exact facial likeness has been obtained, but by the sacrifice of all naturalism and all feeling for texture. Just at the end of the Republican period, as far as we can judge, this style ripens into a very good school of portraiture. These busts are noted for excellent characterization, faithfulness in detail and a fine sense in rendering fleshy surfaces. An air of marked distinction is recognizable, and the bust ceases to be a mere block of marble and begins to live. One of the finest examples of this style...is a faithful and a natural likeness. In character it is humorous and genial, tempered with a certain severity. Also of the period is the group...nicknamed Cato and Portia. The male figure is from stylistic reasons undoubtedly of this time, and thus we can decide the character of a female portrait of the time, and, what is more important, the fashion of doing the hair. We see that this lady parted her hair carefully in the centre and drew it straightly along the sides above the ears to a knob at the back of the neck. Having thus once obtained a date for this fashion of doing the hair, we can place in the same period other busts and so enlarge our knowledge of female portraiture of the republican period. Such busts as we can thus add, shew the style already described, but are not good examples of it: and speaking generally one finds throughout the Roman female portraits are less well executed than the male busts.

Augustan Period 30 B.C.–14 A.D.

We have seen that art in Roman portraiture had just begun to live. It is at once killed by the cold, Hellenic classicism of the Augustan age. Augustus wished to

FIGURE 11–2   Business Family. This family portrait shows a hard-working corn merchant named Ampudias with his equally diligent (and weary) wife and daughter on either side. Roman sculpture did not limit its keen eye to the "fathers" of the senate or the movers of the empire. (British Museum, London)

revive Rome by Greek civilization. Thus Greek art and literature were forced on the Western world. Augustus, as the apostle of Hellenism, is the Alexander of the West. The effect of this is at once apparent in the portraits of Augustus. Cold idealism replaces warm naturalism, the fresh handling of the flesh gives way to classical severity. The eyes stare vacantly, the hair lacks all character, and the academic treatment of the features robs them of all individuality. These characteristics are present also in the private portraits of the period: and we recognize them again in female busts which from the similarity of their hairdress to coins of members of the Julian house must be of this period. This fashion is evolved from the preceding one. The hair is parted in the centre, drawn with slight waves to the back of the neck where it is fastened in a twisted loop.

Julio-Claudian Period, 14–54 A.D.

The spirit of Greek classicism was too dead and academic to exert any prolonged influence on Roman art. We see in the portraits of Tiberius [A.D. 14–37] and members of his family that the Roman feeling for naturalism is working under the veneer of Greek art. In such busts as a rule the hair and eyes remain Greek in character, while the mouth and chin from the closeness of the modelling betray the Roman spirit. Eventually, after a period of transition in which both styles appear together in the same portrait as described, the Roman spirit emerges triumphant. Thus in the portraits of the time of Claudius [41–54 A.D.], the Roman desire for an accurate rendering of every feature, for precision in modelling, for truth in detail is dominant. Portraits of this period are remarkable for the uncompromising faithfulness with which the artist reproduces all, even unpleasant features. Such portraits seem like accurate maps, plotted out with unremitting care and with all the contouring properly indicated. The technical skill of the artist enables him to give distinction to such heads, but he has no inspiration, and they lack life.

Much the same style is to be observed in the female portraits of the period, though the female face from its softness lends itself less readily to such treatment. In the dressing of the hair we note an advance. The general scheme is the same, but over the forehead a few curls make their appearance in the front hair. Occasionally the long curls hang down behind the ears.

Neronian Period 54–68 A.D.

In this brief time of transition the same style of portraiture is followed, but a sense of spirit or of life is begun to be imparted to the bust. This is finely illustrated by one of the few authentic portraits of Nero.... The features are still accurately plotted out, but are less mechanical, and begin to shew life. In the female busts we note the same tendency, which paves the way for the triumph of portraiture under the Flavian dynasty. In the coiffure the same fashion is followed, but the curls over the forehead increase in number, and are rather heaped up. A curious fashion of this period is shown in some heads, in which the hair is arranged in rows of ribbon-like little curls over the forehead.

Flavian Period 69–96 A.D.

Under the Flavian emperors art in Roman portraiture reaches its highest point. The style of the Neronian period ripens, and the result is exceedingly living and natural. This is well illustrated by a fine Vespasian [example where] we see the style is simple and unpretentious; there is great technical skill, but no *bravura* or artistic trickery. All details are present, but rendered smoothly and naturally. And above all these busts actually live. The artist in his inspiration has known how to endow his work with life. His inspired eye caught a momentary expression that entirely characterized his subject, and his marvelous skill has rendered it in marble that seems to live. We are told that Greek art is Poetry, and that Roman art is Prose; If that be true, this Flavian art is the very finest Prose that man could ever make and far more deserving of study and admiration than much of that Poetic Greek art.

Female portraits of this period do not show quite the same high standard as the male portraits. Still here are two very excellent examples.... In them the same perfect living style is at once distinguished. As regards the hair, a new fashion has come into use. The curls over the forehead are built up into a *toupet*, and the back hair is braided into many plaits, which either hang in loops on the back, or are coiled in a knob at the back of the crown. This is the court fashion, but amongst other classes another fashion prevailed, the hair in front, instead of being in a *toupet*, was smoothly parted in the centre and carried away to the sides with grooved undulations, having obviously been crimped up with tongs.

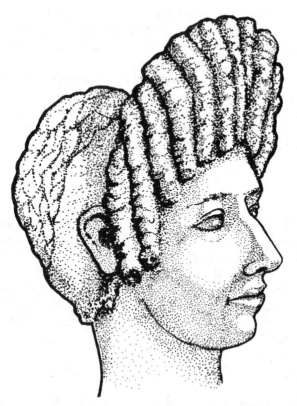

FIGURE 11–3 Julia. Roman realism meant that even such transitory details as a current hairstyle were captured along with the face and expression of the wearer. Greek busts though they show subtle changes in style, give a much stronger impression of timelessness. Here we see what may be Julia, daughter of the popular emperor Titus, as she holds her head (and her curls) high. (Capitoline Museum, Rome)

Trajanic period, 96–117 A.D.

In this period art instead of advancing still further is at a standstill and in some respects declines. If we examine the portraits of Trajan, we observe the same brilliant execution as in the Flavian busts, but a life-like, natural rendering is lacking. We remark a hard, serious style such as perhaps befits this military age, but there is no spirit, no life. There is none of the map-like accuracy of the Julio-Claudian period: all is well and naturally modelled, although a trifle hard in line. The style lacks what we might call atmosphere, and the portrait remains cold, frozen and spiritless. The female portraits of the period are similar in style, and all possess a cold, forbidding appearance, which in some cases does not suit the sentimental pose of the head. The coiffure is a development of the Flavian. The back hair is plaited as before; the *toupet* in front remains a mass of curls or becomes two or more rows of carefully arranged curls rising one above the other. Probably a frame work of some kind, or combs were used in making these erections.

Hadrianic and Antonine Periods, 117–161 A.D.

Hadrian was the first Emperor to wear a beard and thus of course started a fashion. Also he was a dilettante in art without apparently having any real taste for it. This, as natural, influenced the art of portraiture in his times. When we study his portraits, we at once remark a certain Greek feeling. There is a distinct attempt to purify the individual type without generalizing it, and to show the man as he should be and not as he is. It is a peculiar spirit of idealism which we find best illustrated in the heads of Antinous. In these a sulky, spoilt expression is evident and in spite of all divine idealism the individual character is still obvious. The same character is seen in private portraits of the period, of which some are signed by Greek artists.

The portraits which, if conjecture is right, represent Sabina, Hadrian's wife, show the same idealistic treatment. The heads suggest a rather weak attempt at representing a goddess. They may possibly be meant to show Sabina as deified after death. Sabina, to judge from the coins, first used the Trajanic fashion of hairdressing, and then adopted the rather Greek style shown by the heads mentioned. The hair is parted in the centre, waved down the sides to the back, where it is twisted in a knob. Faustina, the wife of Antoninus Pius, started a rather different fashion. She also abandoned the Trajanic *toupet,* at the back made it into a large plait which was coiled on the top of her head. Her busts and other female portraits of the time shew the same tendency as the male portraits. In the reign of Antoninus the Greek influence was still felt, but weakly. The artist retained his technical skill, and set himself a new problem to work out. He modelled the face well, but without any life: the result is accurate, but dull; it lacks inspiration. Instead an attempt is made, by rendering the hair more loosely and using the drill to work it, to emphasize the difference in texture between hair and skin. Consequently the face is polished to some extent.

Aurelian Period, and reign of Septimius Severus. 161–193, 193–211 A.D.

Under Marcus Aurelius and Commodus the style, whose beginning is seen in the Antonine age, continues and develops. From being as at first, a mere attempt to indicate the difference in texture between hair and skin, it becomes a serious effort to realize in sculpture the pictorial effects of light and shadow obtainable in painting. Its aim is "colouristic". The face is smooth, though well modelled, and carefully polished. The curling masses of hair are honeycombed by the drill. Thus the face remains white, or of a pale flesh tint, while the drill-holes in the hair create shadow and thus produce a distinct effect of colour, while still emphasizing the different texture. This is well seen in the portraits of Marcus Aurelius....Under Septimius Severus the "Colouristic" principle is still followed. The face is more carefully rendered, and rather less natural, while the hair with its innumerable drill holes, though effective at a distance, is intolerable when looked at closely.

The female portraits of this period shew another change in the fashion of hair-dressing....The hair was parted in the centre, waved away to the sides with grooved undulations, and at the back fastened in a knob. This is a slight development of the Antonine fashion.

Under Septimius Severus the hair in front was still done in the same manner. It was however carried further down the neck behind, sometimes covering the ears, then twisted into a roll each side; and of these rolls a kind of nest was made.

Naturally from the way the hair is dressed it is almost impossible to work it on the "colouristic" principle. Consequently we find a new method adopted with apparently the same purpose. The hair is rendered by frequent fine lines which cause slight shadow and give some slight colour effect. But this is not very successful from its smooth, even appearance. One point noticeable in the female busts of the time of Septimius Severus is that since the fashion changed frequently, the hair is removable so that as the fashion changed, a fresh top to the head could be made and set on, in order that the lady should always be in the fashion.

Early Third Century, 211–253 A.D.

In this period, the "colouristic" principle is still the artist's chief idea, but he adopts different methods to attain his end. Instead of drilling the hair deeply, he represents it and the beard as being very short, and either blocks them out roughly, as a mass of small, tight curls, or scratches them in with pick-strokes of his chisel over a roughened surface. This method is equally effective; the fine, frequent strokes arrest light and create shadow, so producing the desired colour effect which is heightened by the smooth, polished treatment of the face. This style first appears in male portraits in the young heads of Caracalla; thus we have to consider the time of Septimius Severus as the real period of transition.... It is to be noticed that at first the hair is longer and more curly.... Later it becomes shorter and less rough, the pick-strokes are carefully arranged, so as to give the appearance of carefully brushed hair. All through this style the face is carefully modelled, and accurately rendered, often with great distinction and spirit. Eventually this style of portraiture reaches its high point in the superb bust of Philippus Arabus.... Here we find vivid characterization, and sympathetic rendering coupled with the practice of the "colouristic" effect. The effect is marvelous, and would be perfect, but for the unnatural rendering of the hair, not as hair, but as a rough, coloured surface. A private portrait of the period...shows us how effective is this style even for commonplace subjects....

In female portraits the same style is remarked; it is of course a direct continuation of that of the Aurelian period.

Some splendid, most realistic portraits remain to shew us that the female busts reached the same height as the male. In hair-dressing the fashion of the time of Septimius Severus was at first followed, with occasional variations, such as loose curls handing behind the ears. Later a new fashion was adopted.... The hair in front is treated in exactly the same manner as before; but behind, the twisted rolls are plaited together and carried forward up the head over the crown in a broad, flat band. This fashion lasted till the time of Gallienus, and after that period we have no further trustworthy evidence as to the fashions of hair dressing.

Gallienic Period 253–268 A.D.

In this period it seems to have been the fashion for men to wear their hair longer. This when copied in a portrait makes the head look more natural, and this additional touch with the impressionistic effect of the "colouristic" style succeed

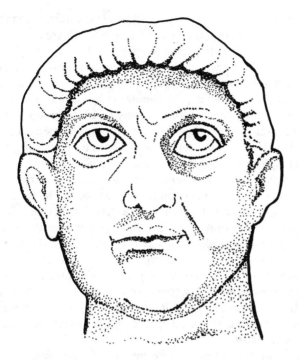

FIGURE 11–4 Constantine. This famous portrait of Constantine not only shows the rough impressionism of the late Empire, but also the enormously muscular and stolid image required of emperors of that age. They promised to protect an increasingly fragmented and threatened culture. The face has become almost an icon for strength; it recalls more of the lion or bull on Croesus' coins than the portraits of the Roman Republic. (Basilica of Maxentius, Palazzo del Conservatori, Rome)

in producing a remarkable series of portraits. To adopt the language of painting, we can say that in the previous period the hair has been rendered by "touches"; in this period we find it treated in a broad, sweeping manner. The result of this style is to produce a fine impressionistic portrait broadly handled, and in its best productions it almost succeeded in giving them a living spirit; and there is no straining of naturalism.

...The true Gallienic impressionism is to be remarked in portraits of Gallienus and the many excellent private busts of his time.... Female portraits of this period are rare; one, which is possibly Salvina, the wife of Gallienus, is a good example of the impressionism already described, its coiffure is of course similar to that of the latest examples of the last period.

Late Third Century and Constantinian Period 268–305, 305–337 A.D.

Portraits of these periods are not common.... A brief examination at once shows us that portraiture has gone back to the pre-Gallienic style. There is the short beard and hair worked on the "colouristic" principle; and in general these heads shew the rough and ready impressionism common in the second-rate portraits of the pre-Gallienic period. But there is yet a further quality in these portraits. The head is set squarely on the shoulders, and turns but little to right or left; and the face looks solidly before it in a monumental manner. This we may call the principle of "frontality", which in the ensuing period of decadence dominates and preserves art.

This principle of "frontality" becomes more marked in the Constantinian age. The head is set perfectly rigid: it is not turned even the smallest degree to right or left. Of this the portraits of Constantine are good examples.... This "frontality" gives to the head a very solid character. The firm, unbroken lines enable the eye to travel all around, from whatever point it is viewed. To adopt Riegl's phraseology the head possesses "cubical individuality." [A. Riegl, *Spatromische Kunstindustrie*, 1901.] Up to this period for all the idea of solidity it conveys, any portrait in marble differs but little from a painting on a flat surface. The head presents only one side at a time to the spectator, and that side always seems flat. However good the modelling, there is no sufficient conception of distance between, for example, the nose and ears. The portrait hitherto has been a painting in the round; the Constantinian portrait first shows the true solidity, the perfect roundness that sculpture should aim at....

It is not to be imagined that the artist had this subtle principle before him. His aim was to produce sculpture, and owing to the fact that mastery over his material had partly left him, he unconsciously made this discovery. And it is a discovery that has been left unnoticed; no subsequent art had made any use of it. Beauty is of course to some extent lacking in this style: we may say it is monumental, or to again adopt Riegl's phraseology, "crystalline."... In [one] colossal head we see how well this style suits monumental sculpture. Also in spite of the crystalline beauty we can discern indications of good modelling in the face; all combines to characterize the subject for us as a proud, self-confident youth.

Henceforward there is no Roman portraiture for us to follow; Roman art is merged in Byzantine. We can trace the principle of "cubical" style and "crystalline" beauty in Byzantine art. It is dominant in the mosaics of Justinian and Theodora at Ravenna; it is to be traced in many mosaics in Roman churches, and survives in the ninth century in mosaics.... From Byzantine art in turn we can trace the beginning of Italian painting, and thus obtain an idea of the continuity of art. Art is by its nature continuous in its evolution. It has good periods and decadent periods. But the former should not be studied for their relative beauty, nor the latter condemned for their inferiority. The true art-critic must study both for the history of art, and never lose sight of the whole field even when confining his attentions to the best part. Thus we are enabled to see how from age to age, from style to style, was the torch of art handed on, though often burning dimly, that finally we might in our turn hold it, worship it, and hand it on.

For historians, art must be a usable tool, not just an end in itself. We might amend Wace's conclusion to ask whether studying art's nature and evolution gives us any insight into the subjects it portrays. Wace stressed continuity: from the earliest examples of portraits, we note an attempt to render every detail faithfully, even to reveal the subject's interior psychology. The question is whether historians can treat the result with any confidence. How reliable are the things we learn (or seem to learn) from portraits in the Roman style? Are there any cautions?

First of all, it is vital to remember that Roman art, like the Roman Empire itself, is a medley of inheritances. As the empire expanded to incorporate the Mediterranean orb and fair chunks of Europe, Asia Minor, Africa, and the Near East, it came into contact with a variety of well-established artistic traditions. Romans discovered art in classical Greek styles as they encountered the old Greek cities of Southern Italy and Sicily. They found it, even by the accounts of the conservatives, appealing. So the idealized, generalized likenesses familiar from Classical Greece are found in the world of Rome as well. Augustus Caesar, as Wace noted, is often portrayed in Hellenic fashion, perhaps echoing a conscious revival of Greek ideas sometimes attributed to him. Roman sculptors were also well schooled in art styles of Hellenistic Greek; Alexander and his successors provided a fund of material upon which the younger imperial world could draw. Sculptors combined the heroic types of great men and women wielding power and wealth with those individual distinctions of inner character that Romans looked for in a face. Any Roman who wished to imitate Alexander might be shown in the same variety of forms that were used to depict the Macedonian conqueror.

From the Egyptian portion of the Hellenistic world came a love for minute detail; from the Levant, a spiritual intensity that was reflected in sculpture as well as in text. Celtic traditions ran into the Roman stream with the expansion into western and northern Europe. We might, before we made this list exhaustive, include every culture the Romans touched with their imperial scheme. And every one of these rivulets flowed with its own artistic and social characteristics into the mainstream that was called *Romanitas*. Each brought some genuine values from its own culture. How do we distinguish the truly Roman from the admixture?

Rome's literary records will help. They are full of descriptions of the virtues that Romans sought to embody: gravity, dignity, respect for custom, discipline, and strength of hard work. These same qualities are apparent in the "realistic" portraits of its leading statesmen and their families. Taken together they form the set of qualities found in the effigies displayed by families on occasions when they celebrated their heritage. Busts of Romans lower in social class show the same characteristics. But is this realism? Perhaps it is a kind of corporate propaganda, meant to instill the obedience of Romans and subjects alike to an ideal?

Certainly propaganda makes itself felt at a great many points. The emperor Nero wanted to impress his world—those contemporaries who left accounts of him make that almost pathetically clear. He had a statue 120 feet high made of himself. Imperial portraits of the late empire, done of men who were struggling against massive problems, emphasize a stern, military remoteness. They seem distanced, ceremonial. In a somewhat lighter vein, the Roman writer Lucian noted that Roman ladies insisted upon flattery in portraits of themselves.

Passing fancies, too, temper portraits. Portraits fashioned during the Antonine period of the second century A.D. offer us some hair styles that are quite amazing while in other periods severity of hair styling is preferred. The emperor Hadrian began a fashion for beards, which then find their way into portrait sculpture. The carved faces of the third century A.D. show so many brooding, doubtful countenances that one suspects a fashionable pose as much as a reflection of real, particular worries.

Artistic technique also shapes the nature of portraits. During the reign of Hadrian, for example, the habit of incising eyes, already practiced on bronze sculptures and on gem cuttings, made its way to marble sculpture. No longer are the eyes of statues sightless and staring but rather they are sharply piercing, alive. During the second century A.D., too, sculptors learned how to reproduce the texture of the skin, giving it a greater naturalism. Some artists were innovators, others more conservative; some were especially gifted, others were not.

Other practices affect our judgment of realism. Many statues were made decades after the death of a person. No death masks were available for the fashioning of Alexander, Sulla, and Hannibal that Caracalla commissioned in the early third century A.D. It is not unusual to find mismatched heads and bodies and, in a number of cases, realistic-appearing faces look out from conventional, stereotypic bodies. There are examples as well of refurbished or recarved statues. Where is the realism in a form originally intended to portray a Roman emperor of the first century that has been remade into the semblance of a fourth century Roman emperor?

And, finally, there is the debate over the meaning of the terms *real* and *ideal* in art. To return to Violet Paget (Vernon Lee), they are "handy terms" at the center of "one of the tangled questions of art-philosophy." Let us follow her own demonstration of the tangle:

> All art is decorative, ornamental, idealistic therefore, since it consciously or unconsciously aims, not merely at reproducing the already existing, but at producing something which shall repay the looking at it, something which shall ornament, if not a place, at least our lives; and such making of the ornamental, of the worth looking at, necessarily implies selection and arrangement—that is to say, idealism. At the same time, while art aims definitely at being in this sense decorative, art may very possibly aim more immediately at merely reproducing, without selection or arrangement, the actually existing things of the world; and this in order to obtain the mere power of representation. In short, art which is idealistic as a master will yet be realistic as a scholar: it decorates when it achieves, it copies when it studies. (3–4)

How can we judge whether an individual artist intended to reproduce or whether he hoped to achieve something worth looking at?

With all these limitations, do we truly sense the immediate presence of the person portrayed, or are we simply swept up, deceptively, in the technique of artists who were drawing, consciously and unconsciously, on a great many varied traditions? Is this Julius Caesar or simply the visage of a man created by a talented artist who had a good many tricks at his grasp and who was constrained only by the societal demand for appropriate characteristics?

We must be cautious, certainly, but it is not necessary to deny all likelihood of understanding the Romans more fully through these portraits. In the earlier examples, especially, we often look on the true face of the individual portrayed. With their fondness for respect for tradition, the Romans collected family statues preserving the likeness of their ancestors. The likenesses were formed from wax masks taken from the very face of the recently deceased. To create a more durable form, bronze casts were then made from the wax molds. The structure of the face was thus reproduced. In the second and first centuries B.C., marble busts also served as funerary portraits. Sculpted rather than cast from molds, these busts did not permit the same exact fidelity that could be gained from wax masks. But if we study the differences between these busts, noticing features like bags under the eyes, crows' feet wrinkles, excessively thin or overly thick lips, and double chins, we can appreciate the continued desire for the true representation with which Roman portraiture began.

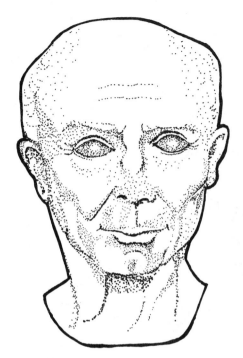

FIGURE 11–5 Waxen Style Image. Roman death bust, carved following a waxen death mask. Romans valued actuality over flattery even in the memory of ancestors they were brought up to revere. It is probably not possible to think from "inside" the Roman mindset until one can find faces like these, or those of Ampudias' family, honestly beautiful. (Rhode Island School of Design)

But what shall we say about the "foreign" influences that captivated the Romans as they expanded around the Mediterranean? Did not Greek influence turn Roman portraiture in the direction of idealism? Yes, it did. The Romans delighted in Greek sculpture and sculptors. Indeed, they transported whole shiploads of Greek work to Italy where these idealizing forms decorated gardens, atriums of homes, and even public places. But the imported sculptures did not replace the Roman tradition; the two coexisted. And even when it is difficult to separate the two traditions, the combined product discloses a good bit about Roman taste. The Romans were selective in their borrowing, telling us, in turn, what appealed to their collective taste and what did not. Let us return to the difference found in portraits of Julius Caesar and Augustus. Examples of the former tend toward verism, even when features are unattractive: sunken cheeks, a bulge in the center of the forehead, crows' feet wrinkles, and an asymmetrical skull. By contrast, many of the representations of Augustus show the simplicity of classical Greek form. Lines of the mouth and hair are beautifully elegant but quite like others of similar type. It is instructive that Julius Caesar refused the crown of kingship unfamiliar to the Romans but entrenched in the Hellenistic East. Augustus, on the other hand, allowed—perhaps encouraged—a ruler cult devoted to Rome and himself, another practice of the Hellenistic kingdoms. In other words, coming to terms with their Greek inheritance was not a simple issue for the Romans, a fact of considerable importance to historians.

Equally revealing are the qualities that mark so many portraits of patricians and ordinary Romans alike. Such qualities as discipline, resolution, respect for tradition, loyalty to family, and attention to duty found their way into portraits because they molded Roman success. The

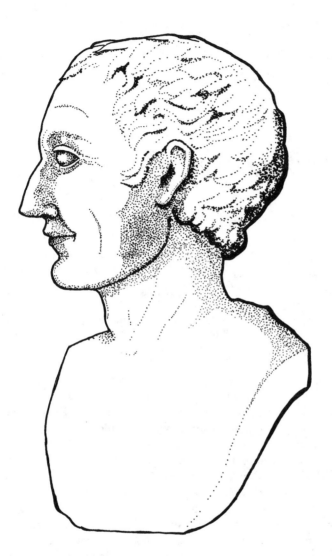

FIGURE 11–6 Caesar. Fame, success, or even a grip on the highest power in the state did not mean a Roman could demand a flattering portrait. Caesar at the height of his career still appeared in stone much as any Roman might, with blemishes, marks of age, and the plain scarring of his wounds. (Naples Museum)

ordinary Roman experienced these qualities in his leaders—on the field of battle, in the forum, and in dealings with others. These virtues made for success; they should be emulated. If we hope to understand the Romans' success in fashioning their empire, we are well advised to look to the character that impelled them, a character that lives in their portraits.

But these are not the only qualities in the faces. After the confident realism of the Republic, many examples from the first and second centuries A.D.—especially portraits of rulers and their families—show the old tendency toward types again. The preference for illusion increases under the Flavian emperors (A.D. 69–96), and, in the second century A.D., a wealth of change finds its way into portraits. Third-century portraits are dogged by worry—the eyes sometimes unfocused, the brows furrowed, the mouths stern. As the third century passes into the fourth, sternness turns to rigid, unapproachable grandeur. This course has its parallels

FIGURE 11–7 Augustus. Augustus carried into his new era a Rome exhausted and horrified by a century of bloodletting. The calm, almost supernatural Hellenizing of his official portraits—full of clarity and quiet in a troubled world, full of health, though he was himself tired—helped reassure the empire that something like normal life was possible again. (Boston Museum of Fine Arts)

in the survey of Roman history with which we began this chapter, every phase of portraiture echoing the spread, and strain, and ultimately the troubled transformation of the empire. Those efforts, largely successful for a time, to standardize and unify the conglomerate out of which the empire had been built, gave in the second century an earnestness to the faces the sculptors carved. That unity, which almost disappeared in the chaos of the third century, was restored by the grip of the iron-willed absolutist monarchy. The late third and fourth centuries harden the eyes, thicken the necks, and muscle the faces of the imperial protectors they portray. Had we known nothing of the history, the portraits would have suggested it to us, and supplied much of flavor and detail.

There are some basic traits that persist in the carved faces from the early Republic through the last days of the Empire. We might justly infer from their portraiture that Romans as a people did not shrink from reality, that they possessed a deep resolve and will to work that marked their demeanors, that they seldom relaxed their guard even for a smile. These were the traits on which they built an empire, and we are haunted by an uncanny sense that we have experienced these traits at first hand. We *have* seen them, in their eyes.

FURTHER READING

The best way to study Roman portraits is by looking at them, as actual objects, *not* photographs. If this course is not practical, discussions of portraiture usually have numerous, good illustrations. The oversized illustrations in Ludwig Goldscheider, *Roman Portraits* (New York: Oxford University Press, 1940) provide fine detail. Two older, standard texts are A. Hekler, *Greek and Roman Portraits* (New York: G. P. Putnam's Sons, 1912) and E. Strong, *Roman Sculpture*, 2 Vols. (London and New York: Duckworth and Scribners, 1907). More recently, J. M. C. Toynbee has written extensively on Roman portraiture: see *Roman Historical Portraits* (London: Thames and Hudson, 1978). *Roman Portraits: Aspects of Self and Society,* which accompanied an exhibition of Roman portraits, is a sensitive treatment of specific examples shown in a 1980 exhibition. It was published in that year through The J. Paul Getty Museum and the Regents of the University of California.

Chapter Twelve

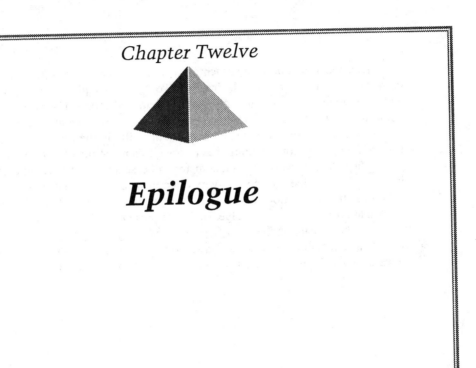

Epilogue

"Out of olde feldes as men seith
Cometh at this newe corn."
—Chaucer

At the outset of *Decoding Ancient History*, we painted a rather dour picture of the road ahead—a trail rather than a paved road, uncertain and twisting, with only a potsherd here and the scraps of an oral memory there as clues to what happened along the wayside long ago. But we did not intend to warn off would-be travelers. We hope that some readers, as they have progressed by case studies through ancient Western Europe and Mesopotamia to Mycenae, Lydia, Greece, Macedon, and Rome, have caught the excitement of this journey. A historian without an easy wealth of ancient written narrative is really no worse off than those real detectives who have no film producers to provide them with a convenient flood of confessions in the closing minutes of a case. Clues remain, but it takes a command like Hercule Poirot's of "zee lettle gray cells" to find them and to read their meaning. And even when ancient narrative exists, whether in the enigmatic symbols on the earliest coins, or in the commentary of a comic mind, or in the very personal revelations of a Roman writing a private letter, it is likely that the sleuth trained to be careful will make the fewest mistakes.

We have hoped by providing this toolkit (there are other tools of course, and yet other uses for those found here) to whet appetites, to pique curiosities about the freshness that remains in so many of the ancient world's mysteries. The clues about Nestor, or the scrawny little farm that inspired Hesiod, are still collecting as this book is written, still stubbornly resisting a neat solution, but waiting perhaps for a new eye to spot the pattern, as Ventris spotted those Greek words lurking behind Linear B.

Alexander conquered a stretch of the ancient world so vast that the shadow of his deed took centuries to die, but the jury is still out on the simplest questions of his character and motivation. The true figure of Socrates seems to become mistier not more distinct as books appear every year explaining or condemning that enigmatic Athenian in great and confident detail. Are those really the bones of Philip in the tomb at Vergina? Are those truly Mycenaeans moving along the shadowed shores in the oldest lines of Homer?

The detective work of ancient history, in case a reader has caught a yen to explore it a little further, does not consist very often in spectacular final-moment discoveries or solutions. Its satisfaction lies rather in that somewhat old-fashioned confidence of all workmanlike researchers that clues to past or present, if collected carefully, if faced with honesty, skepticism, and respect, will gradually begin to give up portions of their real story. Ancient history provides test cases unusually rich and complex and exciting. It still rewards, sometimes even startles, those who know and use their tools.

References

Adams, W. L.

1980 "The Royal Macedonian Tomb at Vergina: An Historical Interpretation." *Ancient World* 3: 67–72.

Andronikos, Manolis

1978 *The Royal Graves at Vergina.* Athens.

1978b "The Royal Tomb of Philip II." Archaeology 31, 33–41.

Bailey, G.

1984, 1985, 1986, 1987, 1988 Report on season's work in *Archaeological Reports* 1983–1984: 40–42; 1984–1985: 38–39; 1985–1986: 52–54; 1986–1987: 29–31; 1987–1988: 40–41.

Barr-Sharrar, B., and E. N. Borza, eds.

1982 *Macedonia and Greece in Late Classical and Early Hellenistic Times. Studies in the History of Art* 10. Washington, DC. National Gallery of Art.

Bengtson, Hermann

1970 *Introduction to Ancient History* (English trans.) Berkeley and Los Angeles. University of California Press.

Bintliff, J., and A. Snodgrass

1986 Report on season's work in *Archaeological Reports* 1985–1986. Hertford, England: Stephen Austin and Sons, Ltd.

Blegen, C. W.

1957 "The Palace of Nestor Excavations of 1956." *American Journal of Archaeology* 61: 129–35.

Borza, Eugene

1987   "The Royal Macedonian Tombs and the Paraphernalia of Alexander the Great." *Phoenix 41: 105–21.*

Bradeen, Donald

1947   "The Lelantine War and Pheidon of Argos" in *Transactions of the American Philological Association* 78: 223–41.

Burn, A. R.

1936 and 1966   *The World of Hesiod* (2d ed.). New York: B. Blom.

Bury, J. B.

1927 and 1935   "The Age of Illumination," Chapter 13 in *The Cambridge Ancient History*: 376–97. Cambridge: Cambridge University Press.

Chadwick, John

1958 and 1967   *The Decipherment of Linear B.* Cambridge: Cambridge University Press.

Chatwin, Bruce

1987   *The Songlines.* New York: Viking.

Cherry, John

1983   "Frogs Round the Pond: Perspectives on Current Archaeological Survey Projects in the Mediterranean Region" in Keller and Rupp, *Archaeological Survey in the Mediterranean Area.* Oxford: British Archaeological Reports.

Clark, L. Pierce

1923   "The Narcism of Alexander the Great." *Psychoanalytic Review* 10: 56–69.

Cocks, Geoffrey, and Travis L. Crosby

1987   *Psychohistory: Readings in the Method of Psychology, Psychoanalysis, and History.* New Haven and London: Yale University Press.

Crawford, Michael

1983   "Numismatics," Chapter 4 in *Sources for Ancient History.* Cambridge: Cambridge University Press.

Crossland, John, and Diana Constance

1982   *Macedonian Greece.* London: B. T. Batsford.

Daniel, Glyn

1968   *The Origins and Growth of Archaeology.* New York: Crowell.

Daniel, Glyn, and Colin Renfrew

1988   *The Idea of Prehistory* (2d ed.). Edinburgh: Edinburgh University Press.

de Lumley, Henry

1969   "A Paleolithic Camp at Nice." *Scientific American*, May: 42–50.

de Romilly, Jacqueline

1985   *A Short History of Greek Literature* (trans. L. Doherty). Chicago: University of Chicago Press.

Dow, Sterling

1968   "Literacy: The Palace Bureaucracies, The Dark Age, Homer" in *A Land Called Crete*: 109–47. Northampton, MA: Smith College.

Ehrenberg, Victor
1968 and 1973 *From Solon to Socrates*. London and Bungay, Suffolk: Methuen.
1938 *Alexander and the Greeks*. Oxford: Blackwell.

Ellis, J. R.
1976 *Philip II and Macedonian Imperialism*. London: Thames and Hudson.

Friedländer, Saul
1978 *History and Psychoanalysis* (English trans. Susan Suleiman. New York and London: Holmes and Meier.

Gardner, Percy
1918 *A History of Ancient Coinage 700–300 B.C..* Oxford: Clarendon Press.

Garlan, Yvon
1988 *Slavery in Ancient Greece* (rev. ed.). Ithaca: Cornell University Press.

Goody, Jack
1977 *The Domestication of the Savage Mind*. Cambridge: Cambridge University Press.

Hammond, N. G. L.
1978 "Philip's Tomb in Historical Context," *Greek Roman and Byzantine Studies* 19 , 331–50.
1972 *A History of Macedonia, I*. Oxford: Oxford University Press.

Harris, Ramon
1968 "The Dilemma of Alexander the Great." *Proceedings of the African Classical Association* 11: 46–54; reprinted in Borza, Eugene, *The Impact of Alexander the Great* (1974).

Havelock, Eric
1963 *Preface to Plato*. Cambridge, MA: Harvard University Press.
1982 *The Literate Revolution and Its Cultural Consequences*. Princeton, NJ: Princeton University Press.

Hexter, J. H.
1966 *The Judaeo-Christian Tradition*. New York and London: Harper & Row.

Higgins, W. E.
1977 *Xenophon the Athenian*. Albany, NY: State University of New York Press.

Jones, Tom B.
1988 "Graecia Capta," 51–75 in *Paths from Ancient Greece*, ed. C. G. Thomas, Leiden: Brill.

Jones, Tom B.
1967 "Numismatics," Chapter 7 in *Paths to the Ancient Past: Applications of the Historical Method to Ancient History*. New York: Free Press.

Kagan, Donald
1960 "Pheidon's Aeginetan Coinage" in *Transactions of the American Philological Association* 91: 121–36.

Keegan, John
1987 *The Mask of Command*. New York: Penguin.

Keller, D. R., and D. W. Rupp
1983 *Archaeological Survey in the Mediterranean Area*. Oxford: British Archaeological Reports.

Killen, John

1985   "The Linear B Tablets and the Mycenaean Economy," 241–305 in *Linear B: A 1984 Survey*, eds. A. Davies and Y. Duhoux, Louvain-la-Neuve: Bibliothèque des Cahiers de l'Institut de Linguistique.

Langer, William

1958   Presidential Address. *American Historical Review.* 63: 282–304.

Lee, Vernon

1884   *Euphorion.* London: T. F. Unwin.

Leroi-Gourhan, André

1965   *Préhistoire de l'art Occidental.* Paris: L. Mazenod.

Levi, Peter

1985   *The Pelican History of Greek Literature.* Harmondsworth, England: Penguin.

Luce, John

1987   Comment in concluding remarks of symposium on *The Function of the Minoan Palaces*, ed. R. Hägg and N. Marinatos. Stockholm, Svenska Institutet: Athen.

Luria, A. R., ed.

1968   *The Mind of Menmonist, A Little Book about a Vast Memory* (trans. Lynn Solotaroff). New York: Basic Books.

Moscati, Sabatino, ed.

1962   *The Face of the Ancient Orient.* Garden City, NY: Anchor.

Parry, Milman

1930   "Studies in the Epic Technique of Oral Verse-Making. 1. Homer and Homeric Style," *Harvard Studies in Classical Philology* 41: 73–147.

Pfeiffer, John E.

1982   *The Creative Explosion: An Inquiry into the Origins of Art and Religion.* New York: Harper & Row.

Prag, A. J. N. W., J. H. Musgrave, and R. A. H. Neave

1984   "The Skull from Tomb II at Vergina: King Philip II of Macedon." *Journal of Hellenic Studies* 104: 60–78.

Redfield, James

1975   *Nature and Culture in the Iliad: The Tragedy of Hector.* Chicago: University of Chicago Press.

Robinson, E. S. G.

1951   "The Coins from the Ephesian Artemision Reconsidered." *The Journal of Hellenic Studies* 71: 157–67.

Samuel, Alan E.

1988   "Philip and Alexander as Kings: Macedonian Monarchy and Merovingian Parallels." *American Historical Review* 93: 1270–86.

Starr, C. G.

1977   *The Economic and Social Growth of Early Greece, 800–500 B.C.* New York: Oxford University Press.

Strong, Eugenie

1907 *Roman Sculpture*, 2 Vols. London and New York: Duckworth and Scribners.

Tarn, W. W.

1913 and 1969 *Antigonos Gonatas*. Oxford and Chicago: Clarendon and Argonaut.

Tredennick, Hugh

1970 Translation of *Xenophon: Memoirs of Socrates and the Symposium*. Harmondsworth, England: Penguin Books.

Tyrrell, R. Y., ed.

1885 *The Correspondence of M. Tullius Cicero*. Dublin: Hodges, Foster and Figgis.

Vansina, Jan

1985 *Oral Tradition as History*. London and Nairobi: James Currey and Heinemann Kenya.

Vlastos, Gregory

1971 "The Paradox of Socrates" in *The Philosophy of Socrates*. Garden City, NY: Anchor.

Williams, E. H.

1985 Report on season's work in *Archaeological Reports* 1984–85. Hertford, England: Stephen Austin and Sons, Ltd.

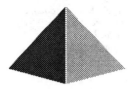

Index